Microsoft®
Power BI

by Jack Hyman

for
dummies®
A Wiley Brand

Microsoft® Power BI For Dummies®

Published by: **John Wiley & Sons, Inc.,** 111 River Street, Hoboken, NJ 07030-5774, www.wiley.com

Copyright © 2022 by John Wiley & Sons, Inc., Hoboken, New Jersey

Published simultaneously in Canada

For general information on our other products and services, please contact our Customer Care Department within the U.S. at 877-762-2974, outside the U.S. at 317-572-3993, or fax 317-572-4002. For technical support, please visit https://hub.wiley.com/community/support/dummies.

Wiley publishes in a variety of print and electronic formats and by print-on-demand. Some material included with standard print versions of this book may not be included in e-books or in print-on-demand. If this book refers to media such as a CD or DVD that is not included in the version you purchased, you may download this material at http://booksupport.wiley.com. For more information about Wiley products, visit www.wiley.com.

Library of Congress Control Number: 2021952556

ISBN: 978-1-119-82487-9 (pbk); 978-1-119-82488-6 (ebk); 978-1-119-82489-3 (ebk)

SKY10099742_031025

Contents at a Glance

Table of Contents

Introduction

Data is everywhere — no matter where you go, and no matter what you do, someone is gathering data around you. The tools and techniques utilized to evaluate data have undoubtedly matured over the past decade or two. Less than a decade ago, for example, the lowly spreadsheet was considered an adequate tool to collect, measure, and calculate results — even for somewhat complex datasets. Not anymore! The modern organization accumulates data at such a rapid pace that more sophisticated approaches beyond spreadsheets have become the new normal. Some might even call the spreadsheet a dinosaur.

Welcome to the generation of business intelligence. And what does business intelligence require, you ask? Consider querying data sources, reporting, caching data, and visualizing data as being just the tip of the iceberg. Ask yourself this question: If you had to address your organization's needs, what would they be? Would taking structured, unstructured, and semistructured data and making sense of it be part of your organizational requirements? Perhaps developing robust business analytics outputs for executive consumption? Or, is the mandate from the leadership the delivery of complex reports, visualizations, dashboards, and key performance indicators? If you're shaking your head right now and whispering all the above, you are not alone.

This is what enterprises today, large and small, expect. And with Microsoft Power BI, part of the Power Platform, you can deliver a highly sophisticated level of business intelligence to your organization, accomplishing each of these business objectives with little effort.

Power BI was initially conceived as part of the SQL Server Reporting Team back in 2010. Then, Power BI made its way into the Office 365 suite in September 2013 as an advanced analytics product. Power BI was built around Microsoft Excel core add-ins: Power Query, Power Pivot, and Power View. Along the way, Microsoft added a few artificial intelligence features, such as the Q&A Engine, enterprise-level data connectors, and security options via the Power BI Gateway. The product became so popular with the enterprise business community that, in July of 2015, Power BI was separated from the Office family, becoming its own product line. Finally, in late 2019, Power BI merged with other Microsoft products to form the Power Platform family, which consists of Power Apps (mobile), Power Automate (workflow), and Power BI (business intelligence).

Whether you're using Power BI as a stand-alone application to turn your data sources into interactive insights or integrating Power BI with applications such as Power Apps, SharePoint, or Dynamics 365, Power BI allows users to visualize and discover what is truly essential in their vast data resources. Users can share data at scale with ease. Depending on your role, you can create, view, or share data using the Power BI Desktop, the cloud-based Service, or the mobile app. The Power BI platform is designed to let users create, share, and consume business insights that effectively serve you and your team.

About This Book

This book is intended for anyone interested in business analytics, focusing as it does on the general platform capabilities across the Power BI platform. It doesn't matter whether you're a novice or a power user — you'll definitely benefit from reading this book. I'm thinking especially of the following business roles:

>> **Business analyst:** As a business analyst, you're tasked with many responsibilities. Maybe you're the requirements-gathering expert, the configuration guru, the designer, or even the quasi-developer. This book can be used as a resource for many of the critical tasks you may encounter in the field.

>> **Data professional:** Data is complex — make no mistake about it. This book doesn't help you tackle the formulas behind the scenes or tell you how to construct and programmatically code many sophisticated reports, dashboards, visuals, and KPIs. It does, however, help you understand the foundational activities across the Power BI platform if this is your first foray into using Microsoft's business intelligence (BI) platform. You'll be able to quickly ingest data, conduct data analysis, and build relatively sophisticated reports after reading this book.

>> **Developer:** This book isn't specifically for you, but you can find plenty of tips, tricks, and techniques you can learn throughout the book. Power BI is a collection of products that require users to understand several fundamental programming languages, including DAX and SQL. In this book, you can see that the surface is scratched ever so slightly in covering these topics. Take a look at the chapters on DAX in Part 4 if you want an introduction or a refresher.

>> **IT professional:** Whether you're a cloud expert, systems engineer, or database professional or you fill another IT role, this book doesn't provide you with all the technical answers you're looking for. Instead, this is a starting point if you want to take a leap into the world of Microsoft enterprise business intelligence.

>> **Manager or executive:** Often, the deliverables created in Power BI are built for managers and executives. Power BI has over 70 data connectors available for data extractions, report development, visualization support, and dashboard creation. Under your guidance, these deliverables are created by analysts, developers, and data professionals. Therefore, reading *Microsoft Power BI For Dummies* may help you better understand the art of the possible.

Foolish Assumptions

Power BI is a pretty big application, as you can probably already tell. Microsoft assumes that its interfaces are relatively simple for users to create reports and dashboards. Here's the truth: Some users find that it can be overwhelming, depending on which product you're using. Admittedly, lots of bells and whistles appear across each platform. As the author, I've written the book for users wanting to learn about those critical features across the three Power BI platforms: Desktop, Services, and Mobile. This book isn't intended to be a crash course for certification or a deep dive into administration or coding for Power BI. You can find specific books on the market for these purposes.

Throughout this book, though, I point you directly to the Microsoft Power BI website, when appropriate, where you can find resources to dig a bit deeper from time to time, on technical capabilities you may need to know about.

Because Power BI is made up of many components, I've made some assumptions about your configuration for this book as you follow along on the journey:

>> **You have downloaded a copy of the Power BI Desktop.** Some things in life are free, and this is one of them. Microsoft actually provides the Desktop client to its users for free! The Desktop client is intended to build the enduser data models, reports, and dashboards for personal consumption. That's where it ends, though. You do need an online account to share and collaborate. About half the steps lists in this book can be completed using the Desktop client.

>> **You have at least signed up for a Power BI Free Services account, but preferably have a Power BI Pro account**. If you want to share and collaborate with others, you need a Pro account. Otherwise, the Free online account will do for now. The purpose of the online companion is to distribute your outputs in read-only format, if you want. Suppose that you want others to edit and manipulate the data. In that case, there's no getting around paying for the Pro or Premium per User version. Also, the larger your dataset, the more likely you will want the upgrade.

>> **You have access to the Internet**: This may sound a bit obvious. Even with the Desktop client, an Internet connection is required in order to access datasets from the Internet.

>> **You have a meaningful dataset**: What does *meaningful* mean? I've created a sample dataset that can be downloaded for you from www.dummies.com to follow throughout the book. However, suppose that you want to use your own data. In that case, a meaningful dataset includes at least 300 to 400 records containing a minimum of five or six columns' worth of data.

Icons Used in This Book

Throughout *Microsoft Power BI For Dummies*, you see some icons along the way. Here's what they mean:

TIP

Tips point out shortcuts or essential suggestions on doing things quicker, faster, and more efficiently in Power BI.

REMEMBER

If you see the Remember icon, pay particular attention because these gotchas can make Power BI a bit difficult to understand. Don't worry, though — I'll help you find a workaround.

TECHNICAL STUFF

Technical Stuff is a way for you to consider exploring the inner workings of Power BI and perhaps how it integrates with other applications a bit more. That means there may be a configuration to a data source that has a nuance or an advanced reporting feature that may help shape your data a smidgen. These items are here to help you on a case-by-case basis.

ON THE WEB

This icon points to useful content available to you out there on the World Wide Web.

WARNING

Do not take warnings as a sign of panic. They appear once in a while, though, to make you aware of a common issue or product challenge many users face. Again, do not fret!

Beyond the Book

In addition to the content you're reading in this book, you have access to a free Power BI Cheat Sheet that can give you a hand when it comes to creating compelling dashboards, valuable reports, and structured DAX code. You also have access to a complete dataset that can be imported into your instance of Power BI Desktop or Services. The dataset is helpful because it can be used across all exercises throughout the book. To find the Cheat Sheet, go to www.dummies.com and enter **Power BI For Dummies** in the Search box. For the dataset I've prepared for you, go to www.dummies.com/go/mspowerbifd.

1

Put Your BI Thinking Caps On

IN THIS CHAPTER

» Figuring out the different types of
data Power BI can handle

» Understanding your options for
business intelligence tooling

» Familiarizing yourself with Power BI
terminology

Chapter **1**

A Crash Course in Data Analytics Terms: Power BI Style

ata is everywhere — literally. From the moment you awaken until the time you sleep, some system somewhere collects data on your behalf. Even as you sleep, data is being generated that correlates to some aspect of your life. What is done with this data is often the proverbial 64-million-dollar question. Does the data make sense? Does it have any sort of structure? Is the dataset so voluminous that finding what you're looking for is like finding a needle in a haystack? Or is it more like you can't even find what you need unless you have a special tool to help you navigate?

I'd answer that last question with an emphatic yes, and that's where data analytics and business intelligence join the party. And let's be honest: The party can be overwhelming if data is consistently generating something on your behalf.

REMEMBER

Dealing with data isn't always a chore — data can be fun to explore as well. Sometimes it's easy to figure out precisely what is needed to solve a problem, but at other times you need to put on your Sherlock Holmes deerstalker cap. Why? Because the data you're working with may lack structure and meaning. Of course, you're bound to take up tools to help you play the role of detective, evaluator, designer, and curator.

In this chapter, I discuss the different types of data you may encounter along your journey. I review the key terminology that you should become familiar with upfront. Don't worry: It's not like you need to memorize a dictionary. You learn a few key concepts to give you a head start in Power BI and business intelligence. Are you ready to go?

What Is Data, Really?

Ask a hundred people in a room what the definition of data is and you may receive one hundred different answers. Why is that? Because, in the world of business, data means a lot of different things to a lot of different people. So, let's try to get a streamlined response. Data contains facts. Sometimes, the facts make sense; sometimes, they're meaningless unless you add a bit of context.

The facts can sometimes be quantities, characters, symbols, or a combination of sorts that come together when collecting information. The information allows people — and more importantly, businesses — to make sense of the facts that, unless brought together, make absolutely no sense whatsoever.

When you have an information system full of business data, you also must have a set of unique data identifiers you can use so that, when searched, it's easy to make sense of the data in the form of a transaction. Examples of transactions might include the number of jobs completed, inquiries processed, income received, and expenses incurred.

The list can go on and on. To gain insight into business interactions and conduct analyses, your information system must have relevant and timely data that is of the highest quality.

REMEMBER

Data isn't the same as information. *Data* is the raw facts. That means you should think of data in terms of the individual fields or columns of data you may find in a relational database or perhaps the loose document (tagged with some descriptors called *metadata*) stored in a document repository. On their own, these items are unlikely to make much sense to you or to a business. And that's perfectly okay — sometimes. *Information* is the collective body of all those data parts, that results in the factoids making logical sense.

Working with structured data

Have you ever opened a database or spreadsheet and noticed that data is bound to specific columns or rows? For example, would you ever find a United States zip code containing letters of the alphabet? Or, perhaps when you think of a first name, middle initial, and last name, you notice that you always find letters in those specific fields. Another example is when you're limited to the number of characters you can input into a field. Think of Y as Yes; N is for No. Anything else is irrelevant.

What I'm describing here is called *structured data.* When you evaluate structured data, you notice that it conforms to a tabular format, meaning that each column and row must maintain an interrelationship. Because each column has a representative name that adheres to a predefined data model, your ability to analyze the data should be straightforward.

If you're using Power BI, you notice that structured data conform to a formal specification of tables with rows and columns, commonly referred to as a *data schema.* In Figure 1-1, you find an example of structured data as it appears in a Microsoft Excel spreadsheet.

	A	B	C	D	E	F	G	H
1	Employee ID	First Name	Last Name	Birth Date	Email Address	Mobile Number	Department	Office Location
2	123-45-453	Joe	Smith	1/3/2000	joe.smith@dataco.com	555.421.9051	Data Management	Seattle
3	123-45-459	Bob	Jones	2/14/1974	bob.jones@dataco.com	555.429.9082	Data Management	Seattle
4	123-49-907	Jane	Richards	3/15/1978	jane.richards@dataco.com	555.904.2852	Data Management	Seattle
5	190-90-223	Sally	Frank	2/28/1967	sally.frank@dataco.com	555.229.1804	Accounting	Atlanta
6	229-29-004	Emma	Donaldson	10/21/2002	emma.donaldson@dataco.com	555.867.5309	Marketing	San Francisco

REMEMBER

Whether you're using Power BI for personal analysis, educational purposes, or business support, the most accessible data sources for BI tools are structured. Platforms that offer robust structured data options would include Microsoft SQL Server, Microsoft Azure SQL Server, Microsoft Access, Azure Table Storage, Oracle, IBM DB2, MySQL, PostgreSQL, Microsoft Excel, and Google Sheets.

Looking at unstructured data

Unstructured data is ambiguous, having no rhyme, reason, or consistency whatsoever. Pretend that you're looking at a batch of photos or videos. Are there explicit data points that one can associate with a video or photo? Perhaps, because the file itself may consist of a structure and be made of some metadata. However, the byproduct itself — the represented depiction — is unique. The data isn't replicable; therefore, it's unstructured. That's why any video, audio, photo, or text file is considered unstructured data.

Adding semistructured data to the mix

Semistructured data does have some formality, but it isn't stored in a relational system and it has no set format. Fields containing the data are by no means neatly organized into strategically placed tables, rows, or columns. Instead, semistructured data contains tags that make the data easier to organize in some form of hierarchy. Nonrelational data systems or NoSQL databases are best associated with semistructured data, where the programmatic code, often serialized, is driven by the technical requirements. There is no hard-and-fast coding practice.

For the business intelligence developer utilizing semistructured languages, serialized programming practices can assist in writing sophisticated code. Whether the goal is to write data to a file, send a data snippet to another system, or parse the data to be translatable for structured consumption, semistructured data does have the potential for business intelligence systems. If the serialized language can communicate and speak the same language, a semistructured dataset has great potential.

Looking Under the Power BI Hood

Power BI is a product that brings together many smaller, cloud-based apps and services with a specific objective: to organize, collect, manage, and analyze big datasets. Big data is a concept where the business and data analyst will evaluate extremely large datasets, which may reveal patterns and trends relating to human behaviors and interactions not easily identifiable without the use of specific tools. A typical big data collection is often expressed in millions of records. Unlike a tool such as Microsoft Excel, Power BI can evaluate many data sources and millions of records simultaneously. The sources don't need to be structured using a spreadsheet, either. They can include unstructured and semistructured data.

After pulling these many data sources together and processing them, Power BI can help you come up with visually compelling outputs in the form of charts, graphics, reports, dashboards, and KPI's.

As you've already read, Power BI isn't just a single source application. It has desktop, online, and mobile components.

REMEMBER

Across the Power BI platforms, you are certain at some point to encounter one (or more) of the following products:

>> **Power Query**: A data connection tool you can use to transform, combine, and enhance data across several data sources

>> **Power Pivot**: A data modeling tool

» **Power View**: A data visualization tool you can use to generate interactive charts, graphs, maps, and visuals

» **Power Map**: A visualization tool for creating 3D map renderings

» **Power Q&A**: An artificial intelligence engine that allows you to ask questions and receive responses using plain language

» **Power BI Desktop**: A free, all-in-one solution that brings together all the apps described in this list into a single graphical user interface.

» **Power BI Services**: A cloud-based user experience to collaborate and distribute products such as reports with others

In the following few sections, I help you take a deeper dive into each product's core functionality.

Posing questions with Power Query

Before Power BI became its own product line, it was originally an advanced query and data manipulation add-in for Excel, circa 2010. It wasn't until around 2013 that Microsoft began to test Power BI as its own product line, with the formal launch of Power BI Desktop and Services in July 2015. One of the justifications for the switch to a dedicated product was the need for a more robust query editor. With the Excel editor, it was a single data source, whereas with Power BI's Power Query you can extract data from numerous data sources as well as read data from relational sources such as SQL Server Enterprise, Azure SQL Server, Oracle, MySQL, DB2, and a host of other platforms. If you're looking to extract data from unstructured, semistructured, or application sources — such as CSV files, text files, Excel files, Word documents, SharePoint document libraries, Microsoft Exchange Server, Dynamics 365, or Outlook — Power Query makes that possible as well. And, if you have access to API services that map to specific data fields on platforms such as LinkedIn, Facebook, or Twitter, you can use Power Query to mine those platforms as well.

Whatever you have Power Query do, the procedure is always pretty much the same: It transforms the data you specify (using a graphical user interface as needed) by adding columns, rows, data types, date and time, text fields, and appropriate operators. Power Query manages this transformation by taking an extensive dataset which is nothing more than a bunch of raw data (often disorganized and confusing to you, of course) and then creates some business sense by organizing it into tables, columns, and rows for consumption. The product produced by the Power Query output in the Editor can then be transferred to either a portable file such as Excel or something more robust, such as a Power Pivot model.

Working behind the Power Query scenes is a formula language called M. Although M never shows its face as part of the graphical user interface, it's definitely there and doing its job. I briefly tackle M in several upcoming chapters so that you can see how the mechanics work as you transform data quickly across structured, semistructured, and unstructured datasets in Power BI.

Modeling with Power Pivot

Power BI's data modeling tool is called Power Pivot. With it, you can create models such as star schemas, calculated measures, and columns and build complex diagrams. Power Pivot leverages another programming language called the Data Analysis eXpression Language — or DAX, for short. DAX is a formula-based language used for data analysis purposes. You soon discover that, as a language, it's chock-full of useful functions, so stay tuned.

Visualizing with Power View

The visualization engine of Power BI is Power View. The idea here is to connect to data sources, fetch and transform that data for analysis, and then have Power View present the output using one of its many visualization options. Power View gives users the ability to filter data for individual variables or an entire report. Users can slice data at the variable level or even break out elements in Power View to focus like a laser on data that may be considered anomalous.

Mapping data with Power Map

Sometimes, visualizing data requires a bit more than a Bar chart or a table. Perhaps you need a map that integrates geospatial coordinates with 3D requirements. Suppose that you're looking to add dimensionality to your data — perhaps with the help of heat maps, by gauging the height and width of a column, or basing the color used on a statistical reference. In that case, you definitely want to consider Power BI's Power Map feature set. Another feature built into Power Map is the use of geospatial capabilities using Microsoft Bing, Microsoft's external search engine technology that includes capabilities for mapping locations. A user can highlight data using geocoordinate latitude and longitudinal data as granular as an address or as global as a country.

Interpreting data with Power Q&A

One of the biggest challenges for many users is data interpretation. Say, for example, that you've built this incredible data model using Power Pivot. Now what? Your data sample is often pretty significant in terms of size, which means that you need some way to make sense of all the data you've deployed in the model. That's why Microsoft created a natural language engine, a way to interpret text, numbers, and even speech so that users can query the data model directly.

Power Q&A works directly in conjunction with Power View.

A classic example of a situation where Power Q&A can be enormously helpful would involve determining how many users have purchased a specific item at a given store location. If you want to drill down further, you could analyze a whole set of metrics — asking whether the item comes in several colors or sizes, for example, or specifying which day of the week saw the most items sold. The possibilities are endless as long as you've built your data model to accommodate the questions.

Power BI Desktop

All these Power BI platforms are great ideas, but the truly stupendous idea was bundling together Power Query, Power Pivot, Power View, and Power Q&A to form Power BI Desktop. Using Power BI Desktop, you can complete all your business intelligence activities under a single umbrella. You can also develop BI and data analysis activities far more easily. Finally, Microsoft updates Power BI Desktop features monthly, so you can always be on the BI cutting edge.

Power BI Services

Over time, the product name for Power BI Services has evolved. When the product was in beta, it was called Power BI Website. Nowadays, you often hear the product referred to as Power BI Online or Power BI Services. Whatever you call it, it functions as the Software as a Service companion to Power BI. Accessible at `https://app.powerbi.com`, Power BI Services allows users to collaborate and share their dashboards, reports, and datasets with other users from a single location.

The version of Power BI you have licensed dictates your ability to share and ingest data.

Knowing Your Power BI Terminology

Whether Microsoft or another vendor creates it, every product you come across has its own terminology. It may seem like a foreign language, but if you visit a vendor's website and do a simple search, you're sure to find a glossary that spells out what all these mysterious terms mean.

Microsoft, unsurprisingly, has its own glossary for Power BI as well. (Those folks refer to terminology as *concepts*, for reasons clear only to them.). Before you proceed any further on your Power BI journey, let's establish the lay of the land. In Microsoft Power BI-speak, some concepts resonate across vendors no matter who you are. For example, all vendors have reports and dashboards as critical concepts. Now, do all other vendors adopt Microsoft's practice and call dataflows a type of workflow? Not quite. They all have their names for these specific features, although all such features generally work the same way.

TIP

Microsoft has done a pretty good job of trying to stick with mainstream names for critical concepts. Nevertheless, some of the more advanced product features specific to AI/machine learning and security adopt the rarefied lingo of Microsoft products such as Azure Active Directory or Azure Machine Learning.

Capacities

What's the first thing you think about when it comes to data? Is it the type, or is it the quantity? Or do you consider both? With Power BI, the first concept you must be familiar with is *capacities*, which are central to Power BI. Why, you ask? Capacities are the sum total of resources needed in order for you to complete any project you may create in Power BI. Resources include the storage, processor, and memory required to host and deliver the Power BI projects.

There are two types of capacity: shared and dedicated. A *shared* capacity allows you to share resources with other Microsoft endusers. *Dedicated* capacities fully commit resources to you alone. Whereas shared capacity is available for both free and paying Power BI users, dedicated capacity requires a Power BI premium subscription.

Workspaces

Workspaces are a means of collaborating and sharing content with colleagues. Whether it's personal or intended for collaboration, any workspace you create is created on capacities. Think of a workspace as a container that allows you to manage the entire lifecycle of dashboards, reports, workbooks, datasets, and dataflows in the Power BI Services environment. (Figure 1-2 shows a My Workspace, a particular example of a Power BI workspace.)

REMEMBER

The My Workspace isn't the only type of workspace available. You also have the option to collaborate. If you want to collaborate, you have no choice but to upgrade to a Power BI Pro or Premium plan. Features that come with collaboration include the ability to create and publish Power BI-based dashboards, reports, workbooks, datasets, and apps with a team.

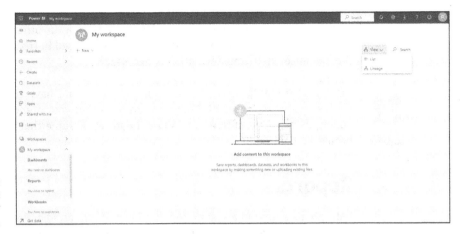

FIGURE 1-2:
My Workspace
in Power
BI Services.

REMEMBER

Looking to upload the work you've created using Power BI Desktop? Or perhaps you need to manipulate the work online without collaborating with anyone? If the answer to either question is yes, My Workspace is all that is necessary. You only *require* the use of the Power BI Online Free License. As soon as you want to collaborate with others, you need to upgrade to a paid Pro or Premium subscription.

So now you know that your work is stored in a workspace. Next question: What happens with the data in that workspace? The answer is twofold: There is what you see as the user, and then there's what goes on behind the scenes as part of the data transformation process. Let's start with the behind-the-scenes activities first.

A *dataflow* is a collection of tables that collects the datasets imported into Power BI. After the tables are created and managed in your workspace as part of Power BI Services, you can add, edit, and delete data within a dataflow. The data refresh can occur using a predefined schedule as well. Keep in mind that Power BI uses an Azure data lake, a way to store the extremely large volumes of data necessary for Power BI to evaluate, process, and analyze data rapidly. The Azure Data Lake also helps with cleaning and transforming data quickly when the datasets are voluminous in size.

Unlike a dataflow (which, you may remember, is a collection of tables), a dataset should be treated as a single asset in your collection of data sources. Think of a dataset as a subset of data. When used with dataflows, the dataset is mapped to a managed Azure data lake. It likely includes some or all of the data in the data lake. The granularity of the data varies greatly, depending on the speed and scale of the dataset available.

The analyst or developer can extract the data when building their desired output, such as a report. Sometimes, there may be a desire for multiple datasets, in which case dataflow transformation might be necessary. On the other hand, sometimes multiple datasets can leverage the same dataset housed in the Azure data lake. In this instance, little transformation is necessary.

REMEMBER After you've manipulated the data on your own, you have to publish the data you've created in Power BI. Microsoft assumes that you intend to share the data among users. If the intent is to share a dataset, assume that a Pro or Premium license is required.

Reports

Data can be stored in a system indefinitely and remain idle. But what good is it if the data in the system isn't queried from time to time so that users like you and me can understand what the data means, right? Suppose you worked for a hospital. You needed to query the employee database to find out how many employees worked within five miles of the facility in case of an emergency. That's when, quickly (not warp speed though) you can create a summary of your dataset, using a Power BI report. Sure, there could be a couple of hundred records or tens of thousands of records, all unique of course, but the records are all brought together to help the hospital home in just who can be all hands-on deck in case of an emergency whether it is just down the block, five miles away, or fifty miles away.

Power BI Reports translates that data into one or more pages of visualizations — Line charts, Bar charts, donuts, treemaps — you name it. You can either evaluate your data at a high level or focus on a particular data subset (if you've managed to query the dataset beforehand). You can tackle creating a report in a number of ways, from taking a dataset using a single source and creating an output from scratch to importing data from many sources. One example here would be connecting to an Excel workbook or Google Sheets document using Power View sheets. From there, Power BI takes the data from across the source and makes sense of it. The result is a report (see Figure 1-3) based on the imported data using predefined configurations established by the report author.

TIP Power BI offers two Report view modes: Reading view and Editing view. When you open a report, it opens in Reading view. If granted Edit permissions, you can edit a report. When a report is in a workspace, any user with administrative, member, or contributor rights can edit a report.

TECHNICAL STUFF Administrative, member, or contributor access grants you access to exploring, designing, building, and sharing capabilities within Edit view. Users who access the reports created by these privileged users can interact with reports in Read-Only mode. That means they can't edit it — they can only view the output. Reports created by privileged users are accessible under a workspace's Reports tab, as shown in Figure 1-4. Each report represents a single-page visualization, which means it's based on only one dataset.

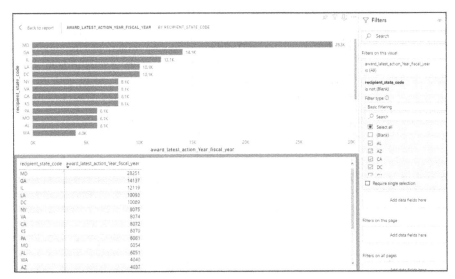

FIGURE 1-3:
A sample Power BI report.

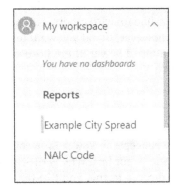

FIGURE 1-4:
The Reports tab in Power BI Desktop.

Dashboards

If you've had any experience with Power BI whatsoever, you already know that it's a highly visual tool. In line with its visual nature, the Power BI dashboard, also known as Canvas, brings your data story to life. If you're looking to take all the pieces of your data puzzle and capture a moment in time, you use the dashboard. Think of it as a blank canvas. As you build your reports, widgets, tiles, and key performance indicators (KPIs) over time, you pin the ones you like to the dashboard to create a single visualization. The dashboard represents the large dataset that you feel covers your topic at a glance. As such, it can help you make decisions, support you in monitoring data, or make it possible for you to drill down in your dataset by applying different visualization options.

To access a particular dashboard, you must first open a workspace. All you need to do then is click the Dashboards tab for whichever app you're working with. Keep in mind that every dashboard represents a customized view of an underlying dataset. To locate your personal dashboards, go to your My Workspaces tab (see Figure 1-5) and then choose Dashboards to see what's available.

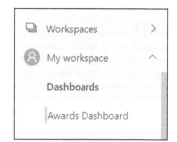

FIGURE 1-5:
Locating your
dashboards.

REMEMBER

If you own a dashboard, you have permission to edit it. Otherwise, you have only read-only access. You can share a dashboard with others, but they may not be able to save any changes. Keep in mind, however, that if you want to share a dashboard with a colleague, you need, at minimum, a Power BI Pro license. (For more on the ins and outs of licensing, see Chapter 3.)

Navigation pane

I talk about a lot of the must-know concepts in Power BI in this chapter, but I've saved the best — the Navigation pane — for last. Why is the Navigation pane the best? Simple. All the capabilities I discuss to this point in the chapter are labels found in the Navigation pane. (See Figure 1-6.) You would, for example, use the Navigation pane to complete actions to locate and move between a workspace and the various Power BI capabilities you want to use — dashboards, reports, work-books, datasets — whatever.

Your Navigation pane options are endless. For example, a user such as yourself can

>> Expand and collapse the Navigation pane.

>> Open and manage your favorite content with the help of the Favorites option.

>> View and open the most recently visited section of content.

FIGURE 1-6:
The Navigation
pane.

Business Intelligence (BI): The Definition

Earlier sections in this chapter are designed to give you a basic understanding of the ingredients that make up Power BI. Now it's time to explicitly define a term that's been bandied about but never truly explained: business intelligence. I've avoided this topic deliberately because many IT vendors define business intelligence differently. They put their spin on the term by injecting their tool lingo into the definition. For example, if you were to go to a Microsoft website, you'd be sure to find a page or two that would have a pure definition of business intelligence, but you'd also find a gazillion pages detailing how you can apply Power BI platform solutions to every conceivable business problem.

So, let's avoid the vendor websites and stick with a no-frills definition of *business intelligence:* Simply put, it's what businesses use in order to be in a position where they can analyze current as well as historical data. Throughout the process of data analysis, the hope is that an organization will be able to uncover the insights needed to make the right decisions for the business's future. By using a combination of available tools, an organization can process large datasets across multiple data sources in order to come up with findings that can then be presented to upper management. Using the enterprise BI tool, interested parties can produce visualizations via reports, dashboards, and KPIs as a way to ground their growth strategies in the world of facts. Many tools allow for collaboration and sharing among groups, because data changes over time.

REMEMBER

Almost every concept I cover in this chapter is part of the definition, which is why I introduce the terminology before presenting the BI definition. Those terms specific to Microsoft Power BI were left out of the definition of business intelligence deliberately. As you continue reading this book and immerse yourself into using Power BI, some of the lessons I present are *tool agnostic:* It doesn't matter which vendor's business intelligence product I'm referring to. At other times, you know when the advice is specific to Power BI, because the comments are instructional.

REMEMBER

Not so very long ago, businesses had to do many tasks manually. Remember those days? BI tools now save the day by reducing the effort to complete mundane tasks. You can take four actions right now to transform raw data into readily accessible data:

>> **Collect and transform your data:** When using multiple data sources, BI tools allow you to extract, transform, and load (ETL) data from structured and unstructured sources. When that process is complete, you can then store the data in a central repository so that an application can analyze and query the data.

>> **Analyze data to discover trends:** The term *data analysis* can mean many things, from data discovery to data mining. The business objective, however, is all the same: It all boils down to the size of the dataset, the automation process, and the objective for pattern analysis. BI often provides users with a variety of modeling and analytics tools. Some come equipped with visualization options, and others have data modeling and analytics solutions for exploratory, descriptive, predictive, statistical, and even cognitive evaluation analysis. All these tools help users explore data — past, present, and future.

>> **Use visualization options in order to provide data clarity:** You may have lots of data stored in one or more repositories. Querying the data to be understood and shared among users and groups is the actual value of business intelligence tools. Visualization options often include reporting, dashboards, charts, graphics, mapping, key performance indicators, and — yes — datasets.

>> **Taking action and making decisions:** The process culminates with all the data at your fingertips to make actionable decisions. Companies act by taking insights across a dataset. They parse through data in chunks, reviewing small subsets of data and potentially making significant decisions. That's why companies embrace business intelligence — because with its help they can quickly reduce inefficiency, correct problems, and adapt the business to support market conditions.

Chapter **2**

The Who, How, and What of Power BI

E nterprise business intelligence (BI) solutions aren't one-size-fits-all, which is why vendors like Microsoft cater to a broad audience in their marketing and distribution of products in the Power BI niche. Stakeholders involved in the business intelligence lifecycle create the data models for analysis and planning, cleanse the datasets, transform and validate datasets into data models, and manage the infrastructure for the data models to run on, day in and day out.

Several years ago, you could probably count on your two hands how many people were involved in managing data across a global organization. Nowadays, as many as a dozen separate teams might be responsible for data management, and one of those teams can easily be dedicated to supporting Power BI efforts and the analytics outputs such as the reports, dashboards, and datasets produced. In this chapter, you can read about the typical power players in an organization who make use of Power BI, how those players shape the data from its start, and what kinds of analytics outputs they might create along the way.

Highlighting the Who of Power BI

There once was a time when you could point to a single person in a company and say, "Tag — you're *it!*" You knew that this one person was responsible for running the reports and accounting for the companywide data on the hard drive, so you knew who to turn to if you had a problem. Those days are long gone.

The new world order now includes departments full of people who handle the management and analysis of data. It's no secret that more money than ever is now being spent on the knowledge economy, and much of that money is being channeled to departments that use Power BI. There, you can find several key stakeholders tasked with spending that money wisely. These days, most vital BI programs include business analysts, data analysts, data engineers, data scientists, and database administrators as part of their teams. Together, these data experts handle evangelizing how to take raw data and use it to tell a compelling story.

Business analyst

The business analyst focuses on the data footprint from a qualitative or functional perspective. When you need a person to interpret data and explain what things mean in words, not numbers, you would ask the business analyst to either gather and document the business data requirements or evaluate the data. A business analyst is the closest member of the Power BI team involved in the day-to-day decision-making process because that person often acts as a business liaison to decision-makers and the data team. When a new report or dashboard requires creation, you often find that a business analyst is the first point of contact that a stakeholder in the business addresses. This person's vision is translatable to a workable dataset, which eventually becomes a data model.

Data analyst

Unlike the business analyst, the data analyst does not approach analysis based on a user or the business need, but rather on the data produced. Once data enters the enterprise information systems, these assets become the analyst's most valuable utility. The data analyst looks to understand value by way of visualization and reporting tools, such as Power BI. As such, the data analyst wears many hats in that role, from profiling, cleansing, and transforming raw data to presenting the data in its finalized form to the appropriate stakeholders.

REMEMBER

A data analyst, in addition to managing the data behind the scenes, also has a hands-on role in the management of Power BI assets. When a business analyst is tasked with translating requirements into actual products, the data analyst is the point person who acts as the developer. That person addresses the data and reporting requirements by turning raw data into relevant, valuable insights.

Think of the data analyst as the gatekeeper. This person must work as an intermediary between the end user and a) the business analyst b) the data engineer and c) the database administrators to confirm operational validity. That's a whole lot of negotiating! The last-named role requires that the data analyst be familiar with the data platform and its accompanying security principles, process management, and general management principles. (Talk about a bit of juggling.) Other roles in the BI ecosystem demand as much commitment, though, so the weight of the world doesn't fall exclusively on the data analyst.

Data engineer

Because data isn't a one-size-fits-all kind of concept, you can imagine that the individuals who implement the data need to know a thing or two about the different flavors of data delivery available to them. For example, the people implementing BI solutions must be able to address data on-premises as well as data in the cloud. Moreover, the data you're managing and securing often requires that you evaluate the flow of both structured and unstructured data sources. Sometimes, it may be just the one source, but more often than not it involves many different sources. The platforms themselves run the gamut, from a typical relational database to nonrelational databases and even from data streams to file stores. One thing is for sure, though: Data must always be secure and seamlessly integrated regardless of the data service.

Just like the data analysts, data engineers are forced to wear many hats — it's just that, while wearing those many hats, they're implementing data tools rather than analyzing processes. That means the engineer must know how to use on-premises service tools as well as cloud data service tools to ingest and transform data across sources. Finally, keep in mind that you can't plan on the sources being bound to just the organization itself, because data sources often live outside your organization's four walls.

TECHNICAL STUFF

Synergies often exist between the data engineer and a database administrator. You might wonder why a data engineer isn't called a database administrator also. The thing is, a data engineer doesn't just supply advisory services, manage the hosted infrastructure, or support operational data needs. That person is also responsible for crafting the agenda for business intelligence and data science initiatives. The role requires the engineer to have a handle on data in all shapes and formats. As such, the data engineer must master *data wrangling*, where you use the latest technology to transform and map data from its raw form to a more streamlined form — a form easier for BI or analytics to exploit, in other words.

REMEMBER

Smaller organizations often look to have a jack-of-all-trades who would be in a position to support as many tasks as possible. As you'll quickly realize, the roles blur a bit. In the real world, data analysts, data engineers, and database administrators work together, often sharing duties and responsibilities. It's not uncommon to have an overseer role with a single title — commonly, data engineer. A database administrator, analyst, or even a BI professional can easily transition into the data engineer role, as long as they grasp the requirements of the people, processes, and technologies used to sift through the data.

Data scientist

Data scientists are seldom responsible for managing infrastructure. Most data scientists don't usually install much software, either. The data scientist is laser focused on creating and executing advanced analytics to extract the data from the systems put in place by the business analysts, data analysts, data engineers, and database administrators. As I explain later in this chapter, the data scientists perform analytics routines on descriptive, diagnostic, prescriptive, predictive, and cognitive data. Whether the analysis conducted is quantitative using statistical tooling or machine learning functionality to detect patterns and anomalies or the data requires qualitative evaluation, the end goal is the same: to create a well-built model.

Building data models with analytics is only part of a data scientist's responsibility. As the world of machine learning and artificial intelligence continues to thrive, the data scientist is tasked with exploring deep learning and performing experiments with complex data problems with various coding languages using algorithmic techniques. They must be heavily vested in understanding programming languages that can transform data that may otherwise be obscure or otherwise difficult to exploit.

REMEMBER

It's no secret that most of the time spent by a data scientist is on addressing issues related to fixing data, also known as data wrangling. By having a team, the data scientist can often speed up the process. Better yet, by using tools, such as Power BI, that automate many of the roles in the business intelligence and data science lifecycle, the data scientist can more easily address the questions that require answers.

Database administrator

Your database administrator handles implementing and managing the database infrastructure. In some organizations, the database is entirely cloud enabled. Legacy organizations, on the other hand, have often kept their database on-premises or in a state of flux, resulting in a hybrid data platform deployment. When using Power BI, you'll likely have your database administrator build solutions on top of Microsoft Azure-based data services, including Microsoft Azure SQL.

Whereas the data engineer or analyst might handle the availability and performance of the database solution, ensuring that stakeholders can identify and implement the policies and procedures they need in order to support the data environment properly, the data administrator has quite a different set of responsibilities. The database administrator is like a doctor: This person ensures the health and wellness of the database as well as the infrastructure that the organization's data runs on.

REMEMBER

When you try to sum up who does what in the Power BI data lifecycle, keep these two points in mind:

» **Your business analyst, data analyst, and data engineer are involved in the creation of data and its manageability.** The key words here are *ingestion, transformation, validation, cleansing,* and *creation.*

» **Your database administrator, on the other hand, handles the systems which ensure that the data remains healthy.** The responsibility isn't just limited to data reliability, but security fitness as well.

Understanding How Data Comes to Life

Data takes time to nurture. Treat the process as though you're starting at the center of a bull's-eye, where the focus is on preparation. As you learn more about the organization's people, processes, and technologies, your data requirements evolve, and those evolving requirements end up informing your data model. As models mature and the data volume proliferates, the visualizations available to you increase in detail, variety, and size. You're in a position to complete far more analyses, which might run the gamut from qualitative to quantitative and occur either sporadically or in realtime. Ultimately, data management is all-encompassing because it overlays every phase of the data lifecycle. Figure 2-1 illustrates what a typical organization's leaders should expect when they nurture data using an enterprise BI solution such as Power BI.

Prepare

Though the preparation stage is the most focused and tedious, the entire data lifecycle is influenced by preparation. Why, you ask? Well, what do you end up with if you start out with insufficient data? Bad reporting or poorly constructed visualizations leading to faulty analyses that can have a catastrophic impact on an organization, that's what.

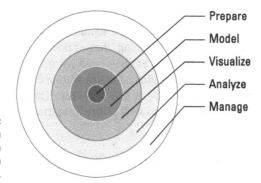

Prepare
Model
Visualize
Analyze
Manage

FIGURE 2-1:
A prototype data
lifecycle for an
organization
using Power BI.

REMEMBER

Data preparation requires a business analyst to evaluate the business's needs and a data analyst to construct an appropriate data profile for cleansing and transformation. The data may come from one source or many sources.

Suppose that either the business analyst or data analyst improperly constructs the expected profile, maps the resultant output poorly, or transforms the data into a subpar result so that the model and visualization present the data incorrectly. In that case, an organization might find that the product delivered by a BI tool has little meaning. Admittedly, the process can be complicated, given that the data may be coming from multiple sources or that it might not be clear how best to connect to your sources — factors, I might add, that can have significant performance implications. The trick is to determine what is needed to ensure that performance isn't impacted negatively and to then ensure that the models and reports meet these predetermined requirements. (Requirement examples here would include data and memory volume or perhaps CPU use for processing.)

TIP

Avoid any temptation to skimp when it comes to meeting these requirements. Such processes include gathering data, looking for patterns, and anomalies, and synthesizing the data into meaningful requirements. Be warned though, that some data workloads might be unable to handle ad hoc querying abilities if memory volume or processing power is insufficient.

Model

Okay, you say your data preparation is complete. Data scrutiny is at a high level, so many eyes have confirmed the data is in its proper state. Now what? Organizations often take this opportunity to model the data. In this context, data modeling can be seen as a process where all those raw pieces of data have been formalized and structured. The goal is to decide how the organized datasets can relate to each other. After you define the relationships, you can then build on the models by creating metrics, calculations, and rule sets.

REMEMBER

The model is a critical component in the data lifecycle. Without a model, the end user cannot produce reports or conduct analyses for an organization. A properly designed model is the key to delivering accurate and trusted results, especially as more organizations begin to work with large datasets.

TIP

Anytime you experience performance issues using Power BI, start by evaluating your model. Examples that may show performance as an issue include report refresh rates taking a bit longer than they should, data loading and preparation lagging, or data rendering from an often-accessed dataset that's taking a tad too long to query.

Visualize

Visualizing data helps organizations better understand business problems in ways that plain text can't convey. Picture the thickness of this book as a single set of data for a report. Do you think it's easy for a person to summarize the contents of this book after reading it for two minutes? How much effort would it take to discretely come up with five or six key data points? (My sense is that it would take a superhuman effort.) The old saying "A picture is worth a thousand words" surely applies here. That's why visualization can make data come alive. Visualizations tell compelling stories, enabling business decision-makers to gain needed insights reasonably quickly.

A good BI solution such as Power BI incorporates many visualization options that make report outputs easier for decision-makers to understand. The visualizations generally aggregate the data to guide the professional through the dataset quickly. Reports built on these visualizations can be crucial aids when it comes to driving decision-making actions and behaviors in an organization. Given that many organizations don't even look at the structured dataset, never mind the raw data that the business or data analyst spends so much time evaluating as part of the preparation and data modeling stage, you need to make sure that your visualizations supply accurate messaging.

TIP

Not all visualizations are proper for a dataset. For example, a treemap requires at least three variables to be a workable visual output. On the other hand, pie charts and bar charts are quite content to settle for just two variables. Given that fact, it pays to take the time to fully understand the business problem you're trying to solve, to see whether all data points are necessary. Too much data may make it more difficult to detect key patterns.

REMEMBER

Power BI has built-in AI capabilities that guide the best-fit visualization for reporting without requiring code. Consider using the Questions and Answers feature, trying out the various visualization options, or using Quick Insights to map your data model with the best-fit solution in Power BI.

Analyze

No two individuals analyze data in the same way. The analysis task is another step in the process when crafting your data model and interpreting your visualizations. Consider analysis as an overarching activity that often coincides across roles. It would be best if you continually had to analyze your data, the model you derived, and your visualization output to make sure that accuracy follows. You should ensure accuracy in finding patterns, noticing trends, communicating with others, and even predicting outcomes based on data, even if you find anomalous tendencies. Platforms such as Power BI make data analysis more accessible because the process is simplified for business stakeholders when it comes to completing each one of those tasks.

REMEMBER

Power BI is a desktop solution as well as a cloud-based one. You can do most of your business analysis, data analysis, data modeling, and visualization activities using Power BI Desktop. You can even analyze the data on your own using Power BI Desktop, assuming that you've connected your data model to the proper data source. However, if you want to share your data or analyze it with others, you must use Power BI Services.

Manage

When you have a chance to look more closely at Power BI, you soon see that, as a platform, it consists of lots of different apps. The outputs produced are plentiful: reports, dashboards, workspaces, datasets, KPIs, and even other apps. On a well-organized team, every member usually manages one or more byproducts supporting the management of the Power BI assets, allowing for the sharing and distribution of data. Whether you're the data analyst who oversees the validation of the data or the database administrator who must ensure the health and well-being of the hardware infrastructure, everyone has a role in managing the platform.

When you complete activities using Power BI Desktop, the eventual intent is to share the deliverable with a larger audience. As soon as the deliverable is made available, the content you've created using the Power BI Desktop fosters collaboration between teams and individuals. Sharing of content means ensuring that the right stakeholders gain access to the product you've created.

REMEMBER

Security can be a bit challenging in large organizations. Your business analyst, data analyst, and data engineer each has a role in making sure that the right people have access to only what they need. The data scientist makes sure that the data assets being created are of high value. And of course, the database administrator ensures that the data house is always open for business by managing the infrastructure that all stakeholders support as part of the data lifecycle for business intelligence using Power BI.

Examining the Various Types of Data Analytics

Earlier in this chapter, I describe those stakeholders in an organization who would typically use Power BI. I've tried to show, at a very high level, how each of these stakeholders takes data that has been created and transforms it into something useful using Power BI Desktop or Power BI Services. The only thing left for you to do before I let you loose in the Power BI forest involves learning the type of analytics produced by Power BI. If you have ever read a generalist book on business intelligence, this section may not hold new information for you. If this is your first foray into BI or learning what makes Power BI different among the analytic product outputs, this section is your one-stop shop to summarize the details.

You can produce five types of analytics using Power BI: x, descriptive, diagnostic, predictive, prescriptive, and cognitive. Depending on the business goal and application within Power BI, the analytic products are a bit different. Table 2-1 describes the five types of analytics, including each one's purpose and where you'll most likely have success using each analytics type.

TABLE 2-1   Types of Analytics Produced in Power BI

Type	What It Does
Descriptive	Helps answer questions based on historical data. Descriptive analytics also summarize large datasets and describe outcomes.
Diagnostic	Explains why events happen. Typically, diagnostic analytics support descriptive analytics as a secondary form of analytics that allows you to discover the cause of events. Analysts look for anomalies in datasets, reports, and KPIs. The use of statistical techniques available within Power BI helps users discover relationships in the data and trends.
Predictive	Helps answer questions about what might potentially happen in the future. Taking historical trends and finding patterns, the resultant output is an observation of what is likely to occur. Techniques used to derive results involve combinations of statistical methodologies and machine learning capabilities available in Power BI.
Prescriptive	Answers the question about which actions one must take to meet a goal. Taking the data gathered, organizations can address issues based on unknown conditions. Such analytics also rely heavily on big data analytics and existing datasets being evaluated by Power BI's machine learning engine to find patterns, which helps deliver on different outcomes.
Cognitive analytics	Referred to at times as inferential analytics; lets the analyst pull together data from across the datasets to detect patterns, develop conclusions, and set up a knowledge bank for future learning. The keyword here is *future* because what is learned and seen is used to self-guide for the future. If conditions change, the knowledge bank adjusts accordingly. Because inferences are unstructured thoughts and hypotheses, it's up to machine learning solutions within Power BI to process the data change, make sense of the existing data sources, and create data correlations.

Taking a Look at the Big Picture

As the data in the organization grows, so does the need for more stakeholders to support the enterprise. Each stakeholder has a unique place in supporting the BI data lifecycle. Though data is often raw when first introduced as part of the data lifecycle, the final product created using Power BI must be refined and crisp. Whether you enable reporting, data visualization, dashboarding, KPI, or another BI choice within the Power BI platform, remember that the data must be free from errors and trusted for any business to be successful. That means the data is consumable, meaningful, accessible, and understood by all parties no matter what the analytics product might be. And, as you now know, people and processes are in place to ensure that the engine operates continuously, no matter which type of analytics product is produced.

Chapter **3**

Oh, the Choices: Power BI Versions

Picking out the correct version of Power BI might be like visiting the world's biggest candy store: You can choose from many alternatives with subtle nuances. The choice boils down to wants, needs, scale, and, of course, money. Some versions are free (well, sort of), and other versions can be expensive. And, of course, the most obvious difference is that some versions are desktop- or server-based whereas others offer online-only capabilities.

If you visit the Microsoft website on any given day and search for products, you notice quite a few versions of Power BI exist. However, the Pricing page and the Products page don't necessarily match. (Thanks for the help, Microsoft!) It isn't clear whether "Free is free" or whether products are inclusive within specific Power BI versions. In this chapter, I clear up any confusion you may have so that, moving forward, you know which product you should use.

Why Power BI versus Excel?

Microsoft markets Power BI as a way to connect and visualize data using a unified, scalable platform that offers self-service and enterprise business intelligence that can help you gain deep insights into data. So, it begs the question:

Doesn't Microsoft Excel do this already? What makes Power BI different? Ask yourself these questions:

>> What level of analytics does your organization need?

>> Is collaboration an issue?

>> What is the size of your dataset?

>> Is there a pricing issue?

>> How meaningful are visualizations to you or your team?

Both Excel and Power BI can handle all five requirements, but Power BI is a significant upgrade, for several reasons. Data volume, breadth of visualization options, cost, and collaboration are differentiators with Power BI.

REMEMBER

>> Power BI supplies an array of high-level analytics offerings that Excel doesn't include, such as the ability to create dashboards, key performance indicators (KPI), visualizations, and alerts.

>> Power BI has significant collaboration capabilities, whereas Excel has limited data collaboration options.

>> Though Excel can help when it comes to creating advanced reports, if you want to build data models that include predictive and machine learning assets, you have to turn to specific versions of Power BI.

>> There is no single free version of Excel. On the other hand, you can start with Power BI for free. You can also purchase premium alternatives if you need advanced features — from a few dollars per month to several thousand.

In summary, Power BI integrates business intelligence (BI) and data visualization so that users can create custom and interactive dashboards, KPIs, and reports. Simultaneously, Microsoft Excel is limited in handling data analytics, mathematical operations, or data organization using a spreadsheet. Power BI can extract and format data from more than a single data source type. Because Power BI handles extensive *data ingestion* — the uploading of data from an external source, in other words —the process is, by nature, much faster. Furthermore, because Power BI can connect with various data sources, the range of outputs, including dashboards and reports, is more interactive, whereas Excel is limited in scope. Above all, Power BI is a tool for data visualization and analysis that allows for collaboration. At the same time, Excel limits sharing and data analysis to a limited number of end users.

Power BI Products in a Nutshell

Microsoft confuses customers like you and me by using the words *version* and *license* interchangeably. Let me clear up these terms before you read any further.

REMEMBER

Licensing refers to the products a customer is procuring, whereas *version* deals with where Power BI runs: on a desktop, from a server, or in the cloud. One or more Power BI products may be required in order to fully support deployments of Power BI. In some cases, you may require a hybrid solution of desktop *and* online versions of the product.

Introducing the Power BI license options

You can choose from four product license options: Power BI Desktop, Power BI Free, Power BI Pro, or Power BI Premium. You might be scratching your head because Microsoft also shows a few other Power BI products, including two versions of Power BI Premium as well as Power BI Mobile, Power BI Embedded, and Power BI Report Server on the Microsoft website. If you're confused, you're not alone. The good news is that some of these products are included with all three product licensing options, whereas others are specific to either the Pro or Premium version. Let's review each product license:

>> **Power BI Desktop**: The free desktop version of Power BI allows a user to author reports and data analytics inputs without publishing them to the Internet. If you want to collaborate and share your desktop output, however, you have to switch to either the Pro or Premium version.

>> **Power BI Free**: Considered the entry-level free cloud version, this version lets you author and store reports online versus the desktop. The only drawback is storage capacity, limited to 1GB, and no collaboration.

>> **Power BI Pro**: The entry-level paid version of Power BI gets you a larger storage allocation, limited to 100GB, as well as the ability to collaborate with Pro licensed users.

>> **Power BI Premium**: The enterprise paid version comes in two editions: per user and capacity. Per-user licensing is intended for those with big data aspirations who also need massive storage scale but who have no global distribution requirements. Capacity is useful for an enterprise that intends to have many users. Keep in mind one catch with capacity licensing: You also need to procure Pro licenses because what you're paying for is the storage and security — Pro's killer feature.

- **Power BI Mobile**: Intended to be a complementary product to manage reports, dashboards, and KPIs on the go, Power BI Mobile has limited, if any, authoring capabilities. Your ability to collaborate on Mobile varies depending on your license authorization.

- **Power BI Embedded**: This version offers a way to integrate real-time reports on public- or private-facing products using the Power BI API service in Microsoft Azure,

- **Power BI Report Server**: A server-based Power BI product intended to produce reporting output offline, its users store their reports on a server, not online. Note that you must still procure some form of Premium license, either stand-alone or using a Software Assurance subscription (an enterprise-based software plan).

REMEMBER

Core functionality, data processing, and handling capacity differ among the four licensing options for Power BI. When it comes to data handling capacity, think of free as a filing cabinet worth of data versus Pro and Premium managing several hundred filing cabinets. Even among the two paid versions, Premium has the most capacity available. Similarly, each version has more reporting options and improved collaboration quality.

TIP

Even if you have a small set of users, the Premium license supplies more storage capacity and higher data limits — which include refresh rates and data isolation options— than the Pro version. The significant difference in price between Pro and Premium is more than justified.

Looking at Desktop versus Services options

The beauty of Software as a Service (SaaS) is that anytime a vendor such as Microsoft wants to add a new feature to a product, it can do so with little effort — a user will see the magic of the new feature instantly and will start using it. That isn't the case with downloadable software. Once an application is configured for the desktop, it's up to the end user to keep track of the updates. Vendors also update downloadable software less often. Whereas cloud-based solutions may be updated daily, a software release for a significant product happens monthly with Power BI.

Power Bi Desktop is a complete authoring tool for analytics and business intelligence designers. You can download Power BI Desktop for free and install it on your local computer. The desktop version allows a user to connect to more than 70 data source types and then transform those sources into data models. You can take the reports you've created and add visuals based on the data models using Desktop. Because Power BI Desktop exists as an application, it's updated each month cumulatively with all the features and functionality made available for consumption on the Services platform.

TIP

To download a copy of the Power BI Desktop application, go to `https://powerbi.microsoft.com/en-us/desktop`.

Except for the Power BI Desktop and Power BI Report Server, all other versions of Power BI fall into the cloud delivery model commonly referred to as Services. Why, you ask? Because each version is delivered as Software as a Service. SaaS cloud delivery allows Microsoft to auto-update features regularly and deliver the product over the Internet using a web browser such as Microsoft Edge, Google Chrome, or Apple Safari. In case of a technical issue, Microsoft doesn't have to wait for the end-of-the-month software release to update the code — it does so immediately. In terms of features, end users and designers can view, manipulate, and interact with reports online rather than have to rely on their desktop. Most designers who use Power BI Desktop publish their reports to the Power BI Service at some point. Suppose that you gain access to the service. In that case, you can edit reports, create visual outputs based on existing data models and datasets, and collaborate with other users requiring access to those reports, dashboards, and KPIs you've made.

Though a small number of features overlap between the Desktop and Services offerings, most users initially start with Power BI Desktop to create their reports. In Table 3-1, notice the commonalities among the Power BI features and the obvious differences. Once users finish building the reports, the Power BI Service is used to distribute the reports to others. A limited Power BI Services is offered for free; true collaboration and expanded storage require a minimum of either the Pro or Premium edition.

TABLE 3-1

Power BI Desktop, Common, Service Features

Power BI Desktop	Common	Power BI Services
More than 70 data sources	Reports	Limited data sources
Data transformation	Visualizations	Dashboarding
Data shaping	Security	KPI management
Data modeling	Filters	Workspaces
Measures	R visuals (big data outputs)	Sharing and collaboration
Calculated columns	Bookmarks	Hosting and storage
DAX	Q&A	Workflow/data flow
Python		Paginated reporting
Themes		Gateway management
RLS creation		Row Level Security (RLS) management

Stacking Power BI Desktop against Power BI Free

So, does *free* mean free with Power BI? The answer is yes, with caveats. I need to clear up another product concept before I spell out the licensing options next, though.

The Power BI Desktop option is a free, downloadable application, as is the Power BI Free version, which is part of the Power BI Services offering. The feature set made available in Power BI Free is supposed to mimic the Power BI Desktop client, except that Power BI Free is in the cloud. All those updates you'd wait a month for in the Desktop version are made available in real time by Microsoft. Power BI Free exposes users to authoring reports on the web as opposed to on their desktop application. Of course, you have to keep one big catch in mind: Limited to no collaboration is available when using Power BI Free. For you to collaborate with others requires a minimum of a Power BI Pro license.

Examining the Details of the Licensing Options

Now, I am about to confuse you a bit, compliments of Microsoft. Power BI may have seven product versions, but only two of them cost money, technically speaking. Well, sort of. *License* in Power BI-speak means a product assigned to a specific user. That product may or may not cost money, depending on which of the three per-user license delivery options — Free, Pro, or Premium — you use. To decide which license is best suited for you, ask yourself these questions:

>> Where is your data stored?

>> How does the user interact with the data?

>> Is there a need for premium features, such as collaboration?

Though the per-user license is the most common, another license type is available for enterprise clients — the capacity-based license. Only the Power BI Premium edition is associated with capacity-based licensing. The significant difference is that a user with a Free license can have complete control of content in workspaces provisioned with Premium entitlement. Unless you have a Premium entitlement, a user with a Free license is limited in their ability to create reports and dashboards and connect to data sources only in their My Workspace. In other words, you cannot share, collaborate with others, or publish content from one workspace to another.

Seeing how content and collaboration drive licensing

The sticking point among all Power BI licensing comes down to content and collaboration access. A Power BI Free license comes with limited content storage and collaboration abilities. To reap the more advanced product benefits, you need a subscription.

With a Power BI Pro per-user license, the ability to store and share content is also limited. You can collaborate only with other Power BI Pro users. The Pro user can access content shared by other Pro users, publish content to an app workspace, share dashboards and reports, and collaborate with other Pro users by subscribing to dashboards and reports. The exception is when you have a Premium Capacity workspace — then Pro users can give content to others who aren't entitled to a Power BI Pro license.

With a Premium per User license, users can only collaborate amongst themselves unless they are provided with a workspace with Premium Capacity entitlement maintaining the content. The bottom line here is that capacity allows for a bit more sharing, and user-to-user entitlement is a bit more restrictive. For an overview of the various licensing options, check out Table 3-2.

TABLE 3-2   Comparison of Power BI Licensing Options

FEATURES	Desktop	Free	Pro	Premium per User	Premium Capacity
Delivery method	Offline	Cloud	Cloud	Cloud	Cloud
Cost	Free	Free	$10 per month per user	$20 per month per user	Minimum of $4,995 per month per vCore
Model size limit		1GB	1GB	100GB	400GB
Refresh rate		8/day	8/day	48/day	48/day
Maximum storage capacity	N/A	10GB/ per user	10GB/ per user	100TB	100TB
Works with Power BI Mobile	No	Yes	Yes	Yes	Yes
Connect to more than 100 data sources	Yes	Yes	Yes	Yes	Yes

(continued)

TABLE 3-2 *(continued)*

FEATURES	Desktop	Free	Pro	Premium per User	Premium Capacity
Connect to Power BI Desktop for report creation and visualization		Yes	Yes	Yes	View only
Integrate with Power BI Embedded		Limited	Yes	Yes	Yes
Sharing and collaboration	Requires publishing	No	Only with Pro users	Only with Premium users	Requires minimum of Pro license
AI visualization				Yes	Yes
Unstructured data (text analytics, image detection, machine learning)				Yes	Yes
XMLA connectivity				Yes	Yes
Data flow integration				Yes	Yes
Data warehousing storage options				Yes	Yes
Security and encryption		Yes	Yes	Yes	Yes
Application lifecycle management		Yes	Yes	Yes	Yes
Distributed geographic deployment					Yes
Bring your own key (BYOK)					Yes
Autoscaling					Yes
Can Be Used with Power BI Report Server for offline access					Yes

Starting with Power BI Desktop

No matter which version of Power BI is in use, you will likely use the Desktop client as part of your BI strategy. The Desktop client lets you create the data models and build reports without requiring a license. Once these assets are available, you'll likely want to share them. That's where a required license using Power BI Services becomes essential. You must, at minimum, sign up for a Free licensed account. Without one, you cannot share any of your work created on the Desktop. Figure 3-1 shows you what a typical Power BI Desktop screen looks like.

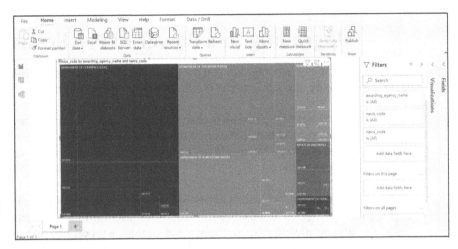

FIGURE 3-1:
The Power BI
Desktop.

Adding a Power BI Free license

Power BI Free is your entry-level license to Power BI. To get the Free license, you must first have a registered user account. Power BI gives a user 10 gigabytes of storage, which helps host Power BI reports and standard content types for analysis, including Excel workbooks.

WARNING

Because Microsoft is supplying the services for free, you also have some hard performance and storage limits. A report cannot exceed a gigabyte. Besides that, the report refresh rate is eight times a day. A user or an organization must wait at least 30 minutes between completing an entire refresh operation to restart the cycle all over again.

Though Power BI Free is full of many free features that competitors charge for, Microsoft limits the products' most crucial components — those that deal with collaboration. You cannot share any of your reports or dashboards with other users using Free services. Additionally, you cannot view any reports or dashboards created by Professional or Premium licensed users.

One last limitation has to do with integration. If you're looking to integrate with Microsoft 365 or export reports to formats such as PowerPoint or CSV files, you must upgrade to the Pro version. Once you're ready to upgrade to Pro, your integration and export opportunities increase.

Why bother with Power BI Free? You can still publish a report to the web. Your Report output will be available at `https://app.powerbi.com`. The result is available to anyone with an Internet connection, which means limited security. Therefore, any corporate data is probably off limits for public viewing, forcing one to upgrade to Power BI Pro.

Upgrading to a Power BI Pro license

You might assume that you now have access to a treasure chest full of new features by upgrading to the Pro license. That is not the case.

The Power BI Pro license is charged based on a per-user license basis. Often, organizations and individuals buy the stand-alone license. (There is one exception: when you buy a Microsoft 365 E5 license, each user gains access to the full version of Power BI Pro.)

REMEMBER

What you unlock with a Power BI Pro license is the ability to collaborate. Users can share reports and dashboards with other users with a Pro license. These users are still entitled to only 10 gigabytes of storage, a report can be a maximum of only a gigabyte, and the report refresh rate is the same as with the Free license. But with Pro, you gain the ability to integrate with Microsoft 365 Groups and Teams, an essential ingredient for secure collaboration not offered with the Free license. That way, you can use collaborative workspaces and configure reports and dashboards for delivery to permissible end users. Figure 3-2 provides you with an example of the Power BI Pro user experience.

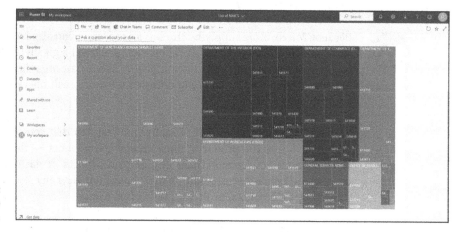

FIGURE 3-2:
The Power BI Pro user experience.

TIP

The Free license undoubtedly limits collaboration and security. If either feature is necessary, you have no choice but to consider the Pro license. Because a user can create and author content beyond just your personal use, most organizations, from start-up to Fortune 100, adopt Power BI Pro for those involved in business intelligence and analytics deployments.

Going all in with a Power BI Premium license

Suppose that your organization has a lot of data. You may even want to host large datasets and require storage for extensive Reports and Dashboard outputs. Additionally, you may have many users collaborating, not just one or two cherry picking data occasionally. That's when you need to consider Power BI Premium.

Until March 2021, Microsoft offered only one version of Power BI Premium. Licensing at that point was consumption based. The Capacity licensing plan offered an organization hosting rights in their premium workspace. A dataset could be as extensive as 50 gigabytes. Also, the organization received as much as 100 terabytes in disk storage capacity.

Fast-forward to 2021, when an additional Premium offering, called Power BI Premium per User, was introduced to complement the consumption plan. Premium per User extended both the capacity requirements as well as the features offered in the Pro license to those who need more storage for big data analytics without being tied to a single location or having rules that tie usage to the storage limits.

TIP

Power BI Pro and Premium per User licenses offer the same core features, except for storage allocation. You can publish reports and dashboard-based content to other workspaces, share dashboards and reports, and subscribe to other user reports and dashboards. Keep one catch in mind: Only users with like-kind licensing can collaborate. Power BI Pro users can collaborate only among themselves. Similarly, only Power BI Premium User licenses can work together. That said, if your organization commits to a Power BI Premium Capacity plan, you must purchase a Power BI Pro license per user to publish content into Power BI Premium Capacity.

Premium per User comes with a few added features intended to accelerate business intelligence scalability. The most obvious difference is that each user can build a data model having up to 100 gigabytes. Refresh rate abilities increase from 8 times per day to 48 times per day. Report outputs can be paginated as well.

What truly separates Free, Pro, and Premium is Microsoft's integration of advanced artificial intelligence (AI) capabilities, including text analytics, image detection, and automated machine learning. These features are exclusive to Premium offerings. Furthermore, adaptability with other models and data repositories is available only in Premium per User or Capacity options. (Features here include XMLA endpoint read/write connectivity, various data flow options, and the ability to analyze data stored in Azure Data Lake or Azure Synapse.) Also, users can begin to enforce business rules with application lifecycle management using the per User license, which isn't available in the Pro license.

Governance, administration, and even more storage allotment separate the Per User and Per Capacity options for Premium. Whereas a Premium per User license is geographically bound, Per Capacity allows for multi-geographical deployment management. Users who want to bring their own key (BYOK) can do so only with the Capacity option. Finally, for those who need autoscaling, should the Power BI Premium Capacity exceed allotment, integration with Azure Cloud is available. Bear in mind that by enabling autoscaling, you also need to obtain an additional account for Azure. With Premium per Capacity, each data model can grow to 400 gigabytes, with a storage cap at 100 terabytes.

On the Road with Power BI Mobile

No matter which license you own, you can access the Power BI Mobile app available for Windows, Apple iOS, and Google Android mobile devices. Those users who want to access and view live Power BI reports, dashboards, and datasets based on their licensed plan can do so with the native mobile BI app. Regardless of which version of Power BI you're authorized for, you can carry out these three business goals:

>> **Connect to data.** Users can monitor their data directly from their mobile devices, whether that data is on-premises or housed in the cloud. Depending on what type of reports and dashboards you've created, you can monitor KPIs and report updates anytime, anywhere. Most important, data is still secure regardless of the device when you integrate with application management features such as Microsoft Intune.

>> **Visualize and extend your search.** Though you author reports and dashboards for users using Power BI Desktop, users can view live dashboards and reports on their mobile devices. Users can leverage built-in AI features that support question-and-answer querying if a user wants to drill down into the data. Data is also filterable based on geography and context of use.

>> **Collaborate from anywhere.** A user doesn't need to be glued to the desktop to collaborate. Assuming that you have the correct permissions, you can collaborate with your team using live data to produce new outputs, including reports, dashboards, and KPIs.

Figure 3-3 illustrates a list of recent reports and dashboards saved to Power BI Pro and accessed using Power BI Mobile. The dashboard titled NAICS lists all contracts issued by four government agencies in fiscal year 2020 and 2021. The data can be updated in real time from the data source, if necessary.

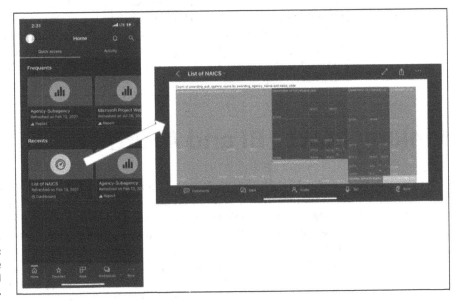

FIGURE 3-3: An example of Power BI Mobile output.

Working with Power BI Report Server

Some organizations — government agencies, healthcare institutes, and finance operations, for example — cannot risk their data being available in a shared data repository. To protect sensitive data while using Power BI, Microsoft developed an on-premises alternative for Premium Capacity users, called Power BI Report Server. Users can use their hardware to host the Power BI platform. The offering allows users to publish and share Power BI reports and native SQL Server Reporting Services outputs within the confines of an organization's firewall.

REMEMBER

Should you require heightened security and want to run your business intelligence operations following your governance practices, including policies and rules, Power BI Report Server is the only option with oomph behind it. If you want to transition from on-premises to the cloud, Power BI Report Server lets you, thanks to numerous autoscaling features. Your ability to map capacity from on-premises to the cloud should be seamless because mapping CPU vCore capacity (the power available per processor) is a known prerequisite.

WARNING

Power BI Premium Capacity licensing can become expensive very quickly. At a minimum of $5,000 per computer processor, plus Power BI Pro licenses, an organization's leaders may want to wait to ensure that it needs the added features. If you're buying Power BI Premium Capacity because of Power BI Report Server, you might have an alternative to procuring Power BI Premium Capacity to save you money. If your organization has an active Software Assurance agreement with Microsoft that includes SQL Server Enterprise Edition, you're entitled to Power BI Report Server at no cost.

Linking Power BI and Azure

Let us not forget that all Microsoft cloud applications ultimately use Azure, the cloud platform that supports storage, security, and application management. With so many modern applications requiring analytic outputs, Microsoft recognized that an API could complement its Power BI offerings with Azure. Called Power BI Embedded, this Premium Power BI feature requires an Azure account to be associated with the enterprise license. Reports and dashboards published in a Power BI workspace can be deployable via API to a web page or application. With Power BI Embedded, end users don't need a Power BI Pro license to view the content so long as they embed the targeted content within the Webpage or Web applications. Reports and dashboards can be customized to meet user experience specifications at the organization level. Best yet, content can be configured based on user identity and row-level security using Microsoft Azure Active Directory, the cloud-based identity management platform.

In summary, there are so many versions of Power BI that in some ways, it is an embarrassment of riches. Microsoft provides end users with the tools their organizations needs based on size to transform raw data into knowledge.

Chapter **4**

Power BI: The Highlights

L ike a state fair judge evaluating a prize cake layered with many ingredients, Power BI requires that its users familiarize themselves with the features baked into the business intelligence (BI) solution. Virtually all users who interact with Power BI start with the Desktop version. Users can mold the data the way they want by following the old saying "Practice makes perfect" by way of ingestion and modeling. Whether you're manipulating the data to make the model just right, tackling data transformation via wrangling, or trying to create beautiful visualizations, the heavy lift is desktop-based. Seldom does the Power BI partici-pant start using online services unless the dataset was previously created for sharing and collaboration. In this chapter, you learn the key features of Power BI Desktop and Services to know precisely when and why you need to use a specific product version.

Power BI Desktop: A Top-Down View

Power BI Desktop is the hub of all self-directed end user activities. The user installs the application on a Windows based desktop to connect to, transform, and visualize data. The data sources users can connect to aren't limited to local repositories — users can aggregate sources locally with third-party data that is structured or unstructured to create data models. The data model lets the user build a visual representation of the stored datasets. When you have many visuals, the user can derive reports or dashboards for analysis. A typical usage of Power BI Desktop is

>> Ingest data across one or more data sources.

>> Model data to create reports and dashboards.

>> Refine, cleanse, and visualize the data by way of analysis.

>> Create reports for individual consumption.

REMEMBER

Though you can complete these activities online, the Desktop platform is purpose-built for individual user consumption or development work — it isn't intended for groups. Not until the user is ready to share the products created using Desktop do you need to expose anything to Power BI Services.

The end user gains access to three distinct views in Power BI Desktop: Report, Data, and Model. Figure 4-1 shows you the left-side navigation to find these views in Power BI Desktop. Though these features are also available in Services, feature richness for personal analysis is significantly greater in Power BI Desktop.

Model view

Data view

Report view

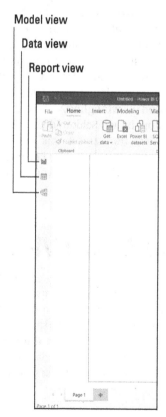

Each Power BI Desktop view carries out specific tasks:

>> **Report:** You can create reports and visualizations after you've ingested and modeled the data. Users spend most of their time here post-data ingestion, transformation, and modeling.

>> **Data:** You can find all data ingested, or migrated, from tables, measures, and data sources associated with reports and visualizations created here. Sources can be local to the desktop or from a third-party data source accessible over the web.

>> **Model:** Like creating a relational data model in Microsoft SQL Server, Azure SQL Server, or even Microsoft Access, you can fully manage the relationships among the structured tables you've created after you've ingested the necessary data using Power BI.

Ingesting Data

Without data, you can't do all that much with Power BI — data truly is the main ingredient of your end-state recipe. Whether you're trying to create a chart or a dashboard or you're posing questions with Questions and Answers (Q&A), you must have data that comes from an underlying dataset. Each dataset comes from a particular data source, either found on your local desktop (if you're using Power BI Desktop) or acquired from other online data sources. These sources may be Microsoft-based applications, a third-party database, or even other application data feeds. In Power BI Desktop, you either use the Power BI Ribbon (shown in Figure 4-2) or click the Power BI Data Navigation icon (shown in Figure 4-3), to access a data source.

Files or databases?

In Power BI, you can create or import content yourself. When it comes to the type of content users can create or import, it boils down to either files or data stored in a database. A word to the wise: Files can be a bit more complicated than databases. You need to get the data, transform the data, and then import the data into a readable form. Suppose that you want to import an Excel or .cvs file that includes many data types. First, you load the data into Power BI. Then you format the data into a Power BI-ready format in conjunction with dataflows, which transforms the data to support a data model. Finally, you query the data using the Get and Transform feature in Power Query.

FIGURE 4-2:
Getting data from
the Power BI
Ribbon.

FIGURE 4-3:
Accessing a data
source using the
Data Navigation
icon and landing
page.

Now, what if the data you're trying to import isn't structured or perhaps you don't want it housed in Power BI Desktop? Your best choice is to use native Microsoft options such as OneDrive for Business. Such a choice offers the most flexibility in mapping data through application interoperability and application integration. If you prefer keeping your data on a local drive, you can do that as well.

Where you store your data makes a difference when dealing with data refresh. Consider the frequency of data updates when selecting the data storage location. When the data is on your local desktop, you'll generally find better performance, even with large datasets. With shared data accessible over the Internet, you are reliant on network connectivity and other users accessing the data source. Data stored on the desktop is managed by one person — you.

You don't always have to store the data directly in Power BI Desktop. You can always use Desktop to query and load data from external sources. If you prefer to extend your data model with calculated measures or a specific relationship, consider importing the Power BI Desktop file into a Power BI Online site for easier manipulation.

Databases are a bit different from files because you connect to a live data source — sources requiring an Internet connection which are made available to either a small subset of users or to many users for consumption. This is especially true when the database is available "as a service," such as Azure SQL Database, Azure Cosmos DB, Azure Synapse Analytics, or Azure HDInsight. Because the data is live, all that a data professional must do is appropriately model the data first. Once satisfied with the intended model, the user can explore the data, manipulate the data, and create data visualizations.

If you want to explore a plethora of data sources beyond those offered by Microsoft, including open source and third-party options, you need to utilize Power BI Desktop. Online Services offers a narrow range of options, whereas Desktop offers over 100 options for you to choose from.

The term *data* gets thrown around a lot — you're probably already confused about data, datasets, dataflows, and even databases. And believe me, I throw lots of data words at you in this book. When it comes to data ingestion, "dataset" and "data source" are treated the same, even though they're actually just distant relatives that support the same mission.

You create a dataset in Power BI whenever you use the Get Data feature. It's what allows you to connect and import data, including from live data sources. A dataset stores all the details about the data source and its security credentials. A data source is where all the data stored in the dataset is derived, which can be a proprietary application data source, a relational database, or a stand-alone file storage alternative such as a hard drive or file share.

Building data models

Some BI tools aren't data-model-dependent; Power BI isn't in that camp. Power BI is a data-model-based reporting tool. First, let me help you understand what makes a data model unique.

These are the key characteristics of data models:

» Tables hold meaningful data.

» Relationships exist between the loaded tables with data.

» Formulas, also known as *measures*, apply business rules to the raw data to extract, transform, and load data to create meaningful business insights.

REMEMBER

Power BI isn't alone in its inclusion of these attributes that create a data model. Other Microsoft products, including Power Pivot for Excel and enterprise BI tools, offer this feature set.

You might wonder why you even need a data model. Going back to my analogy of the cake recipe from the beginning of this chapter, if you follow the recipe, it's easy to make the same cake time and time again. When the cake ingredients vary, though, inconsistency leads to data irregularity and continual rebuild efforts. And, like the cake's failure to win any culinary awards, the data needs handling and refinement. With BI solutions such as Power BI, users are able to streamline business issues with a data model.

To summarize, models are useful for these reasons:

» **Reusability:** Users can solve a reporting requirement or business challenge using a formulaic approach without having to reinvent queries or rebuild datasets.

» **Management:** Business users are in a position to manage the data on their own after models are built. Seldom is a database expert or technical professional needed to handle infrastructure requirements.

» **Adaptive models:** You can build a logical model with minimum code. Changes are accommodative to technical and business requirements, including the use of measures (formulas) and rule sets.

Though you can find many tools on the market, including Microsoft Excel and BI-based reporting tools, not all tools offer to build data models. A BI tool not incorporating data models requires the analyst or data engineer to generate a query to fetch the data. Though many of these tools have graphical user interfaces to support query generation, you need to reinvent the process each time you use it, with little extensibility available. In Power BI, the relationships you need to keep track of are mapped out in the Model Viewer with the help of a data model. (See Figure 4-4, which models a single table named Awards.)

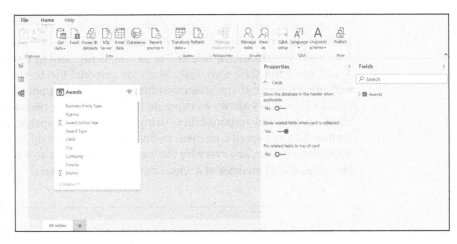

FIGURE 4-4:
Example of a data
Model Viewer.

REMEMBER

You know the old saying "Reuse, reduce, recycle"? It's synonymous with the data model. A *data model* is a reusable asset that, when tweaked a little depending on the business need, can dramatically reduce development efforts and cut costs. Sometimes, you get lucky and can build new assets on top of the existing solution. At other times, recycling the asset with a few enhancements can score you the desired results.

Analyzing data

Before sharing any data with a team, you first have to carry out your own, personal data analysis using Power BI Desktop. You can conduct several forms of analysis. At the most basic level, when the data enters the system, you have to review it to make sure it looks right and appears as it should. If it doesn't, you manipulate the data by cleansing it — a task often carried out by an analyst or engineer. The process often takes a while because it's quite laborious — kind of like preparing a big holiday dinner. Yet when the results are available, they're easy to read in a matter of seconds. As much as this strategy sounds like a hassle, the results are what you want to aim for in business intelligence.

Once the data source has been cleaned up and you've mapped the data into refined datasets, it's time to create the necessary visualizations. Here I'm talking about pictures that can serve as examples of your data sources — charts, maps, indicators, and gauges. You'll find these visuals in deliverables such as reports and dashboards. Even the Q&A feature in Power BI produces visuals after you ask focused questions.

Though Power BI has an extensive catalog of visuals available, you may want more options for complex visuals. Industry-specific options that aren't part of Power BI Desktop or Online may also be available. To see more options, go to the Microsoft AppSource at https://appsource.microsoft.com.

You eventually want to get to a point in your use of Power BI where you can rapidly generate reports and access data using dashboards. A Power BI designer builds out dashboard visualizations, referred to as *tiles*, using data in reports and datasets. A user can build their own dashboards for personal use or share the dashboard with others. (*Note:* If you share dashboards, security credentials are tied to each visual.) Figure 4-5 shows an example of a collection of tiles across a dashboard based on role and responsibility. Using the data in Snapshot format (a way to capture data at a specific moment in time) you've worked up in Desktop or shared with others online, any everyday business user should be able to carry out a quick (and productive) analysis of a whole series of large datasets.

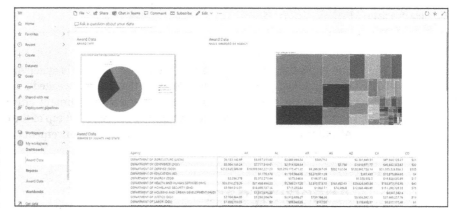

FIGURE 4-5:
A sample
dashboard that
aggregates many
visual sources.

Creating and publishing items

You may want to learn more about Power BI by trying out the free Desktop client to tackle more complex data projects. And, at some point, you might want to post that data project on the web in a read-only format to a limited audience. And you certainly can for free. Suppose, however, that you want others to edit and collaborate with you beyond read-only support. In that case, you must pay for such features.

When you publish items from Power BI Desktop to Power BI Services, the files are workspace bound. Similarly, if you've produced any reports, they appear in Report view. Datasets migrate from the desktop with the same name, as do any reports to the workspace. The relationship is often a one-to-one relationship, with rare exceptions. (For more about importing and publishing various types of data, visualizations, and reports, see Chapter 5.)

In Power BI Desktop, you can publish your files by choosing Publish ⇨ Publish to Power BI from the main menu or selecting Publish on the Ribbon. (See Figure 4-6 and Figure 4-7.)

FIGURE 4-6:
Publishing items using the Power BI Desktop File menu.

FIGURE 4-7:
Publishing items using the Power BI Desktop Ribbon.

REMEMBER When you publish an item from the Power BI Desktop to Services, you're performing the same action as using the Get Data feature. That means connecting to a data source, uploading a file from Power BI Desktop, and sending it to Services.

WARNING Saving in Power BI Services doesn't make changes to the original Power BI Desktop file. Therefore, don't expect any updates when you or your colleagues add, delete, or change any dataset, visualization, or report.

Services: Far and Wide

Services aren't intended for a single user, whereas Desktop supports individual usage exclusively. The purpose of Services is to allow the individual user to publish data from the desktop and then share it with user groups. In a perfect Microsoft world, some users want to manipulate that data over time. The data grows, requiring either a Pro or Premium license.

REMEMBER

The Desktop user can continually update their data product, whether it is a dataset, data model, or report, after they publish it online using Power BI Services. However, Power BI Services doesn't refresh the data at the desktop level. Therefore, it's up to you to keep data in sync.

Services offers four significant product features beyond Desktop for multiuser access that Desktop doesn't support: the ability to view and edit reports, access to dashboards based on credentials, collaboration among users, and data refresh options depending on product type purchased.

Viewing and editing reports

The report lifecycle generally begins when a user sets up a dataset and builds a functional data model in Power BI Desktop. The user also crafts one or more reports. Once a report is developed, you can then publish it to Power BI Services. The workflow is typical, as refinement with complex data makes it easier to build a report deliverable offline. You can assume that you don't need an Internet connection to access the dataset.

Sometimes you might require online services access because you have large datasets from third-party applications. Everyday use cases include when you have a subscription to CRM or ERP solutions requiring data connections. Assuming that you are part of an organization and have access to a service (SaaS) app, you'll find someone in your organization whose job it is to publish apps. That person generally distributes the app, granting you access to specific features and data. With Power BI Services, you connect to these apps to generate reports specific to your business need.

REMEMBER

Though you can directly connect to data sources such as databases, files, and folders in Power BI Desktop, applications are different. You need Power BI Services to access app data.

Sharing your results

With Power BI Services, you publish your data to the Internet for a reason: You want to share with colleagues and collaborate. Once you create reports or dashboards, you can share them with users who are given Power BI Services accounts. The type of license in force dictates how the user can interact with the data, of course. Some users may be able to view only the reports and dashboards, and others may be able to collaborate fully. For you and your colleagues to manage a report or dashboard, a workspace may be established. You bundle and distribute the deliverable as an app. Once you share the dataset, it becomes the basis for a new set of dashboards or reports.

REMEMBER

A Power BI report, by default, supplies a holistic view of a dataset. It has visuals representing findings from one or more datasets. Reports may hold a single visualization or many.

Seeing why reports are valuable

The basis of a report is a single dataset, whereas a dashboard collects many reports. With reports, you get a laser-focused view of a topic. Moreover, data is static in a non-data-model-based application; such is not the case in a tool such as Power BI. The visuals are dynamic because, as the underlying data updates, so do the reports in real time. In addition, a user is free to interact with the visuals as little or as much as they want in a report. They can also use reports to filter and query in a variety of different ways within Power BI. Reports are highly interactive and even customizable based on your organizational role and responsibility.

Accessing reports from many directions

You should consider two basic scenarios when it comes to report access: Either you created the report yourself and imported it from Power BI Desktop or someone has shared a report with you. Any report that you imported is on your My Workspace. (See Figure 4-8.)

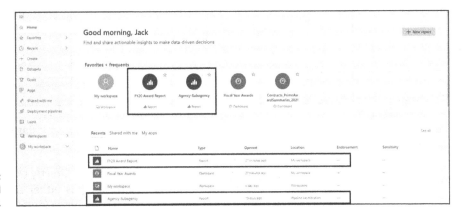

FIGURE 4-8:
Reports imported to the workspace.

Within the framework of these two scenarios, access might come about as

>> Reports shared directly, for example, by email

>> Reports shared as part of an app

>> Reports accessible from the dashboard

>> Recent or favorite reports, dashboards, apps, and workspaces accessible from the Services Navigation pane.

Among these options, the three most common ways users view and edit reports when collaborating are a) sharing directly b) sharing as part of an app and c) accessing the dashboard.

To open a report that is shared with you, follow these steps:

1. **Open Power BI Services, located at** https://app.powerbi.com.

2. **Select Home in the Navigation pane.**

   The Home canvas appears.

3. **Click the Shared with Me icon.**

4. **Then, select a report found on the Shared with Me page.**

   In Figure 4-9, you can see one dashboard and one report. The report is named FY20 Award Report. While you only see one report on the canvas, there are in fact several reports available upon clicking the Report Card. In Power BI, a single report can contain many sub-reports.

FIGURE 4-9:
Accessing
reports directly.

Report   Dashboard

The second choice is receiving an app from someone directly or accessing the app using Microsoft's AppSource. You access these apps either from the Power BI home screen or from the Apps and Shared with Me items found on the Navigation pane.

Someone who wants to open an app must first either acquire a Power BI Pro license or have an app workspace stored in a Power BI Premium capacity. In other words, if you're looking to use apps under the free model, it isn't possible.

WARNING

To access reports from an app, you need to navigate to the app source. Here's one example of how you'd do it:

1. **Point your browser to the app source's location, such as** https://appsource.microsoft.com.

2. **Select the Power Platform check box.**

3. **Using the Search box at the top of the screen, search for** *Microsoft sample Sales and Marketing*.

4. **Click the Get it Now button.**

5. **On the new page that appears, choose Continue ⇨ Install to install the app in the Apps canvas.**

6. **Open the app in the Apps canvas or Home canvas.**

   You should see the assigned app under Apps. (See Figure 4-10.)

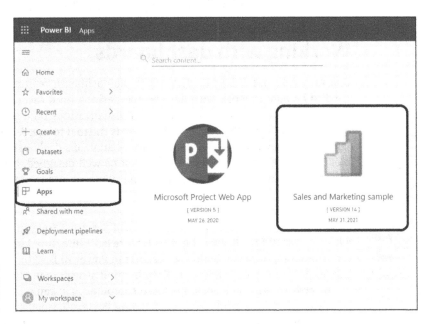

FIGURE 4-10:
Access app from
Apps menu in
Power BI.

You can also open reports from a dashboard. Most times, a tile is a snapshot of a pinned report. When you double-click the tile, a report will open. To open a report from a dashboard, follow these steps:

1. **From the dashboard, select any tile.**

   In the example (see Figure 4-11), the tile selected is NAICS Awarded By Agency using the treemap.

2. **Drill down into a more granular view of the report data by clicking on data points within a report.**

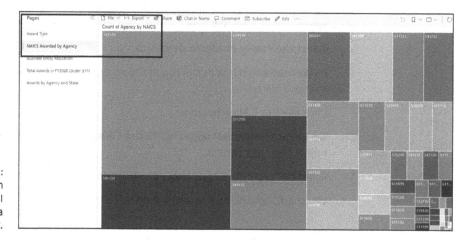

FIGURE 4-11:
Drill down from
the Power BI
dashboard for a
report.

Working with dashboards

One reason to use Power BI Services is the dashboard feature. It's all well and good to be able to work with data on the desktop on a case-by-case basis, but suppose that you want to aggregate your visualizations on a single page using a canvas. In that case, the Dashboard feature is the tool to use. A dashboard lets you tell a story from a series of visualizations — think of a dashboard as a single-page menu at the restaurant. A dashboard must be well designed, because it contains the critical highlights so that a reader can drill down into related reports and view details later.

REMEMBER

Dashboards are available only with Power BI Services. You can create dashboards with a Power BI Free license, but this feature isn't integrated into Power BI Desktop. Therefore, once you build your reports in Power BI Desktop, you need to publish outputs to Power BI Services. Keep in mind as well that, although dashboards can be created only on a desktop-based computer, you can view and share dashboards on all device form-factors, including Power BI Mobile. When you want to create a dashboard, you need to have at least one or more reports pinned to a blank canvas. Each tile (see Figure 4-12) represents a single report based on a single dataset.

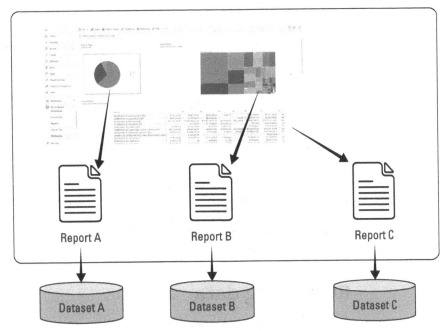

FIGURE 4-12:
Architecture of a
dashboard.

Collaborating inside Power BI Services

The transition from Power BI Desktop to Power BI Services is partially due to collaboration — you're unable to collaborate with others using Power BI Desktop. You may want to share with a small subset of users, or perhaps the group of users you're looking to share information with is distributed. Depending on the Power BI Services option you're working with, you have these options:

» **Using workspace:** The most common way to share reports and dashboards is by using the workspace. Suppose that another user is given access to a report or dashboard. In that case, the user either views or edits the workspace area in Power BI Services.

» **Using Microsoft Teams**: Using the Chat feature in Teams allows for collaborating on reports and dashboards with Power BI.

» **Distributing your reports and dashboards via an app**: If your results are focused, the user can build a single app and create a working executable for sharing among other users.

» **Embedding reports and dashboards on websites:** Sometimes, the reports and dashboards you create might be helpful for targeted public consumption on an external or internal facing website. You can create an iteration of a Power BI report or dashboard that's viewable. Any user who visits that website may view the data if they're assigned permission to do so.

>> **Printing reports:** When in doubt, you can always print your reports and distribute paper copies. Of course, each time the data is refreshed, you need to print a new copy of the report. For dashboards, each output is printed separately.

>> **Creating a template app:** If your deliverables are repetitious, distribute them so that Power BI users can access them using the Microsoft AppSource. One must assume that these items are publicly consumable for other businesses to use.

No matter which collaboration options you select, a Power BI Pro license or higher is required. The license is nonnegotiable because content needs to be implemented in a Premium capacity. Though license requirements can vary for viewing items, the ability to edit and manage the outputs mandates, at minimum, a Power BI Professional license.

Refreshing data

Every time you access a report or a dashboard on Power BI Services, you must query the data source. If there are new data points, the results are updated in the dataset as part of the visualization. Depending on the refresh requirements, one or more processes might be needed. The refresh process consists of several phases, depending on the storage operation required for the dataset. You have two concepts to consider: storage mode as well as data refresh type.

Storage modes and dataset types

Power BI offers several modes for allowing access to data in a dataset:

>> **Import mode:** Datasets are imported from the original data source into the dataset. Power BI can query the reports and dashboards submitted to the dataset and return results from the imported tables and columns. You may find this to be a snapshot copy — a dataset representing a moment in time, in other words. Each time Power BI copies the data, you can query the data to fetch the changes.

>> **DirectQuery/LiveConnect:** Two connection types that don't rely on importing data directly are DirectQuery and LiveConnect. Data results come in from the data source whenever the report or dashboard queries the dataset. Power BI will then transform the raw data into usable datasets. Only DirectQuery mode, though, requires that Power BI not use queries using the Power Query Editor Extract Transform Load (ETL) engine. The reason for this is that the queries are processed directly using Analysis Services, without having to consume resources. Data refreshes aren't required because no imports occur in the

Power BI Desktop environment. Features that are still updated include tiles and reports, whereby the data updates about every hour. The schedule can be changed to accommodate business needs.

>> **Push mode:** In Push mode, there's no formal definition for a data source, so there's no requirement for a data refresh. Instead, you push the data into the dataset through an external service, which is quite common for real-time analytics processes in Power BI.

Data refresh types

For a Power BI user, data refreshes are defined as importing data from the original data sources into one or more datasets. The refresh is based on a schedule or can be in real time. Depending on the procured Power BI license, the refresh rate varies from 8 updates to as many as 48 per day. You're limited to 8 daily dataset refreshes for shared capacity, which are executed by the schedule using a plan. The updates reset daily at 12:01 AM.

REMEMBER

Licensed users are limited to eight refreshes per day for Power BI Services Free and Power BI Services Pro. If you buy Power BI Services Premium Capacity or Power BI Services Premium per User, your refresh allotment increases to 48 refreshes per day.

A Power BI refresh operation can have multiple refresh types, including a standard data refresh, OneDrive refresh, query cache refresh, tile refresh, dashboard refresh, and course visualization refresh. Power BI decides the individual refresh steps with each of these examples. A precedence must be applied based on operational complexity, as you can see in Table 4-1.

TABLE 4-1   Comparison of Power BI Refresh Types

Storage Mode	Data Refresh	OneDrive Refresh	Query Caches	Tile Refresh	Report Visuals
Import	Scheduled and add-on	Yes, for connected data	If enabled on Premium Capacity	Automatic and on-demand	No
DirectQuery	Not applicable	Yes, for connected data	If enabled on Premium Capacity	Automatic and on-demand	No
LiveConnect	Not applicable	Yes, for connected data	If enabled on Premium Capacity	Automatic and on-demand	Yes
Push	Not applicable	Not applicable	Not practical	Automatic and on-demand	No

REMEMBER

Regardless of the refresh approach, you must ensure that reports and dashboards use current data for a business to be successful. If, for some reason, you find that your data is stale, address the problem with the data owner or the gateway administrator.

When refreshing data, keep the following points in mind:

» For optimal performance, schedule refresh cycles for off-peak business hours, especially if you use Power BI Premium.

» Consider the number of refreshes your organization is allowed with your license and the volatility of your data. Refresh only when you know it makes sense.

» Make sure the dataset refresh doesn't exceed the refresh duration, or else the data won't refresh properly, causing business issues with your options.

» Optimize your data by including only the data needed to operate in the environment necessary for your reports and dashboards. Any extra overhead can be costly, especially when it comes to memory and processing overhead consumption.

» Apply the appropriate security settings for both Power BI Desktop and Power BI Services. The settings don't carry over from one environment to another.

» Be mindful of the visuals used as more outputs result in performance degradation and potential data refresh issues down the line.

» Use only reliable data gateways to connect data sources, whether on-premise or cloud-based. If data refresh failures happen, you may need to deploy additional infrastructure to handle needed capacity.

» If data refresh failures happen, put a notification method in place so that you can quickly deal with any technical concerns.

2

It's Time to Have a Data Party

Chapter **5**

Preparing Data Sources

The modern organization has a lot of data. So, it should go without saying that enterprise software vendors such as Microsoft have built data source connectors to help organizations import data into applications such as Power BI. You quickly realize that connecting to data sources isn't necessarily the tricky part — it's often the data transformation that takes a bit of time. After you figure out which method is best to prep and load the data into Power BI, you're well on your way to analyzing and visualizing the data in your universe. In this chapter, you learn the methods you can apply to prep and load data using Power BI Desktop and Services.

Getting Data from the Source

Without a data source, it's hard to use Microsoft Power BI. You can connect to your own data source or use one of the many connectors Microsoft makes available to users as part of Power BI Desktop or Services. Before you begin loading data, you must first grasp what the business requirements are for your data source. For example, is the data source local to your desktop with occasional updates? Is your data perhaps coming from a third-party data source that supplies real-time feeds? The requirements for both scenarios are vastly different.

Microsoft continually adds data connectors to its Desktop and Services platform. In fact, don't be surprised to find at least one or two new connectors released monthly as part of the regular Power BI update. As a result, Power BI offers well over 100 data connectors. The most popular options include files, databases, and web services.

You can find a list of all available data sources at

https://docs.microsoft.com/en-us/power-bi/connect-data/power-bi-data-sources

To correctly map your data in Power BI, you must determine the exact nature of the data. For example, would you use the Excel Connector if the document type were meant for an Azure SQL database? That wouldn't produce the results you're looking for as a Power BI user.

Throughout *Microsoft Power BI For Dummies*, you find the use of a few supplemental datasets. You can find these datasets on the Dummies.com website by going to www.dummies.com/go/mspowerbifd. In addition, in the downloadable Zip file, you will find an Excel file named FiscalYearAwards.xlsx used for most exercises.

To connect to the FiscalYearAwards.xlsx file using the Excel Connector with Power BI Desktop, follow these steps:

1. **On the Excel Home tab, click either the Excel button or the Get Data button, and then choose Excel from the drop-down menu that appears, as shown in Figure 5-1.**

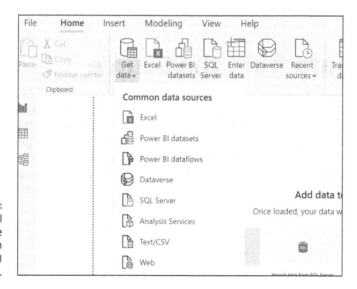

FIGURE 5-1: Finding the Excel Data File Connector in Power BI Desktop.

2. **In the Open window, navigate to the** `FiscalYearAwards.xlsx` **file, click to select it, and then click Open.**

3. **With the file open, head to the Navigator and select both check boxes on the left: Prime Awards and Sub Awards.**

   The window should now look like Figure 5-2.

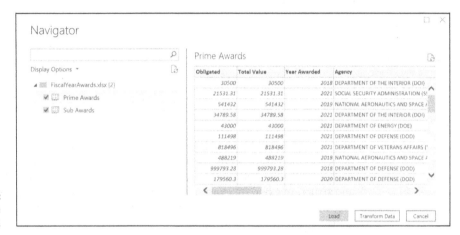

FIGURE 5-2:
Selecting data in
the Navigator.

4. **Click the Transform Data button.**

   Notice that I didn't tell you to press the Load button. If you'd gone with Load, you'd have to make modifications to your dataset manually. With Transform, Power BI does the difficult work on your behalf. (I talk more about data transformation in Chapter 7, but for now the focus is on knowing how to prepare and load data.)

   After you click Transform Data, a new interface appears called the Power Query Editor. It's what loads the data from the two Excel spreadsheet tabs you just clicked on from the previous Power BI screens. You'll find the experience to be like the one shown in Figure 5-3.

REMEMBER

When you load data into Power BI Desktop, the data is stored as a snapshot in time. To ensure that you view the latest data, you click the Refresh Preview button on the home screen every so often.

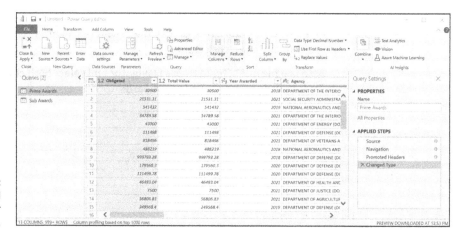

FIGURE 5-3:
Your data, loaded
into the Power
Query Editor.

Loading folders with data inside them can present a few unique challenges. Though you can point to a folder and ingest just about any type of file, it's another matter to replicate a folder structure using the Power Query Editor. When you load data in Power BI stored inside a folder, you should ensure that the same file type and structure exist. An example is a series of Microsoft Excel or Google Sheet files that would be complimentary. To make sure that happens, be sure to follow these steps:

1. **Go to the Home tab on the Ribbon and click the Get Data button.**

2. **Choose All ⇨ Folder from the menu that appears.**

   Want to try another way? Go to the Home tab on the Ribbon, click New Source, choose More from the menu that appears, and then choose Folder.

3. **Whichever way you select Folder, your next step is to click the Connect button. (See Figure 5-4.).**

   Pressing the Connect button enables access to a single data source.

4. **Locate the folder path specific to where you've stored files on your desktop, then browse to the location where you've placed the file similar to** C:\DummiesFiles\TrainingNAICS.

   The files from the folder you just selected load into a new screen, as shown in Figure 5-5.

5. **Select one or more tables that have loaded.**

6. **Once the tables have been selected, click the Combine and Transform Data button.**

   The datasets from the TrainingNAICS.xlsx are now loaded into Power Query Editor.

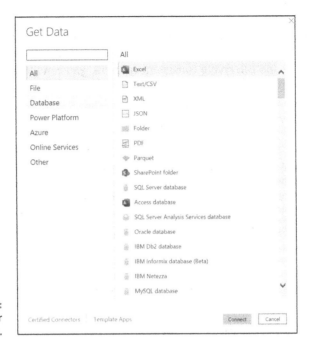

FIGURE 5-4:
Selecting Folder
from Get Data.

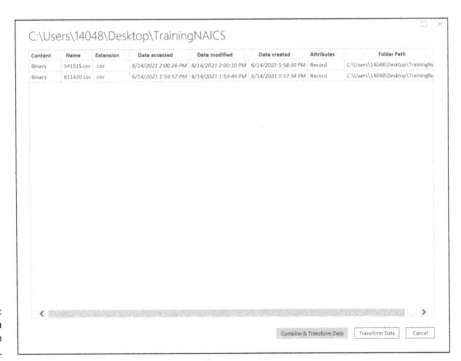

FIGURE 5-5:
Files from a
folder load into
Power BI.

The difference between the Combine and Transform Data option and the Transform Data option comes down to the file type and structure. Assuming that each file is similar and can create consistent columns, you can likely use the Combine and Transform Data option to bring everything into a single file. Otherwise, you're better served using the Transform Data option, since there is usually a single file structure.

By now you can tell that you don't need to do much in order to load a file, folder, database, or web source into Power BI. Most users, if they can point to the file path or if they know the database connection and security credentials or if they know the URL and associated parameters, can configure their data sources in no time. Power BI's Power Query feature automatically detects the nuances in the connection and applies the proper transformations.

Managing Data Source Settings

Commonly, your dataset requirements change over time. That means if the data source changes, so will some of the settings that were initially loaded when you configured Power BI. Suppose that you move the TrainingNAICS folder with the files 611420.xlsx and 54151S.xlsx from C:\Desktop to C:\Documents. Such a change in folder location would require you to modify the data source settings. You can go about making these changes in one of two ways:

1. **Select each query under Queries on the left.**

2. **Locate Query Settings on the right side of the interface.**

3. **Under Applied Steps, click Source, as shown in Figure 5-6.**

   Doing so brings up a window pointing to the file path and file source.

4. **Make the updates necessary to match the new requirements.**

   Change the file type or path of the original file for each query with this option.

FIGURE 5-6:
Using the Applied Steps area to update the data source settings.

Though the steps outlined here may seem easy at first blush, they might become laborious because you need to make a change to each file listed for each query. That process can be pretty time-consuming, and, if you have a lot of queries, you're bound to make errors, given the tedious nature of the work. That's why you want to consider an alternative option — one where you can change the source location in one fell swoop rather than tackle each query independently with this option. Follow these steps for the other method:

1. **On the Power Query Editor's Home tab, click the Data Source Settings button. (It's the one sporting a cog — see Figure 5-7.)**

   A new window opens to make the source location change.

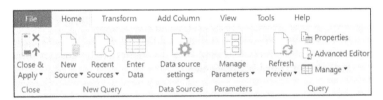

FIGURE 5-7: The Data Source Settings button.

2. **Select all files requiring a change in location by choosing Change Source.**

3. **Make the changes you want to the source location.**

4. **(Optional) Change and clear associated security credentials by selecting Edit Permissions or Clear Permissions in this interface.**

Working with Shared versus Local Datasets

So far, the focus in this chapter has been on local datasets that you handle creating and managing by using Power BI Desktop. After the dataset is published and shared with others — by way of either your own workspace or a shared one — the dataset is referred to as a *shared dataset*. Unlike with Power BI Desktop, where you have to continually update the dataset on the local hard drive, a shared dataset is stored on the cloud, which means that, whether it's stored in your workspace or with others, updates can be more consistent.

You can find many other benefits to using a shared dataset over a local dataset, including

>> Consistency across reports and dashboards

>> Reduction in dataset copying due to centralization of a data source

>> The ability to create new data sources from existing sources with little effort

REMEMBER

Though you may have your own needs with a dataset, after a dataset is shared with a team, the desired outputs might be different. In that case, you may want to create a single dataset and allow the other users to develop reports and dashboards from the single dataset.

TIP

Connecting to a published dataset in Power BI Services requires a user to have Build permission. You can also be a contributing member of a shared workspace where a dataset exists. Make sure the owner of the dataset provisions your access according to your business need.

You can connect to a shared dataset using either Power BI Desktop or Power BI Services. To accomplish this action, follow these steps:

1. **Using Power BI Desktop, either click the Power BI Datasets button on the Home Tab or click the tab's Get Data button and then choose Power BI Datasets from the menu that appears. (See Figure 5-8.).**

   The data is transferred from Power BI Desktop to Power BI Services for you to consume.

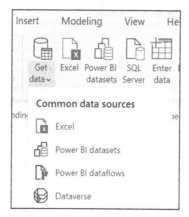

FIGURE 5-8:
Power BI datasets
navigation.

2. **With Power BI Services, you would first go to the workspace you've published your data to and then choose New ⇨ Report, as shown in Figure 5-9.**

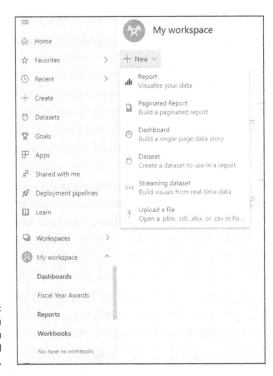

FIGURE 5-9: Connecting to a shared dataset in Power BI Services.

Whether you're using Power BI Desktop or Power BI Services, your ability to connect to a dataset without having to worry about data refresh issues or version control becomes a bit easier. You also have the choice to select Save a Copy in the Power BI Service next to any report in My Workspace or a shared workspace without having to re-create a dataset. This action is similar to connecting to a dataset using Power BI Desktop, because you create a report without the base data model.

WARNING

Don't be alarmed if you decide to use a shared dataset and then some buttons become inactive in Power BI Desktop. It happens because you're no longer able to make changes using Power Query Editor. As a result, the data view is also no longer visible. You can tell whether your dataset is shared or local, however, by looking in the lower right corner of the Power BI Desktop interface, where you can find the name of the dataset and the user accessing the data.

If you ever need to change from a shared dataset to a local dataset, follow these steps:

1. **Click the Transform Data label.**

2. **Select the Data Source Settings option.**

3. **Modify the data source settings to the dataset you want to connect to instead of the shared dataset.**

4. **Click the Change button once complete.**

Storage Modes

As you may have already guessed, you can consume data in many ways using Power BI Desktop and Power BI Services. The most common method is to import data into a data model. By importing the data in Power BI, you're copying the dataset locally until you commit to a data refresh. Though data files and folders can only be imported into Power BI, databases allow you to use a connection that supports more flexibility. Two alternatives exist with database connectivity:

>> **Import the data locally.** This supports data model caching as well as the ability to reduce number of connections and lookups. By ingesting the model, a user can use all Desktop features offered with Power BI.

>> **Create a connection to the data source with DirectQuery.** With this feature, the data isn't cached. Instead, the data source must be queried each time a data call is required. Most, but not all, data sources support DirectQuery.

You can use one of two other methods. One is called Live Connection: With this method, the goal is to use the analysis services integrated with Power BI Desktop or Power BI Services. Live Connection also supports calculation-based activities that occur within a data model.

The second alternative uses composite models. Now, suppose that a user must combine both importing data and DirectQuery, or there is a requirement to connect to multiple DirectQuery connections. In that case, you apply a composite model. You face some risks, though, when dealing with model security. Suppose, for example, you open a Power Bi Desktop file that is sent from an untrusted source. If the file contains a composite model, the information that someone retrieves from a single source using credentials from a user opening the file can be sent to another data source as part of the newly formed query. Therefore, it's vital to ensure that your data sources are correctly assigned to only those who need access to the sources.

Dual mode

The four storage modes — local storage, DirectQuery, Live Connection, and composite models — have data housed in a single location. It's either local to the user or bound to some server on a network in a data center or the cloud.

Looking back at the composite model, the storage mode property prescribes where tables are stored in the data model. To view the properties of a table, you can hover over a table. In Power BI, you can do this in either the Fields pane of a report or by accessing the Data view. You can also change the Model view in the Properties pane by finding the Advanced section.

You can choose one of three options for the storage model: Import, DirectQuery, or Dual. You might be wondering why you can't choose Live Connection or Composite as well. Simply put, those particular options are hybrid modes of Import and DirectQuery.

Dual mode isn't a hybrid mode — instead, it allows for a table to be cached and retrieved in DirectQuery mode when necessary. If another storage mode is used for another table, DirectQuery doesn't need usage. You'll find that Dual mode is beneficial when tables are similar between those imported and exclusively available using DirectQuery mode.

WARNING

If you must change storage modes, you might face some complications. For example, you won't revert later if you decide to go from DirectQuery mode or Dual mode to Import mode. Furthermore, if you decide to take the plunge and change to Dual mode because of changes in table storage, you need to create the table first with DirectQuery.

Considering the Query

In my Power BI discussions, I always stress the fact that you can choose from various methods to prepare and load data into Power BI. When you're in doubt, the method that ensures you and your organization the most accuracy is Import mode — hands down. In some use cases, though, the user experience for direct import isn't the best. Consider the circumstances described in this list:

>> DirectQuery may be the better choice when dealing with a very large dataset. However, the performance of the import correlates directly to the system that the import is coming from.

>> Data frequency and freshness are two reasons to use DirectQuery. This is the case because data sources must always show the return of results in a reasonable length of time.

>> Suppose that the data must reside in its original data source and that the location of the source cannot change. In that case, DirectQuery is better suited for data movement.

DirectQuery isn't the best lifeboat if you think that direct importing doesn't solve your problems. You face an uphill battle at times using DirectQuery under the following conditions:

>> **The state of your infrastructure dictates the results for DirectQuery.** That means slow or old hardware won't work the way you think it will when dealing with large datasets.

>> **Not all query types are usable with DirectQuery.** This is especially true for native queries that have table expressions or stored procedures.

>> **Data transformation is limited, unlike direct import.** You must interact with the interface each time a change is required.

>> **Data modeling limitations exist, especially when you're addressing calculated tables and columns.** As you will see in Chapter 14, DAX functionality is limited when you use DirectQuery to import data.

Data querying varies, depending on the data connectivity mode used in Power BI. Table 5-1 explores the differences between Import, DirectQuery, and Live Connection.

TABLE 5-1   ## Comparing Data Connectivity Modes

	Import	DirectQuery	Live Connection
Maximum size	Based on how you're licensed	Limited by your infrastructure.	Services have dataset size limits like Import Data. Otherwise, infrastructure limits your size.
Number of sources	Unlimited	Unlimited.	One
Security	Row level based on user login	Row level security. Security is defined as the data source for some sources. However, row level security can still be used in Power BI Desktop.	Can use data source security based on current user login

	Import	DirectQuery	Live Connection
Refresh cycle	Based on license: Pro — eight refreshes per day; Premium — unlimited refreshes per day	Shows latest data available in the source.	Shows latest data available in the source
Performance metrics	Optimal	Varies based on data sources.	Optimal
Data transformation	All features	Limited based on data source transformation language.	Not applicable
Modeling requirements	All features	Significant limitations.	Analysis services and Power BI Services measures created with limitations

Addressing and correcting performance

At some point you connect to a data source and stare at the screen and wonder, "Why are things so slow!"

There are a few reasons for slow performance in Power BI, many of which can be diagnosed and corrected in no time.

Power Query transforms your data sources using a native query language pre-configured by Microsoft within the product. A translation language example such as SQL in Power BI helps convert the data source. The language conversion process is referred to as *query folding*. Though query folding is usually quite efficient, hiccups do occur. An example where query folding may result in issues is when a dataset is only partially retrieved from the data source. As a result, rather than load all columns, the dataset loads a subset of the data, making it more difficult for you to pick and choose what you want to keep and what you want to remove.

TIP

If you're looking to see just how Power Query loads the data into Power BI, there's an easy way to review the query sent to the data source: To view the query, right-click a query step in the Power Query Editor under Applied Steps, and then choose View Native Query from the menu that appears.

REMEMBER

Native Query isn't always available. For example, some data sources don't support query folding. In addition, the query step may not be translated, given the native language used, which means that the option is grayed-out.

Diagnosing queries

Power BI includes a query diagnostic toolset that allows you to address any performance issues that might arise. The tools are helpful if you need to review queries you author and produce during a dataset refresh cycle, including those where you may want to better evaluate query folding anomalies. To access the Query Diagnostics toolset, you must first have a data source in place. Ideally, you've already transformed the data, not just loaded it. With that done, follow these steps:

1. **Click the Ribbon's Tools tab.**

2. **Click the Start Diagnostics button to start the process and click Stop Diagnostics to stop. (See Figure 5-10.)**

3. **(Optional) To analyze a single step, click the Diagnose Step button on the Tools Ribbon or right-click a step and choose Diagnose. (See Figure 5-11.)**

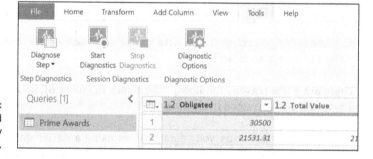

FIGURE 5-10: Start and Stop query diagnostics.

```
{
  "version": "0.1",
  "connections": [
    {
      "details": {
        "protocol": "file",
        "address": {
          "path": "c:\\users\\14048\\desktop\\power bi\\examples\\fiscalyearawards.xlsx"
        },
        "authentication": null,
        "query": null
      },
      "options": {},
      "mode": null
    }
  ]
}
```

FIGURE 5-11: The step process for query diagnostics.

TIP

Query diagnostics is excellent for static data. However, suppose that you have *dynamic* data — data that incrementally requires a refresh. In that case, you never know whether performance will go downhill. If you know that your data will be updated often, implement an incremental refresh policy. That way, your legacy data stays intact. At the same time, only the new data is evaluated during a data load-and-refresh cycle.

Exporting Power BI Desktop Files and Leveraging XMLA

Suppose that you've already connected to data in Power BI Desktop. You can use this connection to export the Power BI Desktop (PBIDS) file, with all data details embedded inside the file. The file is valid when you're looking to create repeatable connections to specific data sources.

To export the PBIDS file for use in another context, follow these steps:

1. **With the file open in Power BI Desktop, choose the Options and Settings option from the File menu.**

2. **Choose Data Source Settings from the Options and Settings menu.**

3. **At the bottom of the page, click the Export PBIDS button to generate your PBIDS file.**

   The file is saved to the location you select, whether it is your desktop or a hard drive. The PBIDS compresses all your data, including data sources, data models, and reports into a file that can reused by others with access to Power BI Desktop or Services.

With Power BI Services Premium, another option for endpoints, called XML for Analysis (XMLA), is available to connect your endpoints. With XMLA, you can pull data from Power BI data and use virtually any other desktop client tool besides Power BI Desktop to manipulate a dataset. For example, if you want to use Excel to edit a dataset, that's definitely a possibility. To use XMLA endpoints, you must configure the XMLA endpoints with the on-premises dataset to be enabled using the Power BI administration portal.

REMEMBER

XMLA endpoint settings require Power BI Premium capacity to operate. To be successful, you must configure the environment to read-only or read-write. For editing a dataset, read-write is necessary.

XMLA endpoint connectivity is treated as connecting your workspace to a server, with a dataset as the database. To ensure that your dataset connects appropriately, go to the workspace connection address and find the workspace settings. Ensure that you have access to the features, by following these steps:

1. **Go to the Power BI Services portal at www.powerbi.com/.**

2. **Select Workspaces from the navigation menu on the left side of the screen.**

3. **Identify the workspace you want to modify by selecting one of the options from the drop-down list.**

4. **Click the vertical ellipses and choose Workplace Settings from the menu that appears.**

5. **Modify the settings to accommodate your environment needs, as shown in Figure 5-12.**

FIGURE 5-12:
Premium
capacity
configuration
for XMLA.

Chapter **6**

Getting Data from Dynamic Sources

D ata can be a bit complicated at times. Admittedly, uploading a single file containing a few spreadsheets or perhaps a feed with a single stream of data to load and transform is child's play. What happens, though, when you have a dataset housed in a corporate-wide enterprise application that continually has transactions written to it? That scenario is quite different. And corporations should be concerned (for good reason) with the integration and output of business intelligence (BI) results. With Power BI, organizations don't need to worry about complex technical manipulations when it comes to their data systems or their communications with third-party data feeds. As you can see in this chapter, the integration is fluid — Power BI has the power to use a standardized connection process, no matter the connectivity requirement.

Getting Data from Microsoft-Based File Systems

In Chapter 5, I talk about loading data directly from the Power BI Desktop and even from folders stored on your desktop. Now I want you to focus your attention on integration with Microsoft-based applications such as OneDrive for Business and SharePoint 365, both of which are Microsoft 365-based applications.

REMEMBER

When using OneDrive, you need to be logged in to Microsoft 365. As long as you're logged in, you can access files and folders as though you're accessing your local hard drive. The only difference is that your hard drive is Microsoft OneDrive. In Figure 6-1, you can see that the path to a OneDrive for Business folder is no different from the path for a standard file or folder on your hard drive.

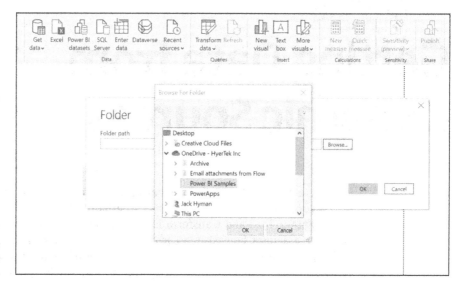

FIGURE 6-1:
OneDrive
file path.

On the other hand, SharePoint 365 offers a variety of options for document management and collaboration. The first option is to search a site collection, site, or subsite (referred to in Power BI as a SharePoint Folder). In this case, you must enter the complete SharePoint site URL. For example, if your company has an intranet, the site might be `http://asite.sharepoint.com`. An example of what you'd see after you enter a complete URL and log in with your Active Directory credentials appears in Figure 6-2.

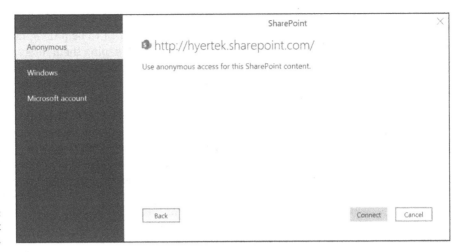

FIGURE 6-2:
SharePoint
Folder path.

You can also collect, load, and transform one or more SharePoint lists in Power BI. (In SharePoint, a *list* looks like a simple container — kind of like an Excel spreadsheet — but acts more like a database.) Using a list lets users collect information — especially metadata — across a SharePoint site where documents might be collected. With a list, data is gathered in rows, with each row represented as a row item similar to a database or spreadsheet item. To load a SharePoint list, you must know the URL path of the SharePoint site collection, site, or subsite. Once a user is authenticated, all available lists are loaded for that person.

TIP

When you're first starting out with Power BI, you might be tempted to keep all your files on the desktop as a way to manage your data. After a while, though, dealing with numerous versions of the same dataset becomes unmanageable. That's why you should use a cloud option such as OneDrive or a SharePoint site to manage your files and datasets, reports, dashboards, and connection files. It helps keep all of it streamlined.

Working with Relational Data Sources

Many organizations use relational databases to record transactional activity. Examples of systems that typically run relational databases are enterprise resource planning (ERP), customer relationship management (CRM), and supply chain management (SCM)-based systems. Another type of system might be an e-commerce platform. Each of these systems has one thing in common: All can benefit from having a business intelligence tool such as Power BI evaluate data by connecting with the relational database instead of extracting individual data files.

Businesses rely on solutions such as Power BI to help them monitor the state of their operations by identifying trends and helping them forecast metrics, indicators, and targets. You can start using Power BI Desktop to connect to virtually any relational database available in the cloud or on-premise on the market.

In the example shown in Figure 6-3, I have Power BI connect to an Azure SQL Server, Microsoft's web-based enterprise database. Depending on your relational database solution, you have a few choices. One would be to choose the Get Data ⇨ More . . . command from the Ribbon's Home tab, then look for Database. Here you will find Microsoft-specific databases. Otherwise, if you are looking for another type of data source, choose Get Data ⇨ More . . . and look for Other. You'll find 40+ alternate database options under this section.

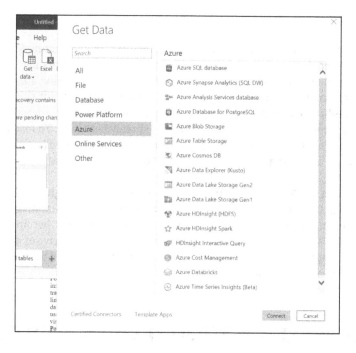

FIGURE 6-3: Azure SQL database location.

In this case, because the selected solution is a Microsoft Azure-based product, you can either search for the product in the Search box or click the Azure option after selecting More.

After you select the database source type under Get Data, you must enter the credentials for the relational database. In this case, you enter the following info:

- » Server name

- » Database name

- » Mode type — Import or DirectQuery

Figure 6-4 gives an example with the fields correctly filled out. (You don't need to add unique command lines or SQL query statements unless you're looking for a more granular data view.)

SQL Server database

Server ⓘ

textbooksamples.database.windows.net

Database (optional)

dataforpowerbi

Data Connectivity mode ⓘ
⦿ Import
○ DirectQuery

▷ Advanced options

OK   Cancel

FIGURE 6-4:
Entry of credentials for relational database.

REMEMBER

In most cases, you should select Import. The circumstances where you select DirectQuery are for large datasets. The data updates are intended for near real-time updates.

After you've entered your credentials, you're prompted to log in with your username and password using your Windows, database, or Microsoft account authentication, as shown in Figure 6-5.

Importing data from a relational data source

Connecting to the data source is often tricky because you need to make sure your database source and naming conventions are just right. However, once you get past these two facts, you often have smooth sailing — well, at least until you need to pick the data to import. Then you might become overwhelmed if the database has a lot of tables.

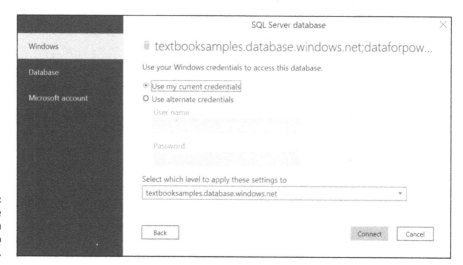

FIGURE 6-5:
Selecting the
authentication
method to
connect.

After you've connected the database to Power BI Desktop, the Navigator displays the data available from the data source, as shown in Figure 6-6. In this case, all data from the Azure SQL database is presented. You can select a table or one of the entities to preview the content.

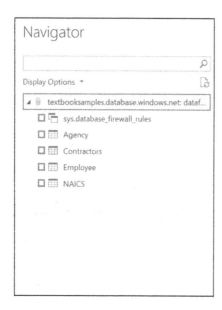

FIGURE 6-6:
Selecting the
tables from the
Navigator for
import.

The data loaded into the model *must* be the correct data before moving on to the following dataset. To import data from the relational data source that you want to ingest into Power BI Desktop, and then either load or transform and load the data, follow these steps:

REMEMBER

1. **Select one or more tables in the Navigator.**

   The data selected will be imported into Power Query Editor.

2. **Click the Load button if you're looking to automate data loading into a Power BI model based on its current state with no changes.**

3. **Click the Transform Data button if you want Power BI to execute the Power Query engine.**

   The engine performs actions such as cleaning up excessive columns, grouping data, removing errors, and promoting data quality.

The good ol' SQL query

You probably shouldn't be surprised, but Power BI has an intelligent SQL query editor. Suppose that you know precisely which tables you require from the Azure SQL database. In this case, all you need to do is call out the tables in a SQL query with just a few keystrokes, rather than request all tables from the Azure SQL Server. For example, Figure 6-7 presents a representative SELECT query for a table found in the dataforpowerbi database.

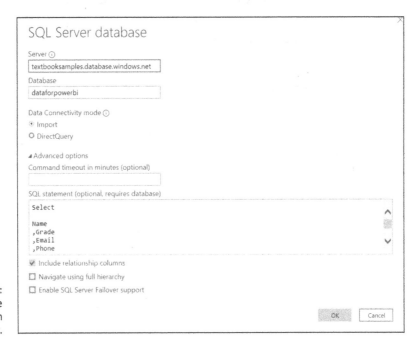

FIGURE 6-7: Representative query data from Azure SQL Server.

Importing Data from a Nonrelational Data Source

Some organizations use nonrelational databases such as Microsoft Cosmos DB or Apache Hadoop to handle their myriad of significant data challenges. What's the difference, you ask? These databases don't use tables to store their data. Data might be stored in a variety of ways in the case of nonrelational (NoSQL) data. Options run the gamut from document, key-value, wide-column, and graph. All database options provide flexible schemas and scale effortlessly with large data volumes.

Though the need still exists to authenticate to the database, the querying approach is a bit different. For example, with Microsoft Cosmos DB, the NoSQL database created by Microsoft that is complementary to Power BI, a user must identify the endpoint URL and the Primary key and Read-Only key so that a connection can be created to the Cosmos DB instance in the Azure portal. To connect to the Cosmos DB, follow these steps:

1. **Choose Get Data ⇨ More . . . from the Home Tab in Power BI.**

2. **In the submenu that appears, locate the Azure submenu.**

3. **Click to select the Azure Cosmos DB option, as shown in Figure 6-8, allowing you to create a nonrelational database connection.**

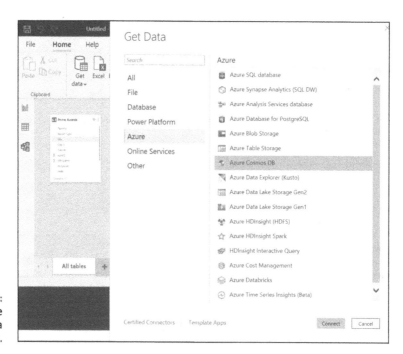

FIGURE 6-8: Selecting the Cosmos DB data source.

4. **Enter the URL of the Cosmos DB in the URL field and then click OK. (See Figure 6-9.)**

FIGURE 6-9:
Connecting to the
Cosmos DB, a
Microsoft NoSQL
database.

WARNING When you're using a NoSQL database, you need to know the keys in order to authenticate. For Cosmos DB, you can find those keys in the Azure portal under the Cosmos DB Instance Settings, Key Link. Be sure to copy down the primary and secondary read-write keys and the primary and secondary read-only key.

Importing JSON File Data into Power BI

JSON files don't look at all like structured data files. Why is that the case? JSON — short for JavaScript Object Notation — is a lightweight data-interchange format. Neither structured nor unstructured, the JSON file type is referred to as *semistructured* because the file type is written by default as a key-value pair. With JSON-based records, the data must be extracted and normalized before becoming a report in Power BI. That's why you must transform the data using Power BI Desktop's Power Query Editor.

If your goal is to extract data from a JSON file, you transform the list to a table by clicking the Transform tab and selecting To Table in the Convert group. Another option is to drill down into a specific record by clicking on a record link. If you want to preview the record, click on the cell without clicking on the link. Doing so opens a data preview pane at the bottom of Power Query Editor.

Need to get a bit more in the weeds? You can click on the cog wheel next to the source step in Query Settings which opens a window to specify advanced settings. There you can specify options such as file encoding in the File Origin drop-down list. When you are ready for show time and your JSON file is transformed, click Close and Apply to load data into the Power BI data model. In the example found in Figure 6-10, employee records have been transformed from the JSON file.

FIGURE 6-10:
JSON file, transformed by the Power Query Editor.

After the Power Query Editor has transformed the file, you might still need to edit specific fields. In this example, the Country field has all null entries, so it's a prime candidate for field deletion. Such a choice is easily carried out with the help of the drop-down menu, as shown in Figure 6-11, where you can drill down and delete specific records.

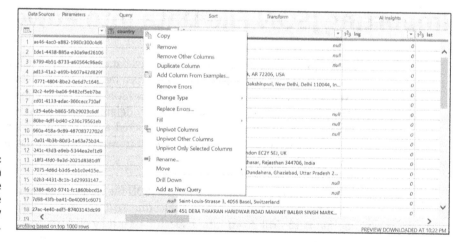

FIGURE 6-11:
Modifying a JSON file using the Power Query Editor.

Importing Data from Online Sources

Enterprise applications and third-party data feeds are widely available in Power BI. In fact, Microsoft has over 100 connectors to applications developed and managed by other vendors, including those by Adobe, Denodo, Oracle, and Salesforce, to name a few. Of course, Microsoft also supports its own enterprise application solutions, including those in the Dynamics 365, SharePoint 365, and Power Platform families. Online sources can be found across several categories using the Get Data feature in Power BI Desktop, but your best bets are under the Online Services heading or the Other heading.

In the example, as shown in Figure 6-12, I've set up a connection to Dynamics 365 Business Central.

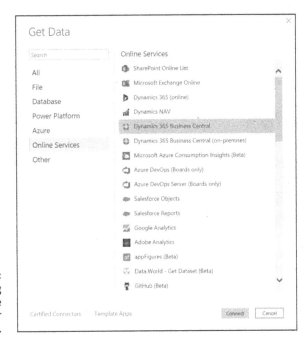

FIGURE 6-12:
Connecting
to an online
service in Power
BI Desktop.

To connect to an online service, follow these steps:

1. **Go to Get Data from the Home Tab of Power BI.**

2. **At the bottom of the Go Data menu, choose the More . . . option.**

   Selecting More provides users with more data source options.

3. **Choose Online Services from the More . . . submenu.**

   Online Services include enterprise applications, where large datasets are available (assuming user credentials are accessible).

4. **On the right side, click Dynamics 365 Business Central (see Figure 6-13).**

   Doing so allows for a connection to Microsoft's Small Business ERP Solution.

5. **At the bottom of the screen, click Connect.**

   The end result is a connection has been established to Microsoft Dynamics 365 Business Central.

FIGURE 6-13: Interface to authenticate with Online Services.

You're then asked to enter your online organizational credentials. Generally, this part is already prepopulated because it's your Single Sign-On login associated with Azure Active Directory. (Refer to Figure 6-13.)

Once you authenticate a session, all data available from the database for the specific source is loaded in the Navigator pane within the Power Query Editor, as shown in Figure 6-14. Power Query transforms the data before loading it in Navigator.

FIGURE 6-14:
Data displayed in
the Navigator
pane within the
Power Query
Editor.

Creating Data Source Combos

When data comes from multiple sources, things can get complex. Creating relationships between data in the hope of yielding calculations and rules on the data creates a new set of "gotchas." In Power BI, calculations are built using the Data Analysis Expression language (DAX). So, it goes without saying that when you need to bring together multiple sources containing calculations, functions, and rule sets, the process can be an arduous activity. However, Microsoft, with its Azure Analysis Services, has reduced the burden considerably.

Azure Analysis Services is similar to the data-modeling-and-storage offering in Power BI. When an organization needs to integrate data from multiple data sources, including databases and online sources, Azure Analysis Services can help an organization streamline the data into a single package. Once the data is organized and consumable in what is known as an Azure Analysis Services cube, a user can authenticate, select a cube to access, and query one or more tables.

Connecting and importing data from Azure Analysis Services

As with other data sources, you click the Power BI Desktop Home tab's Get Data button to access Analysis Services, as shown in Figure 6-15.

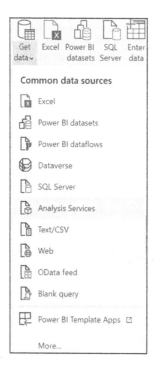

FIGURE 6-15:
Accessing
Analysis
Services.

Once you select Analysis Services, you need to supply the Analysis Services server address as well as the database name. Additionally, you're asked to select whether to import the data or use a live connection. An optional parameter is entering an MDX or DAX parameter. (Figure 6-16 shows the fields you need to fill out.)

TECHNICAL STUFF

You *must* know the difference between DAX and MDX. The MDX concept is associated with *multidimensionality* — several aspects of the same data, in other words. Therefore, you can query the Azure Analysis Cube to get data dimensions and measures as results. With DAX, though, the results you can query are calculations and measures exclusive to Power BI.

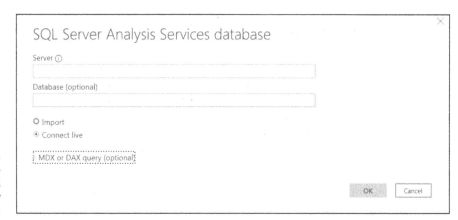

FIGURE 6-16:
The Azure
Analysis Services
connectivity
interface.

Accessing data with Connect Live

Don't confuse Connect Live with Live Connection mode. Connect Live is specific to Azure Analysis Services, which uses a table model and DAX to build calculations. Building such models is comparable to Power BI. With Connect Live, though, you're keeping the data and DAX calculations in their original hosted locations, which means there are no reasons to import them to Power BI natively. Because Azure Analysis Services offers a high-speed refresh rate, the data refresh cycle in Power BI is almost immediate. You never have to worry about hitting the Power BI data refresh threshold, which helps improve data quality for your organization, especially when delivering reports.

Connect Live also allows you to directly query tables within Azure Analysis Services using DAX or MDX, similar to a relational database. That said, most users will likely import data directly into Power BI across all of the data they want, whether it's from a file, database, or service using the Azure Analysis Services model. The other choice is to use Live Connection mode. By using both data modeling and DAX measures, all activities can be performed centrally, allowing for similar data maintainability.

Dealing with Modes for Dynamic Data

The tried-and-true method of importing data reliably with no restrictions is to use the Direct Import method. *Importing* data means that the data is housed in a Power BI file and gets published with reports to the Power BI Services from the Power BI Desktop by a user. Thus, you can rest assured that, if it's possible to interact directly with the dataset, the data is transformed and cleansed the way you want it to be transformed and cleansed. Sometimes, of course, this approach may not be suitable for you or your organization.

Don't use Direct Import in either of these two instances:

>> An environment with complex security requirements

>> Large, unmanageable datasets where the potential for bottlenecks is high

In such cases, go with DirectQuery for dynamic data because you can query the data sources directly without worrying about importing a copy of the dataset into Power BI — a dataset that can potentially be excessively large. Using DirectQuery also helps you avoid another issue that Direct Import often poses as a challenge: data recency and relevancy. You always know that your data is fresh with Direct-Query. In contrast, with Direct Import, you need to update the dataset on your own.

REMEMBER

If you ever needed to switch storage modes, you can do so by going to Model view from the Power BI navigation. First, you select in the Properties pane the data table that requires modification. Then you change the mode from the Storage Mode drop-down menu found at the bottom of the list. There are three options: Import, DirectQuery, and Dual.

Fixing Data Import Errors

Along the way, don't be surprised if you find yourself coming across an import error or two. Most of the time, the culprit has to do with query time-outs, data mapping errors, or data type issues. These problems are easy to fix after you understand the error message. This section describes each of the conditions.

"Time-out expired"

You've read about systems that experience heavy traffic and others that are barely touched. When you have heavy use of a database, administrations often cap the bandwidth of a given user to ensure that no single user consumes all the infra-structure capacity. Suppose that a Power BI query requires a significant dataset.

At the same time, there's a heavy load on a system, and the dataset cannot be fully returned in the distributed time that's set by the system. In that case, the result is a query time-out because the system expires the query.

"The data format is not valid"

Suppose that you import a table into Power BI, and then you see a message stating, "We couldn't find any data formatted as a table." What does this mean, exactly? When you import data from Excel, Power BI expects that the top row of data will hold column headers. If that isn't the case, you need to modify the Excel workbook so that the first row is considered a header. Otherwise, you continue to receive this error until the first line is formatted correctly.

"Uh-oh — missing data files"

Anytime you change the directory or path of your files, whether it's on your local desktop or in a cloud directory, expect to get an error in Power BI Desktop. Though Power BI is an intelligent application, it doesn't track every move your file makes.

Another potential case where a missing data file may appear to be the problem is when changing a file's security permission. Don't assume that Power BI will let you access the application because you were previously granted access — it's just the opposite, in fact. To rectify this issue, follow these steps:

1. **Click the Transform Data button to open the Power BI Query Editor.**

2. **Upon opening the Power BI Query Editor, locate the Queries pane.**

   You'll find one or more of your errors here.

3. **Highlight the query that is reporting an error.**

4. **On the right side of the screen, under Query Settings, locate Applied Steps and select Source.**

   You'll be reconfiguring the Source settings.

5. **Modify the source to match the new location by clicking on the Settings button (the cog icon) next to source and making any permission adjustments as needed.**

6. **Press OK once complete.**

"Transformation isn't always perfect"

It might be hard to believe, but even technology can create data errors when imports occur. (Wait — technology is fallible? Really?) This might happen when you try to import data into Power BI. After all your efforts, a column is blank or filled with a variety of erroneous data types. When the system has a hard time interpreting the data type in Power BI, an error is thrown. The way to fix the problem is unique to each and every data source. Though one source may require data conversion, another source may require complete removal.

REMEMBER

Always specify the correct data type at the data source from the get-go. Completing a direct import versus a DirectQuery also eliminates many of the standard data source errors.

Chapter **7**

Cleansing, Transforming, and Loading Your Data

For any data cleansing and transformation to take place, your organization needs analysts and engineers — and detectives. The idea here is that you must first analyze the data before entering the system or after it exists in its intended data store. Simply glossing over the data alone doesn't cut it. You need to follow a rigorous process as you look for those needles in your data haystack. Without a rigorous process, you can't ensure data consistency across all columns, values, and keys. By following a meticulous analysis process, you can engineer optimized queries that help load the data into the system without issues. This chapter helps you develop that process by evaluating the whole lifecycle and the supporting activities the Power BI professional must undertake in order to make their data shine for visualization consumption.

Engaging Your Detective Skills to Hunt Down Anomalies and Inconsistencies

Anomalous data comes in many flavors. Using Power Query, you can find unusual data trends that you might be on the lookout for — even those slight ambiguities you'd have trouble catching on your own. For example, you can see how an out-of-context dollar amount or error can be traced back to missing values that skew the data results. These are all real-life scenarios that you can address using Power BI.

The easiest and most obvious way to spot errors is to look at a table in the Power Query Editor. You can evaluate the quality of each column by using the Data Preview feature. You can, among each column, review data under a header value in order to validate data, catch errors, and spot empty values. All you need to do is choose View ⇨ Data Preview ⇨ Column Quality from the Power Query main menu. In Figure 7-1, you notice right off the bat that the Agency column has data missing, as shown by the <1% number reported as empty. Such behavior is consistent with data anomalies.

FIGURE 7-1: Addressing column quality issues.

ON THE WEB

Throughout this chapter, you can follow the exercises using the `FiscalAwards.xlsx` file, which can be loaded into Power BI Desktop. To access the file, go to `www.dummies.com/go/microsoftpowerBIfd`.

Notice that all columns except for the Agency column have 100 percent validity. In this case, that <1% means you have either a null value or mistaken data. The purpose of investigating data quality issues using Power Query is best exemplified with this sampling because all other columns show an error percentage of 0. You learn how to correct such ambiguities later in this chapter.

Checking those data structures and column properties

Evaluating data goes beyond column quality. Another measurement you can use to better identify data structure issues involves *column value distribution*, which is a measure of all distinct values in the selected column as well as the percentage of rows in the table that each value represents. You enable this measurement in the Power Query Editor by choosing View ⇨ Data Preview ⇨ Column Distribution. In Figure 7-2, notice that the Total Value columns have a high number of distinct and unique values.

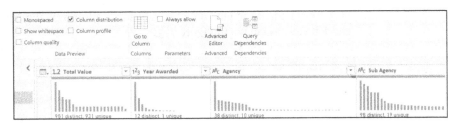

FIGURE 7-2: A look at column distribution.

Here's what *distinct* and *unique* are telling you:

>> **Distinct number:** The number of different values in a column when duplicates are omitted

>> **Unique number:** The number of values that occur precisely one time

By using the Column Distribution command, you can determine the number of distinct and unique values in each column. As noted, the distribution of columns of values is visible under the column header. Regardless of the analysis goal, column profiling is available for all data types.

Each column shows the shape of data — the distribution of values, say, or the frequency with which a specific data type appears. The value 2021, for example, is seen most, whereas the values for 2011 through 2020 are distributed in a proportional amount per the chart, as shown in Figure 7-2, under the Years Awarded heading.

If you want to evaluate the data outside of Power BI and the Power Query Editor, right-click the columns of choice and then select Copy Value Distribution from the menu that appears. You're supplied a list of distinct values and the number of times the data appears in the columns.

TIP

REMEMBER

Column distribution is a valuable utility: If certain columns offer little business value, you can omit the columns. An example might be where you have a limited number of distinct values. Removing columns as you conduct analysis can build more powerful queries, because you're getting rid of clutter by deleting unwanted datasets.

Finding a little help from data statistics

Statistics can sometimes be your best friend, which is why you want to consider using them for profiling and understanding the nature of your data. To enable data preview for statistics, go to the Power Query Editor, choose View ⇨ Data Preview from its main menu, and then select the Column Quality and Column Profile check boxes, as shown in Figure 7-3.

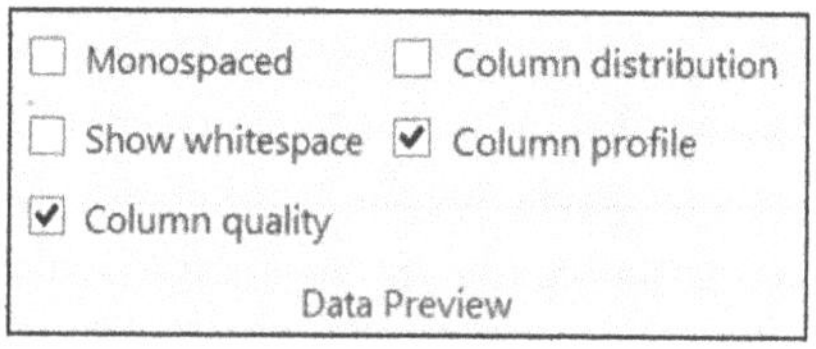

FIGURE 7-3:
Data preview options in the Power Query Editor.

> ☐ Monospaced   ☐ Column distribution
> ☐ Show whitespace ☑ Column profile
> ☑ Column quality
>   Data Preview

After enabling the features, select a column header requiring further statistical analysis. In Figure 7-4, you find the profile of the Total Value and Year Awarded columns from the Excel spreadsheet labeled Fiscal Year Awards. Notice the general-statistics panel on the bottom and then the individual column statistics. Your options aren't limited to column profile and column quality, either. You can also review data for whitespace, monospacing, and column distribution.

These are the key column statistics you can evaluate:

>> Total count of value

>> Number of errors

>> Empty columns

>> Distinct columns

>> Unique values

>> Minimum, maximum, and average values

>> Number of zero, odd, or even values

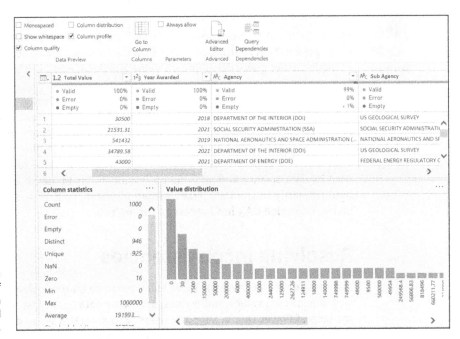

FIGURE 7-4:
Data preview of
the column
profile and
column quality.

REMEMBER

If the column has text, the statistics vary in comparison to numerical columns. With text columns, the number of empty strings and values is highlighted. In contrast, in numeric columns, you're limited to empty values alone.

Stepping through the Data Lifecycle

Data is seldom perfect. Unless you're connecting to a prepared dataset where you have limited control over what has been created for you, there's a good chance you need to do some data cleansing and data transformation before you can load anything for analysis.

Power BI offers an incredibly powerful tool to help guide you through the entire data lifecycle, emphasizing data cleansing and transformation. That tool is Power Query. Within Power Query, a user can extract, transform, and load (ETL) their data using the Get command as well as the Transform Data command. In this book, you use Power Query to connect, transform, ingest, and evaluate available data when connecting to a data source. Power Query is the infrastructure behind the Power Query Editor found in Power BI.

Power Query isn't new to Power BI. In fact, the product is integral to Excel as well. Other products, in addition to Power BI and Excel, include Power Query as a means of modernizing query development using a low-code approach.

Rather than go with SQL, Power Query uses another programming language, called M. M — short for *mash-up* — is a functional, case-sensitive query formula language. As part of the Power BI Query Editor, the language helps prepare data before it's loaded into a Power BI model. M is specific to querying, and DAX, the Data Analysis Expressions language, is an analytical data calculation language used by data science and analysis professionals for in-depth analysis. Unlike M, used primarily in the Data Transformation phase, DAX is used in the Data View phase. I describe DAX in Chapters 14 through 16.

Resolving inconsistencies

The more data you have, the more you have to be on the lookout for inconsistencies, unexpected values, null values, and other data quality issues. Power BI, with the help of Power Query, supports users with several ways to deal with inconsistencies. These include replacing values, removing rows, and completing root cause analysis.

Replacing values

Users can replace mistaken values with desired outcomes directly in the Power Query Editor interface. You would use this approach wherever errors occur in the data sources you create or import into Power BI. An example of such behavior is replacing null values with an updated, unique value. There's a catch, though, when using this technique: A user must fix the error in the source or else the values during a refresh may be written over. You can access your options by right-clicking a column and then choosing an option, as shown in Figure 7-5.

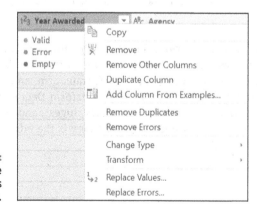

FIGURE 7-5:
Look for the Replace Values menu option.

To replace errors, follow these steps:

1. Right-click a column header and choose Replace Errors from the menu that appears in the Power Query Editor.

2. Enter the values you want to replace in the Value box.

3. Click OK.

Replacing values in a column follows a similar process, as shown in Figure 7-6. Follow these steps:

1. Right-click a column header and choose Replace Value from the menu that appears in the Power Query Editor.

2. On the new screen that appears, fill in the Value to Find and the Replace With fields.

3. When you finish, click the OK button.

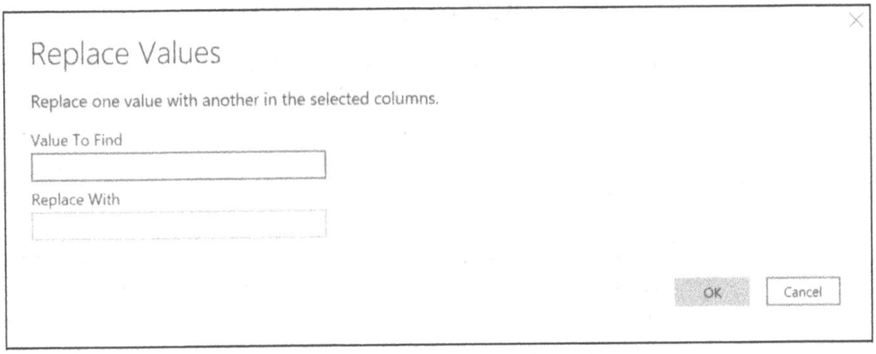

Replace Values

Replace one value with another in the selected columns.

Value To Find

Replace With

OK   Cancel

FIGURE 7-6:
Replacing values.

TIP

After selecting the Replace Value menu, you're prompted to make several updates. Under Advanced, you see two options: Match Entire Cell Content and Replace Using Special Character Codes. If you try to replace text in a column, you need to match an entire cell's content. If you enable the Match Entire Cell Content option, the Power Query Editor won't replace values where the Replace With value is limited to the Value to Find value. Furthermore, suppose that you're looking to replace a unique character. In that case, you need to select the Replace Using Special Character Codes check box. Otherwise, the value isn't entered into the box.

If you want to replace data across multiple columns simultaneously, you must press the Control key (Ctrl) and then select each column that has values you want to replace. If you want to select a range of columns following a specific order instead, press the Shift key and then select each of the columns in the chronological order of preference. Remember that the data type entered in the replacement fields must match across all columns or else errors will appear.

Removing rows using Power Query

From time to time, you find that you must remove entire rows of data because something in the rows is creating an abundance of errors. To remove a row, you would assume that correcting the error should be as simple as right-clicking the column and choosing Remove Errors from the contextual menu. Using this method removes only rows where known errors are present. Suppose that you prefer to remove all rows in a table that meet a particular condition that can lead to errors. In that case, you'd click the Table icon to the left of the column header, select the affected rows, and then choose Remove Errors from the menu that appears.

Digging down to the root cause

Every time an error occurs in a column, you can review the message behind the error. To review the error, select the cell in question. The error message appears in the Preview panel at the bottom of the page. Using this method enables a user to see various content types from tables, records, lists, and of course, embedded errors.

Figure 7-7 shows that an error has been introduced after a new custom column was added to the dataset. The issue presented is a mismatch of data types. Neither a text field nor a numeric field can create a typical column value. It turns out that type conversion is often one of those root causes triggering an error message.

FIGURE 7-7:
An error, as presented in Power Query.

> ⚠ Expression.Error: We cannot apply field access to the type Number.
> Details:
>   Value=30500
>   Key=Year Awarded

From time to time, you may need to convert a column from one type to another (from Text to Number, for example). In Power BI, this is referred to as a *type conversion*. Most times, you make type conversion changes immediately after data is transformed using Power Query.

Evaluating and Transforming Column Data Types

Few data sources are ready for prime time. You need to shape them to be ready for use by Power BI and the Power Query Editor. (Admittedly, such behavior is more often true for files than for structured database systems, but that's beside the point.) As you work through datasets, you need to add query steps as you either add or reduce rows and column data. Even when you try to transpose column data, it should come as no surprise that evaluating and transforming data can be a complex process. In this section, I have you focus on topics that help transform data into its purest possible state. Of course, you need to perform a little bit of magic along the way.

Finding and creating appropriate keys for joins

Power BI supports users by combining data from tables in a number of different ways — but no matter which way you choose, you have to use a join in your query. (A *join* is a way to combine data from multiple tables; it brings together these tables using a common key from two or more tables.) Using Power Query Editor, you can complete this action using the Merge functionality. If you want to create relationships using a model outside of Power Query, you create implicit joins. The use of a join depends on the business requirements.

REMEMBER

Of all the many join types out there, the two you most often hear about are implicit and explicit joins. An *implicit* join performs a left outer join with a table field, pulling from another table. *Explicit* joins specify the integration of two tables. There are many benefits to using implicit joins. A key benefit is syntax because it's a useful substitute for explicit join syntax. In fact, an implicit join can appear in the same query that maintains an explicit join syntax.

Joining tables requires that a criterion be set up. One clear criterion is to identify the key in each table. If you were to look at the Primary and Sub Awards in the sample FiscalAwards.xlsx file, you'd see that one obvious choice to play this role is the Agency Key column for each table. (Though data often appears cleaner if your keys are named the same way, it's not a requirement.)

TECHNICAL STUFF

Tables can be represented by one or many join statements. If a table is represented on the One side of the join, the key in the table is unique in every row. If the table is represented by the Many side of the join, not all keys are unique, which yields some duplication. As you may have guessed, the One side is represented as a primary key, and the Many side can be a foreign key. One-to-one (1:1) and many-to-many (M:M) relationships do exist at times; however, the results produced in Power Query may not be suitable; one-to-one relationship may produce a narrow result set, whereas many-to-many often produces too many results.

Here are two key terms to remember when data modeling:

>> A *relationship* is the connection between entities in a data model, which in turn reflect business rules. Relationships between entities can be either one-to-one, one-to-many, or many-to-many.

>> A *join* is a bit different, in that you're setting up a relationship between two or more tables to pull data. The data is commonly mapped together using a primary key, a foreign key, or a combination, which is referred to as a *composite key.*

Consider the following information as it relates to joins and relationships:

>> **Keys for joins:** You can perform joins based on one or more columns at a time. Creating composite keys isn't a requirement to merge tables using Power Query. When you create joins in Power Query, pay particular attention to the column type. You must match the data type with one another or else a join won't work.

>> **Keys for relationships:** Power BI will try its best to resolve different data types, including converting data types, if possible. Ideally, though, you should make sure, when creating a join, that the data type in the relationship is the same.

Power BI only allows for physical relationships between two tables on a single column pair. This statement means that if you have a composite key in a table, you have to combine the key columns into a single column in order to create the necessary physical relationship. You can carry out this task by either using Power Query or setting up a calculated column with the help of DAX.

You can combine columns in two different ways: Create a new column or merge a column in place. To add a new merged column, first select the columns you're looking to combine and then choose Add ⇨ Column ⇨ From Text ⇨ Merge Columns from the Power Query Editor Ribbon. If you'd prefer to merge columns in place, you replace the original columns. Select the columns you want to merge and then choose Transform ⇨ Text Column ⇨ Merge Columns from the same menu.

Whether you select one of the two options, the outcome is ultimately the same. Figure 7-8 presents the Merge interface. You can combine one or more columns from Prime Awards and Sub Awards. Then, you select the type of join. The result is a new column that merges the two columns.

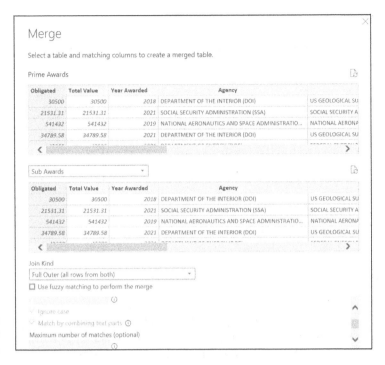

FIGURE 7-8:
The Merge
Columns option.

A final step in the process is defining separators from the Separator drop-down menu, found on the Merge interface. You can either select a predefined separator or come up with your own, by choosing Custom from the menu. If you choose the latter method, you're given a choice to enter a new column name. Once you complete it, click OK.

In the example, a colon is being used as a separator. Finally, the new column is called Agency-Sub Agency, as shown in Figure 7-9.

Shaping your column data to meet Power Query requirements

Not every data source you ingest may have the proper data type. Power Query does its best to detect the data type based on characteristics found in the available dataset. For example, you may be using a US-based zip code as part of your dataset. Power Query may (incorrectly) treat zip codes starting with zeros as though they were whole numbers. As a result, those starting values get cut off. Why? Because a whole number cuts off the zero. In this example, the zip code should be a Text data type, not a whole number.

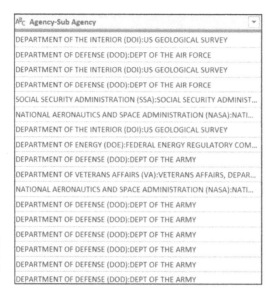

FIGURE 7-9:
Columns that have been merged.

As you begin evaluating your data in columns, keep in mind that Power Query tries to convert any data it receives as one of the data types shown in Figure 7-10. You can keep Power Query on the right track by making sure you're using the correct data type in the first place.

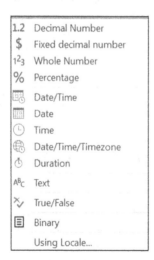

FIGURE 7-10:
The available data types.

REMEMBER

You see complex data types like functions, lists, records, and tables every so often. Keep in mind that not all data types may be available after loading data.

If you want to change the data type, you can do so by right-clicking a column header and selecting Change Type from the menu. Then select the type you want, as shown in Figure 7-11. After changing a data type once in a column, you then see a prompt asking whether you agree to change the column type and insert a step. Figure 7-12 shows an example of inserting a step.

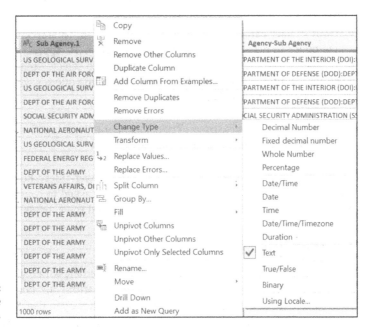

FIGURE 7-11:
Changing the
data type.

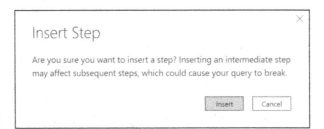

FIGURE 7-12:
Inserting a step.

Combining queries

In Power BI, you can combine queries using Power Query in one of two ways. First, you can append queries. That means you add other queries to an existing set of queries as though you're stacking the data. When you create appended queries, you often use patterns such as SQL's UNION ALL operator. On the other hand, combining queries using the merge structure is based on the supplied primary and foreign keys. You need to set up JOIN statements with Merge queries.

Appending queries

You can always make tables taller or wider. When you append, the table is taller. The reason is that your queries include the same number of columns. In some cases, the resulting tables have columns from all queries; in other instances, columns that were not present in an original query may populate in the dataset. Under these circumstances, each of the rows keeps null values.

A Power BI user can either append a query in its as-is statement or it can create a new query to accommodate the aggregate data. To append queries, you make this choice when there are one or more queries to select. No new queries need to be built — simply reuse whatever exists. Appending queries without creating new ones is the default choice in Power BI.

When you take many new rows of data and string them together using the original query, you should choose Append Queries As New.

To access Append Queries as New, go to the Power Query Editor Home Ribbon. Then select Append Queries as New. You're then asked to concatenate rows from two or more tables. Once you select the tables and rows, press OK.

Merging queries

When you merge queries, you combine them together, which yields a wider table. Because you inherit more columns, it's only natural for horizontal growth to occur. The critical consideration is which set of keys you use. The columns must have matching values in both tables to ensure that one table can be combined with the rows in the second table.

Much like when appending queries, you have two merge options — create a new query or merge two queries and call them new. Merging queries involves creating one of six join types using Power Query, as shown in Table 7-1.

TABLE 7-1 Join Types

Join Type	Direction
Inner	Only matching rows are visible.
Left Outer	All items in the first table appear, but only matching items from the second.
Right Outer	All items in the second table appear, but only matching items from the first.
Full Outer	All rows appear.
Left Anti	Returns all rows from the first table where a match in the second table does not exist.
Right Anti	Returns all rows from the second table where a match in the first table does not exist.

When you try to use one of these queries, you may realize that your data isn't perfect. To alleviate some of the quality concerns, Power Query supports fuzzy matching when performing merges. *Fuzzy matching* occurs when you can compare items from separate lists. A join is formed if there's a close match. You have the ability to set the matching tolerance and similarity threshold when establishing a fuzzy match. Your fuzzy matching options include those described in Table 7-2.

TABLE 7-2   **Fuzzy Matching Options**

Fuzzy Matching Option	Description
Similarity threshold	Values are from 0 to 1. When values are 0, values are said to match each other, no matter how far apart they are. With 1, you get a match only when the match is exact.
Ignore case	Treats upper- and lowercase the same.
Maximum number of matches	Limits the number of rows from the second table that matches the first, which is helpful when the result set produces multiple matches.
Match by combining text parts	Attempts to combine separate words into a single entity, looking to find matches between keys.
Transformation table	Equivalent of a to-and-from, which means there must be at least two columns.

To merge a query, follow these steps:

1. **On the Home tab of the Power Query Editor Ribbon, locate Merge Query.**

2. **Select Merge Queries, not Merge Queries As New.**

3. **Select the tables and columns you want to combine in the Merge Queries interface.**

4. **Select the key that is common to both tables.**

   Notice that the appropriate key column is highlighted.

5. **Select the type of join you want from the Join Kind drop-down list.**

6. **Click OK.**

In Figure 7-13, you can see that you're merging the Prime and Sub Awards queries. The common key selected is Obligated. The type of join kind selected is Full Outer.

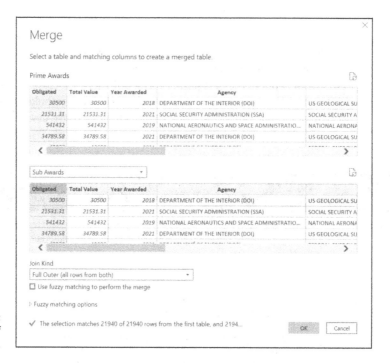

FIGURE 7-13:
An example of
merged columns.

Notice that a new column, Sub Awards, appears in Figure 7-14. Each row is high-lighted and says Table. To view the Sub Awards data, you'd click on the Table link to drill down. When you merge two tables, you may

» Add a new table

» Have the table represented by hyperlinks

» Have a double-arrow button instead of the Filter button as part of the column

   The double arrow is another filter type that allows users to search data from two or more table datasets.

When you select any cell in the new column, a preview of the content contained in the merged table appears.

When expanding a table, you can either *expand* or *aggregate*:

» **Expand:** Here you'd select a column from the merged table that you want to add to the current table. If the merged table has more than one matching row, the current table's row is the one duplicated.

» **Aggregate:** If you want to combine rows without duplication in the current table, this is your best choice. Using DAX, supplying the function that's most appropri-ate for each column is one way to ensure that data is properly combined.

ABc Award Type	▾	123 NAICS	▾	⊞ Sub Awards	⬇⬆
● Valid	100%	● Valid	100%	● Valid	100%
● Error	0%	● Error	0%	● Error	0%
● Empty	0%	● Empty	0%	● Empty	0%
PURCHASE ORDER		541511		Table	
DELIVERY ORDER		541715		Table	
DELIVERY ORDER		541519		Table	
DELIVERY ORDER		541519		Table	
DELIVERY ORDER		541519		Table	
DELIVERY ORDER		541519		Table	
PURCHASE ORDER		541715		Table	
DELIVERY ORDER		541519		Table	
DELIVERY ORDER		541611		Table	
DEFINITIVE CONTRACT		541715		Table	
DELIVERY ORDER		541512		Table	
DEFINITIVE CONTRACT		541715		Table	
PURCHASE ORDER		541715		Table	
DELIVERY ORDER		541519		Table	
BPA CALL		611430		Table	

FIGURE 7-14:
Adding a column.

To expand a merged column using the Fiscal Awards dataset, follow these steps:

1. **In the Prime Awards query, click the double-arrow button in the newly created column.**

   You see a screen that allows you to filter based on Expanded view or Aggregate view.

2. **Clear the Select All Columns check box on the Expanded Merge Columns tab.**

3. **Click to select the Agency check box and the Sub Agency check box.**

4. **Uncheck the Use Original Column Name as Prefix check box.**

5. **Click OK.**

   You should now see an expanded set of columns, showing the values of both tables you just merged.

6. **Right-click the Agency Key column and select Remove Column.**

7. **Right-click the Agency.1 column and select Rename.**

8. **Rename the Agency.1 column to Agency.**

The output of what was produced after all those changes appears in Figure 7-15. There is only one Agency column and a Sub Agency column labeled Sub Agency.1

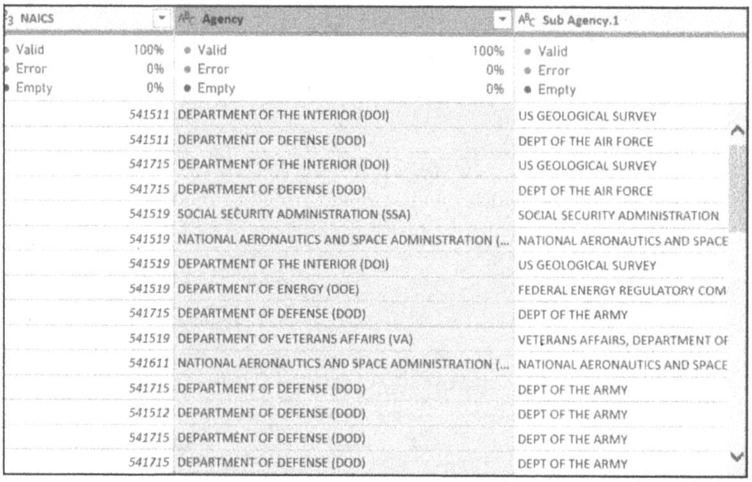

FIGURE 7-15:
The expanded
Merged Columns
example.

USING USER-FRIENDLY NAMING CONVENTIONS FOR COLUMNS AND QUERIES

Whether you bring data into Power BI from an external source or create the data model internally, there are no hard-and-fast rules related to column- and query-naming conventions. That doesn't mean you should get sloppy, however. Just the opposite!

When you create a user-friendly naming convention, it becomes easier to handle data in a model and reduces confusion for users who access data. Microsoft strongly encourages Power BI users to follow a disciplined protocol when naming tables, columns, and measures. You want to apply a naming convention that doesn't require much, especially for those with a limited technical background.

It's not uncommon to retrieve data from a database that may carry a naming convention that isn't desirable. For example, if the field Total Obligated Amount was named fin_Total_Obligations, it may create some confusion. Therefore, simplifying the naming convention to a meaningful one is important when creating and managing a data model.

Tweaking Power Query's M Code

The Power Query Editor in Power BI is quite powerful. Still, it has its limits when it comes to writing queries. That's where human intervention comes in. Writing M queries isn't tricky. Just remember that all queries are case-sensitive and all have to follow the rules behind the Power Query code engine.

REMEMBER

Power BI supports two languages: M and DAX. These languages help manipulate, filter, and analyze data. Whereas DAX is used to analyze data after its loaded into a Data View model, M is used to preprocess the data inside the Power BI Power Query Editor.

To view and edit M queries, you must fire up the Power Query Advanced Editor. To do so, click the Advanced Editor button in the Query area of the Ribbon's Home tab. (See Figure 7-16). Another option is to right-click any query in the Queries pane and then select Advanced Editor from the menu that appears, as shown in Figure 7-17. Whichever method you choose, you're greeted by an editor pane displaying the M code for the query selected, as shown in Figure 7-18.

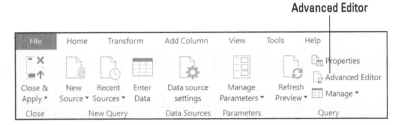

FIGURE 7-16: The Advanced Editor button on the Ribbon's Home tab.

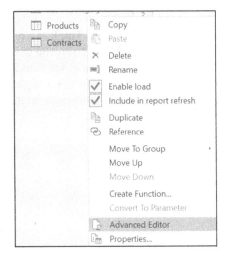

FIGURE 7-17: Getting to the Advanced Editor via the Queries pane.

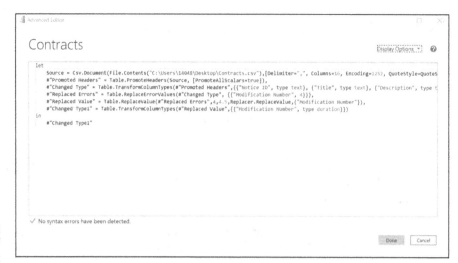

FIGURE 7-18:
The M Query
Editor interface.

**TECHNICAL
STUFF**

All M queries start with let and end with in. Between these two, you can have multiple steps in a query. With the let construct, you can see variable definitions that correspond to query steps.

Here's an example of a let and in statement:

Let   a = 2 + 2, (step 1)

    b = 4 + 4, (step 2)

    c = b + 6 (step 3)

in

    a + b +c (final step)

The first time a query runs, a reference is created. Think of a reference as a starting point to the query. If you make a modification to the query, Power BI asks whether you want to create an added step, or another *iteration*, in your query. Depending on how you view the query steps, you see a slight variation in how steps appear. If you review the Queries Steps pane, you might find step names such as

» Source

» Navigation

» Promoted Headers

» Change Type

When you look at the Query Steps pane, locate Applied Steps. Each time you make a transformation from the reference point in your data, you find such changes on the Applied Steps list. Applied Steps helps track the number of transformations that have happened in the data from the get-go. As with version control, you can return to the previous state using Applied Steps. In Figure 7-18, you can see the historical context for a query that has Applied Steps.

TIP

If you're thinking that M coding can prove a bit unwieldy, you have another possibility to choose from: You can view the code of a query and even manipulate the formulas by taking a step-by-step approach that makes use of the standard Formula bar. First, however, you have to enable it: Go to the Ribbon's View tab and click the Formula Bar button, as shown in Figure 7-19. Whatever would have been shown as the query in the Advanced Query Editor is replicated in the Formula bar. As you make changes to a query, you notice the M Query language output changes in real time.

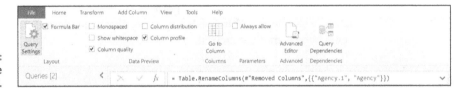

FIGURE 7-19:
Enabling the
Formula bar.

ON THE
WEB

If you want to learn more about the M query language and all its syntax features, go to https://docs.microsoft.com/en-us/powerquery-m.

Configuring Queries for Data Loading

When developing a Power BI data model, users can take advantage of the fact that Microsoft gives them the ability to use Help queries. These helper tools are available by processing your model using the Get Data option and the Transform Data option. Also, when you're trying to combine files or even merge datasets, Power Query supports helper queries.

REMEMBER

Helper queries are embedded into Power BI Power Query in order to assist users in creating query strings. Rather than make the coding process complex, you can use the built-in API to simplify the most difficult parts of query development. In fact, helper queries support common terms, phrases, ranges, and geospatial functions.

Of course, you may have queries you don't need or want to load, because not all data may be helpful. In this case, right-click the Queries pane and then clear the Enable Load section. When queries are already loaded, you may get errors. Otherwise, select which queries you want to omit from the load process.

One common scenario occurs when you don't want to load queries that are appended or merged with other queries. To segregate queries that should not be included, follow these steps:

1. **Right-click the first query you want to omit.**

2. **Choose Enable Load from the menu that appears in the Queries pane.**

3. **Make sure each table you want to omit from the query is deselected.**

4. **Repeat this process for each query you don't want to load.**

The result is removing unwanted entities from the data model for future querying and loading. In Figure 7-20, you can see an example of the drop-down menu to select or deselect Enable Load. Any query that's deselected isn't loaded, and it's noted by text that's italicized.

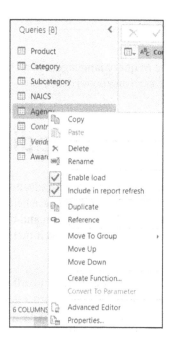

FIGURE 7-20:
Removing queries.

After you've modified the entities to be included in the queries, save your changes by pressing the Close & Apply button on the Ribbon's Home tab. (See Figure 7-21.)

FIGURE 7-21:
Close & Apply
in the Power
Query Editor.

Resolving Errors During Data Import

Every so often, when you load data, you might encounter query errors in Power BI. Don't panic!

Errors come in many forms. Values alone don't cause a query to blatantly fail. Power BI lets you know the total number of errors for each query. *Error values*, or values ignored during querying, are considered blank values. Simply put, they have no text in the field — not even a zero.

To get to the bottom of what's actually causing errors in Power Query, make use of the View Error hyperlink, which can be found in the Power Query Editor column throwing the specified error. When you click the hyperlink, you can see the specific details related to the query. Common reasons why errors are thrown in Power Query often are linked to data conversion. For example, a value originally N/A, which is considered text, would not work in a column intended for numbers.

To correct an error such as this one, you need to change the column type. To make such a modification, follow these steps:

1. **In the Power Query Editor, select the query in question.**

2. **Right-click the column presenting an error.**

3. **Choose Change Type from the menu that appears and then change the selection from Number to Text.**

4. **Select Replace Current when the pop-up appears to validate that you want to change the column data type.**

   You have now changed the column data type from Numerical to Text. Now, alphanumeric values, not just numeric values, can be added to the column for the specific dataset. After you click the Close & Apply button for a dataset that's been corrected, the error messages disappear.

3

The Art and Science of Power BI

Gain firsthand insight into how to load, transform, and extract data to support the data analytics lifecycle in Power BI.

Understand how to perfect datasets without compromising integrity, quality, and reliability using Power BI Desktop tools.

Craft visualizations using Power BI Desktop and Power BI Services to collaborate and share with others in the form of reports and dashboards.

Grasp the technical nuances to enhance your reporting as well as your dashboards as you make the transition from Power BI Desktop to Power BI Services.

Chapter **8**

Crafting the Data Model

You probably thought that, after the data is transformed by Power BI, you'll have smooth sailing. In some instances, this is correct. Of course, when you have created a detailed model with many tables, a bit of work is required to refine the dataset. Data modeling is both an art and a science because you're constantly trying to shape data so that the insights gained are as precise as possible. Once you load and transform the data, the real fun begins — the "trying to perfect it" part. That's where modeling is introduced. In this chapter, I describe schema designs that provide you with the information you need in order to design and develop data models that support visualization and reporting.

An Introduction to Data Models

Data models are the building blocks of visualization and reporting. A data model consists of one or more tables and several relationships — assuming that more than just one or two tables exist. Well-designed data models help users articulate their data and build on insights. As such, data modeling requires some hard work — it cannot be done in one fell swoop. You first have to load your data and then you have to define the relationships between tables after the data is transformed into a table with the help of Power BI.

REMEMBER

The best time to build a model is at the beginning phase of the Power BI report or visualization development. If you want to create efficient measures, you hone the data model, emphasizing table and relationship management.

Working with data schemas

You've imported all this data that was transformed into one or many tables — now what? Your first business aim is to address how to overcome creating complicated data models. In Power BI, data modeling can be streamlined.

Your first goal is to start with the data schema. If you start there, you likely soon recognize that your data is coming from one or more transactional systems. Under these circumstances, having many tables will likely overwhelm you. You don't want data clutter — you want to organize and simplify your understanding of the data. That's where schemas come in.

With Power BI, you have three approaches to data schema design and simplification: flat, snowflake, and star schema design. Understanding when to use each model type can help support data performance and granularity across visualization and reporting. The next few sections are designed to help you gain that understanding.

Flat schemas

Consider a listing of sales transactions, customer identities, or awards. What do all these have in common? Suppose that you were to lay out the data in an Excel spreadsheet. In that case, you'd likely need only a single table to present the essential data. When that's the case, you'd want to use a *flat schema,* — the one that uses just a single table, similar to the one you see in Figure 8-1.

CustomerID	CustomerName	POCName	DateCreated
U123X456	The Art School Inc.	Michael Angelo	1/3/2021 05:00 PM
U123X567	Music Academy LLC	Fred Chopin	2/4/2021 04:00 PM
U123X789	Sports Stadium Inc.	Babe Ruthie	3/7/2021 03:00 PM
U123X678	Bookbinder Corp.	Bill Bookman	4/9/2021 02:00 PM
U123X987	Jingle Cleaning LLC	Jana Jingle	5/8/2021 01:00 PM
U123X756	Gentle George Air Inc.	George Gentle	6/7/2021 12:00 PM
U123X911	Milkman Foods Corp.	Deborah Milkman	5/7/2021 11:00 PM

FIGURE 8-1:
A flat schema.

Note the four columns in Figure 8-1. Each of these data columns may have a unique identifier: a specific time/date stamp showing when the customer data was entered, the company name, the customer ID, and the company point of contact. Each of these data points can be used as a lookup to better assess detailed customer information independently. When you look at the model, though, it can stand on its own. You would consider a flat schema when reporting requirements are linear and unsophisticated, requiring no more than a single table.

TIP

Flat schemas tend to have a limited use value. When you're looking to bring information from a spreadsheet into Power BI for the purpose of fundamental analysis — a task that may involve adding a column of values or filtering of data — this approach is perfectly adequate. As soon as you introduce many tables, you have to go with an alternative approach.

If you deploy just one table, it can be used for reporting, but the scope is limited. Perhaps you can filter data or extract one or two data points to build simplified visuals or basic calculated outputs. That's where the usefulness of a flat schema ends.

Star schemas

Most organizations have a model that is representative of the star schema approach. You often find models with one or two large tables known as fact tables, and then a few dimension tables. When data modeler plans a model, it's a common practice to model tables as either dimensions or facts. Here's how they differ:

>> **Fact tables** are representative of observations or events. Consider patterns such as sales transactions, account balances, and personnel records. The fact table connects to one or more dimension key column that relates to a given dimension. For example, a transaction table with a sales transaction (fact table) might map to a manufacturer (dimension table). The dimension key column decides an item's *dimensionality* — the details within a fact table. Dimension key-values offer product granularity.

>> **Dimension tables** describe the business entity in granular detail. These are attributes of the product, people, places, and concepts that are part of the fact table. Think of a dimension as a quality attribute that can provide a greater level of granularity.

REMEMBER

Dimension tables often have a finite number of rows because these are widely used descriptors. Fact tables can hold many rows and grow over time because these are the transaction records. Consider that the dimension table is an excellent utility for filtering and grouping, whereas the fact table is an example of summarization.

Whenever a Power BI report visualization is generated, you notice that a query is generated against the Power BI model (also referred to as the *dataset*). The query is designed to filter, group, and summarize the model data. Your main goal is to create a model that can meet each of these particular business goals. Figure 8-2 presents the fact-versus-dimension-tables concept, whereas Figure 8-3 presents a prototype star schema.

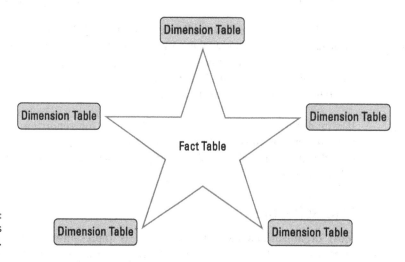

FIGURE 8-2:
Facts versus dimensions.

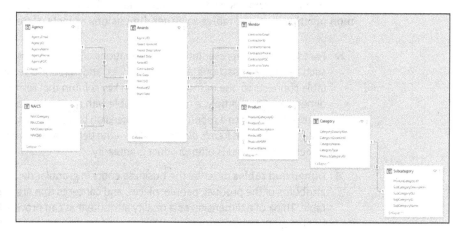

FIGURE 8-3:
A star schema prototype.

REMEMBER

With a star schema, no properties exist to classify a table as a fact or a dimension. The relationship itself decides the model behavior. A model relationship is set up between two entities and the attributes maintained within the entity.

Cardinality — the property of the relationship, in other words — determines the table types. Common relationships are one-to-one, one-to-many, or many-to-many. One side is always the dimension table, whereas the Many side is always a fact table. However, seldom do you ever find a one-to-one relationship within a star schema, because the fact table tends to repeat dimensions more than once.

With data modeling, a well-structured model design includes distinct tables that are either dimension-type or fact-type. Don't mix table types to create a single table. If you create a single table, you realize quickly that the data in place is poorly formed. That's why you should evaluate your data to ensure that you have the right number of tables with the correct relationships in place.

Good data modeling design is both an art and a science. You try to follow all the rules, but sometimes your data doesn't allow you to be a perfectionist. Try to stay the course and do your best to create the purest data model possible.

Snowflake schemas

Another type of schema where you have a set of normalized tables that drill down against a single business entity is the *snowflake schema*, which is an extension of a star schema. Normalized data helps you reduce data redundancy and promotes data integrity. Suppose that each of your products falls into a category or subcategory. The branching outward from the single business entity, products, to its associated category and subcategory reminds some people of a snowflake. (Okay, you do have to squint at it sideways for a few minutes before its snowflakeyness becomes evident — try it with Figure 8-4.)

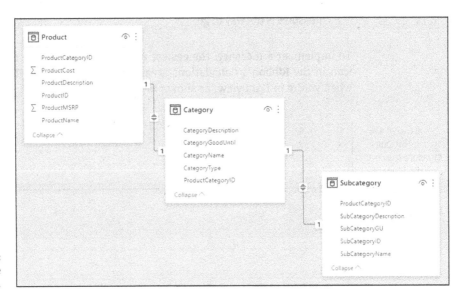

FIGURE 8-4: A snowflake schema.

Storing values with measures

Measures are, generally speaking, a type of fact table column you can use to store summarized values. When you use a Power BI model, a measure has a similar definition. You're creating a formula using DAX to achieve a summary column. Measures often used in DAX are associated with aggregation functions such as SUM, MIN, MAX, and AVERAGE to produce values upon data querying.

There is a second approach to achieve summarization, however. Any column that is numeric can be summarized by a visualization as represented in reports and dashboards or question and answer (Q&A). The second type of measure is an implicit measure. You can create a column that summarizes data in many ways without having to create several aggregation types.

So, when would you use measures, even for basic column summarization? Here are some situations where it makes perfect sense:

>> **When a report author intends to query a model by using multidimensional expressions (MDX):** These models require explicit measures, which require the use of DAX.

>> **When the report author creates Power BI paginated reports using the MDX query design:** The model needs to include explicit measures.

>> **When the report author must use Power BI to conduct the analysis versus the original dataset.** The author must use the MDX query designer.

>> **When summarizing data must be completed in a specific way:** When you're using the aggregation function available in Power BI, for example, using measures is the way to go.

To implement a measure, the easiest way to do so is to click the Quick Measure icon in the Ribbon's Calculations area. (That area is on the Ribbon's Home tab when you're in Data view, as shown in Figure 8-5.)

You can deploy a variety of calculations using Quick Measure, including formulas you've built using predefined calculations. These are the calculation categories:

» Aggregate per category

» Filters

» Mathematical operations

» Text

» Time intelligence

» Totals

Figure 8-6 lists some of the choices under the Aggregate Per Category heading as well as the Filters heading.

FIGURE 8-6:
Some Quick
Measures
options.

Another choice is to create your own formulas using New Measure. To create a New Measure, follow these steps:

1. **Under the Data Tab, either right-click a column or click the ellipses in the Fields Pane and choose New Measure from the menu that appears.**

   Selecting New Measure let you start a new measure with a new pre-defined formula. (By default, a New Measure Starts as Measure =.) Some data might be prepopulated on the Formula bar, as shown in Figure 8-7.

2. **Replace "Measure =" with the name of a new column and an equal sign and then add a prebuilt DAX formula. (I cover this more in Chapter 15.)**

   An example measure could be `TotalBid = Sum(Awards[Bids]`.

The resulting product is a DAX-based formula if you're using New Measure. Otherwise, the Formula bar has the code generated.

Working with dimensions and fact tables (yet again)

With Power BI, you'll notice a theme when preparing data models: You often refer to entities such as Product, Manufacturer, or Company as *dimension tables*. These tables connect to a fact table such as Customer, Sales, or Invoices. Now, a dimension is a qualitative way of describing data, but fact tables are primarily quantitative in nature, where you perform mathematical functions. In the model presented earlier, in Figure 8-2, you notice one fact table and many dimension tables. Each dimension table, commonly referred to as just a dimension, will have many descriptive fields but a few rows. That is not the case with a fact table, where you find that the table has few fields but many rows.

When planning the design of your data model, you have several approaches when it comes to creating dimensional data. Table 8-1 describes each approach.

TABLE 8-1:

Dimensional Data Approaches

Approach	Description
Slowly changing	Manages change of dimensions over time.
Role-playing	Filters facts against many criteria.
Junk	Appropriate to consider when you have many dimensions with few attributes. There are also few values, making the data potentially limited. Examples may include gender and age group.
Degenerate	Requires an attribute to a fact table that is needed for filtering. In this case, a primary key is an example.
Factless fact	Contains no measures, only dimension keys.

Flattening hierarchies

A *hierarchy* is a set of fields categorized in a way where one level is the parent of other levels. The value of the parent level can be drilled down to a lower-level category. A parent-child hierarchy shows data about accounts, customers, or salespeople in a retail environment. Hierarchies are based on variable depth. For example, you might illustrate data based on country, state, or street when describing a business territory. An organization may also be tied to a region. In this case, you have a four-level hierarchy.

A common practice in Power BI is to *flatten* the hierarchy — make the hierarchy structure a single level, in other words — so that a regular hierarchy is made up of one column for the hierarchy. Each node is represented in a separate, distinct column. In Figure 8-8, you can see how the product category ID is tied to the product name and product ID. This represents a two-level hierarchy, because each item is mutually exclusive to a common factor, the product category ID.

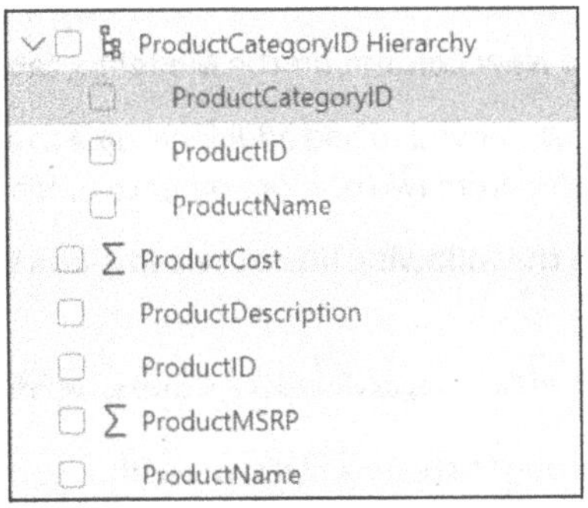

FIGURE 8-8:
Flattening a
hierarchy.

You have a couple of options when creating a hierarchy. The following set of instructions is the most efficient way to create a parent-child hierarchy — you need to be in Report view to complete this series of actions:

1. **Right-click a field and choose Create Hierarchy from the menu that appears.**

   A top-level hierarchy is created.

2. **Right-click the field of an item you want to add to the newly created hierarchy and then choose Add to Hierarchy from the menu that appears.**

3. **In the listing that appears, select the hierarchy you want to add.**

   In this case, I added ProductsName to the ProductName Hierarchy.

To change the order of fields in the hierarchy, follow these steps:

1. **Right-click the field within the hierarchy.**

2. **Choose either Move Up or Move Down from the menu that appears.**

TIP

You can also drag the field to the required position if no existing relationship is in place yet.

An alternative method for creating a hierarchy is to use Data view in connection with the Formula bar. In this example, I use the Subcategory table to show you how to create a hierarchy. Follow these steps:

1. **In Power BI Desktop, choose Data View in the Navigation pane found on the left side of the screen.**

2. **Once you've selected Data view, select a table.**

   I am selecting the Subcategory table.

3. **From the Ribbon, choose New Column on the Modeling tab.**

   Adding a new Column allows for you to add additional data to an existing table, perhaps a formula generated from two or more other columns.

4. **In the Formula bar, type the following line as one line and then press Enter:**

   ```
   Path = PATH (Subcategory[SubcategoryName], Subcategory[ProductCategoryID])
   ```

   You're using the PATH function to create a hierarchy path.

5. **From the Ribbon, choose New Column on the Modeling tab yet again.**

   Keep in mind that you are adding another level to the existing hierarchy you've already created.

6. **In the Formula bar, type the following line and press Enter:**

   ```
   Level 2 = PATHITEM(Subcategory [Path],1)
   ```

   Here you're using the PATHITEM function, which retrieves the value for the particular level in the hierarchy. In the example, you have three levels. It's time to add the remaining two columns of the hierarchy. You'll repeat this to create a three-level hierarchy. Each time you are pressing Enter, you are establishing a new hierarchy level.

7. **In the Formula bar, type the following line and press Enter:**

   ```
   Level 2 = PATHITEM(Subcategory [Path],2)
   ```

8. **Again, in the Formula bar, type the following line and press Enter:**

   ```
   Level 3 = PATHITEM(Subcategory [Path],3)
   ```

   Figure 8-9 shows the output of using the PATH Function and PATHITEM function on the Formula bar.

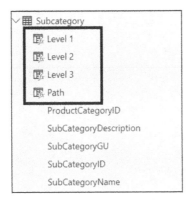

FIGURE 8-9:
Example of a
multi-level
hierarchy.

Dealing with Table and Column Properties

Earlier in this chapter, I briefly discuss designing tables and columns. One commonality is that there are many properties that users can configure, all of which can be set in Model view. To *see* the properties of a column or table, however, you first need to select an object. Once selected, the properties for the object are visible in the Properties pane.

To see how this works, choose Model View from the navigation bar on the left side of the Power BI interface. Once in Model view, click on the object for a table property to view its properties. If you're looking to see a specific column property, click on the column within the table. You can see examples of the table and column properties in Figures 8-10 and 8-11.

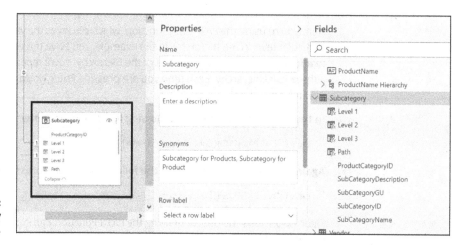

FIGURE 8-10:
Table property
selection.

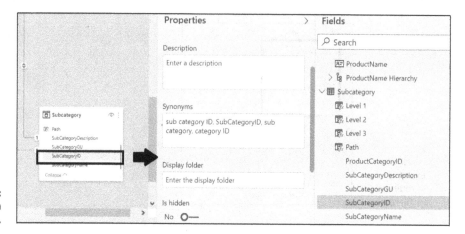

FIGURE 8-11:
Column
properties.

Here are the table property options:

» Name

» Description

» Synonyms

» Row label

» Key column

» Is hidden

» Is featured

And here are the column properties:

» Name

» Description

» Synonyms

» Display folder

» Is hidden

» Data type

» Format

» Sort by column

» Data category

» Summarize by

» Is nullable

TIP

Although most of the measure properties can also be configured as column properties, some column properties — including Sort By, Summarize, or Is Nullable — cannot be made into measures.

Managing Cardinality and Direction

In earlier sections of this chapter, I briefly discuss the relationships between fields and tables. The important thing to remember is whether you're trying to set up a one-to-one, one-to-many, many-to-one, or many-to-many relationship, these are all referred to as relationships *between* tables — its cardinality, in other words. To edit the relationship between tables, click on the relationship link in a model. Doing so brings up a window you can use to better set up the cardinality, as shown in Model view. (Figure 8-12 provides an example of such an editable relationship.) You can change the relationship cardinality on this page. You see a preview of each dataset to select a column that becomes part of the relationship.

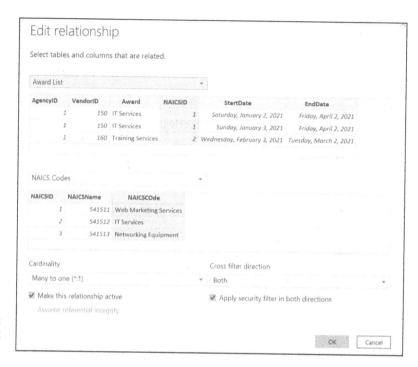

FIGURE 8-12:
Editing
relationships.

To ensure that a relationship is active, be sure to select the Make This Relationship Active check box. (Again, see Figure 8-12.) There can be only one active relationship between two tables. Furthermore, if you choose to use Direct Query, you should check the Assume Referential Integrity check box. (Referential integrity helps improve query performance.)

Cardinality

The relationship between two tables comes in four flavors: one-to-one, one-to-many, many-to-one, or many-to-many. Most times, with Power BI, you use many-to-one relationships to implement parts of a data model. Table 8-2 describes the difference among the four relationship types.

Cross-filter direction

Just because you have set up a relationship type between two tables doesn't mean that the data will flow the way you want. In fact, if you look back at Figure 8-12, you also notice a Cross Filter Direction drop-down menu in the lower right corner of the screen. When setting up a relationship, you can also show the direction in which filters flow. For one-to-many or many-to-one, you have the choice of selecting Single or Both.

TABLE 8-2 **Cardinality and Relationship Description**

Relationship Type	Description
One-to-one (1:1)	Key data appears in both tables only once.
One-to-many (1:M)	*Many* refers to the fact that a key may appear more than once in a select column. *One* means that a key-value appears only once in the selected table. When you have a 1:M relationship, one key on the left side of the relationship acts as a unique identifier, whereas many items on the right side can match.
Many-to-one (M:1)	Similar to a one-to-many (1:M) relationship, many items can often be tied to a single key. The only difference is the direction and order of the key data.
Many-to-many (M: M)	A relationship exists between two tables; however, there is potentially no unique value between both tables.

So, what do Single and Both mean exactly? Here's a clue:

» **Single:** Filters data from the table on the One side to the table data on the Many side. A single arrow points to the relationship line in Model view.

» **Both:** Filters from both tables in both directions. These relationships are bidirectional. Two arrows appear in the relationship line in Model view.

TECHNICAL STUFF

When selecting Both for Apply Cross-Filter Direction, you can also select Apply Security Filter. Adding such features introduces row-level security, a way to implement restrictions on data based on row access.

In Figure 8-13, notice the bidirectionality between the NAICS Code table and the Award List table. On the other hand, there is a many-to-one relationship — hence, a single cross-filter direction — between the Agency Contacts table and the Award List table. That means that many agency contacts can be tied to a single Award List entry. The number of records between both tables varies, given 1:M or M:1 with and without bidirectionality.

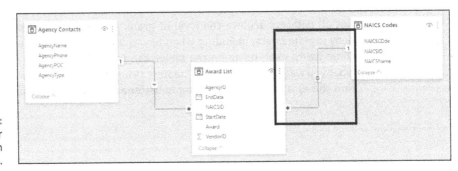

FIGURE 8-13: A cross-filter direction example.

Data Granularity

The details behind your data matter. That's why *data granularity* — the specificity of your data — matters. Take another look at the Award List table shown in Figure 8-13. You can see that the example provides NAICS Code ID to address the refined classification of an award. Filtering the data by a field with a lower granularity, such as StartDate or EndDate, might be helpful. Still, it doesn't supply a definitive result set. The range of responses is broad, as shown in Figure 8-14. Filtering by NAICS Code ID provides a more refined dataset, given the relationship with the table NAICS Codes.

✕ ✓ *fx*	= Table.TransformColumnTypes(Source,{{"AgencyID", Int64.Type}, {"VendorID",			
▦ **Award** ▾	1²₃ **NAICSID** ▾	▦ **StartDate** ▾	▦ **EndData** ▾	
Valid 100%	● Valid 100%	● Valid 100%	● Valid 100%	
Error 0%	● Error 0%	● Error 0%	● Error 0%	
Empty 0%	● Empty 0%	● Empty 0%	● Empty 0%	
distinct, 1 unique	5 distinct, 2 unique	17 distinct, 17 unique	15 distinct, 13 unique	
1 Services	1	1/2/2021	4/2/2021	
2 Services	1	1/3/2021	4/2/2021	
3 aining Services	2	2/3/2021	3/2/2021	
4 aining Services	2	2/4/2021	11/1/2023	
5 otography Equipment	2	2/5/2021	11/1/2023	
6 od	2	2/6/2021	11/15/2025	
7 od	3	2/11/2021	11/3/2022	
8 od	4	5/1/2021	4/1/2025	
9 fice Supplies	4	5/2/2021	4/2/2023	
10 fice Supplies	5	5/24/2021	3/2/2024	
11 Services	1	6/22/2021	3/4/2025	
12 Services	1	6/21/2021	5/1/2025	
13 aining Services	2	7/1/2021	5/12/2022	
14 aining Services	2	4/3/2021	5/19/2023	

FIGURE 8-14: Granularity of NAICS ID, StartDate, and EndDate in the Award List table.

Not all datasets achieve the level of granularity you want. Examples where you need to refine data, including when new columns are introduced, are common. In some cases, even unsupported tables can be filtered, but the results don't yield what you want. As I discuss in Chapters 15 and 16, the use of the ISFILTERED function comes in handy when trying to better assess data granularity.

Chapter **9**

Designing and Deploying Data Models

Manipulating data after it's in Power BI is both an art and a science. Data you've imported into any application requires you to pay attention to not just your dataset but also how the data has been defined. If you learn one thing about data, you need to refine it from the get-go. That means exploiting tables, creating new hierarchies, establishing joins and relationships that make sense, and classifying the data. Of course, you want your outputs to be meaningful, so you have to pay close attention to how you arrange the data in the data model. In this chapter, you discover how to craft your data in Power BI Desktop so that you can design and deploy effective data models for visualization, reporting, and dashboards. This chapter starts out by teaching you how to design and develop a basic data model in the Power BI Desktop environment and then shows you how to publish the model to Power BI Services when you're ready for showtime.

Creating a Data Model Masterpiece

Creating visualizations requires a data model — it's just one of those things. Your data source also needs to be correct, specific, and well crafted. It's true that Power BI can do some amazing things, by transforming data across multiple datasets by utilizing its ETL (extract, transform, and load) framework to support development and design activity. After the data is safely in the Desktop application, though, the accessible data still needs your attention. You need to take some specific actions to prepare the data so that the model can be crafted and work as a well-oiled dataset for visualization and reporting. A well-defined dataset helps you analyze the data as well as gain prescriptive and descriptive insights.

REMEMBER

Model creation doesn't stop at data ingestion. It requires defining data types, exploiting table design, creating hierarchies, crafting joins and relationships, and classifying the data in the model.

Working with Data view and Modeling view

After importing data into the Power BI Desktop environment, your goal is to now manipulate the data so that it works the way you need it to for your models. The first stop on your journey is to explore the Data View tab and the Model View tab. The difference between the two is that the Data View tab presents all data imported into the data model. In contrast, the Model View tab is the visualization of the model based on what Power BI believes the model is at a point in time.

You are responsible for updating the model, because it's part of your responsibility after importing the data. You can do this on either the Data View tab (by viewing all data instances) or the Model View tab (by reviewing the model itself). An example of the output on the Data View tab is shown in Figure 9-1; Figure 9-2 shows the output on the Model View tab.

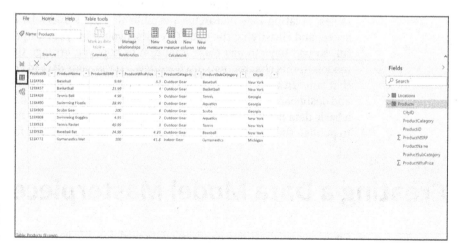

FIGURE 9-1:
The Data
View tab.

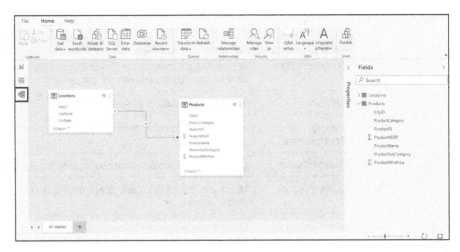

FIGURE 9-2:
The Model
View tab.

The Home Ribbon for the Model View is considered the cockpit for managing many of your data actions, no matter which view you're in within the Power BI Desktop. As you can see in Figure 9-3, the Home Ribbon for the Model View is broken down into distinct areas: Data, Queries, Relationships, Calculations, Security, and Share. Each area has its own set of features, as listed in Table 9-1.

FIGURE 9-3:
The Home Ribbon
in Model View

TABLE 9-1

Buttons On the Power BI Model View Home Ribbon

Button	What It Does
Get Data	Gets data from a data source. You can choose from more than 100 data source options, both relational and nonrelational.
Excel Workbook	Gets data from an Excel File, a common Microsoft data source
Power BI Dataset	Gets data from a previously created Power BI dataset
SQL Server	Gets data from a SQL Server connection
Enter Data	Creates new tables inside Power BI
Dataverse	Connects to an environment from Power BI using a query string, including those supported by DirectQuery
Recent Sources	Allows users to access those data sources most recently created in Power BI

(continued)

TABLE 9-1 *(continued)*

Button	What It Does
Transform Data	Serves as a gateway to the Power Query Editor with tools that can be found to edit and transform datasets
Refresh	Refreshes the data in an easy way
Manage Relationships	Establishes cardinality among tables in Power BI
New Measure	Creates a new calculated measure using the Formula bar
Quick Measure	Using predefined calculations against fields, builds out the specific fields for the user
New Column	Creates a new column for a specific table
New Table	Creates a new table
Manage Roles	Determines who should be able to view specific data models
View As	Limits the dataset to specific users
Publish	Publishes the dataset to Power BI Services

The Power Query Editor shares many of the same features shown in Table 9-1, although it also has (unsurprisingly) specific features for query editing, as shown in Figure 9-4.

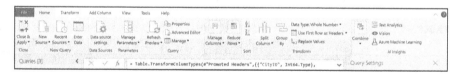

FIGURE 9-4:
The Power Query
Editor Ribbon.

A noticeable difference between Model View and Power Query Editor is that Power Query Editor allows you to set data source settings, manage parameters, configure editor parameters, configure rows and columns, group by, sort by, and handle data types. It also focuses on artificial intelligence features for text analytics. As you begin to manage the design of your datasets, you naturally want to know more about row and column management because configuring rows and columns to behave as you see fit is integral to dataset behavior. Therefore, as you probably guessed you have a few more bells and whistles to play with under the Power Query Editor because you are manipulating queries versus model building.

Importing queries

I walk you through importing Excel files in a number of chapters, but it never hurts to practice importing one or more Excel files to establish fresh queries — I'm giving you another chance. Keep in mind that you can import your queries into Power BI Desktop using one of several import options. Start by using the Navigation pane on the left side of the screen to switch to Data view, where all existing tables are available. If you want to start fresh, open a new file by choosing File ➪ New from the main menu. If, however, you want to import, follow these steps:

1. **Select the type of file or source you want to import into Power BI under Get Data.**

   Once you select your data source, the Navigator window opens, as shown in Figure 9-5.

2. **To load data, pick one or more datasets and then click the Load button.**

3. **To transform data, pick one or more datasets and then click the Transform Data button**.

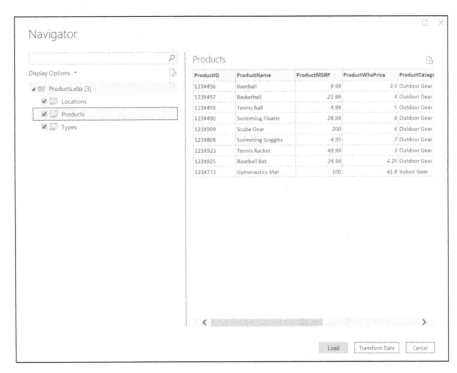

FIGURE 9-5:
The Navigator
window in
Data view.

REMEMBER

If you choose Load, that means the data won't be mapped to a specific data type. If you choose Transform Data, Power BI does its best to map against the proper data type based on ETL properties.

TECHNICAL STUFF

Though Data view is similar to the Power Query Editor, keep in mind that only a sample of your data is shown in the Power Query Editor, whereas all data is available in Data view after it's imported into the data model. In Data view, you're working with your entire dataset, and modifications are made live with the dashboard requirements and specifications. Both Data view and the Power Query Editor can handle the creation of calculated columns in real time, though.

After the data is loaded, you can manipulate it, add queries, add or delete columns, or manage the existing relationships. The following sections explain in detail how to complete each of these activities.

Defining data types

When Power BI imports a dataset, it defaults to a specific data type. For example, in Figure 9-6, you can see that the Products table has several columns, two of these columns indicate decimal numbers as options. The column represented here is ProductMSRP and ProductWhsPrice. The data type may not be accurate because these columns are monetary in nature. You have the choice of decimal number or fixed decimal number. In this case, monetary values require decimal number. A user can also place formatting in the column to better represent the context of the data in each of the cells.

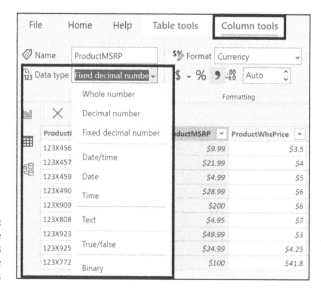

FIGURE 9-6:
Using the Column Tools tab to change the data type.

To review the data types for a given column, follow these steps.

1. **Go to Data view.**
2. **Select the column you want to review and highlight it.**
3. **Make sure you're on the Column Tools tab. (Refer to Figure 9-6).**
4. **On the Column Tools tab, check the Name property to make sure.**
5. **Check to make sure the Data Type drop-down menu (see Figure 9-7) is set to the correct data type.**

   In this case, it's set to Decimal Number.

6. **Switch the option to Fixed Decimal Number.**
7. **Using the tab's Format drop-down menu (again, see Figure 9-6), switch the option to Currency.**

FIGURE 9-7:
A list of data
type options.

This process is consistent throughout Power BI for modifying data types whether you're trying to change numerical data to text or text to numeric.

Handling formatting and data type properties

Depending on whether the column is text or numeric, you can use the Format drop-down menu on the Column Tools tab to also apply specific properties to a column to ensure specific behaviors. At the end of the previous section, I applied the Currency format to my columns, but if the column is numeric, you can also apply other behaviors, including decimal numbers, whole numbers, percentage, and scientific number formatting. (See Figure 9-8.)

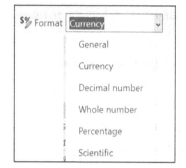

FIGURE 9-8:
Numeric
formatting
options.

Suppose you're looking to apply properties such as Measures, Geographic markers, or Mathematical Behaviors against a column. In that case, you can apply a *summarization* (a way to further evaluate data mathematically) or a data category (a way to classify geographically-based data). Summarization options for the Column Tools tab are shown in Figure 9-9, and the Data Category options are displayed in Figure 9-10.

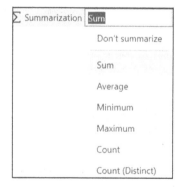

FIGURE 9-9:
The Summariza-
tion options on
the Column
Tools tab.

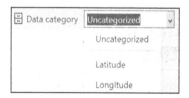

FIGURE 9-10:
The Data
Categories
options.

REMEMBER

Summarization options allow for any column of numeric data in a table to be summarized as a single value. Data Category options are applicable for Power BI mapping — latitude and longitude or degrees, in other words.

Managing tables

You've imported at least one table and created a dataset. Sometimes, the name of the table may not be exactly what you want. Or maybe you want to delete a table. These are all common actions that a data expert faces in Power BI Desktop as they work their way through the design, development, and deployment of their data model.

Adding tables

There may be times when you need to add one or more tables to your data model after you've imported the dataset into Power BI Desktop. Perhaps you want to create an additional fact table for the transactional activity or a dimension table to support a new lookup. Both scenarios are pretty standard, but, luckily, adding a table is straightforward. You' still need to do a bit of configuration after you set the column names, though.

In any event, here's how you add a table:

1. **In Model view, click the Enter Data button on the Home tab of the Model View Ribbon, as shown in Figure 9-11.**

    The Create Table Interface appears.

FIGURE 9-11:
The Enter
Data button.

2. **Enter the column names and data you want into the appropriate table cells.**
3. **Enter a table name in the Name field.**

    The table should look something like the one shown in Figure 9-12.
4. **Click Load once you are finished creating your table.**

The result is a brand-new table that appears as part of the data model you're able to access in Data view as well as in Model view.

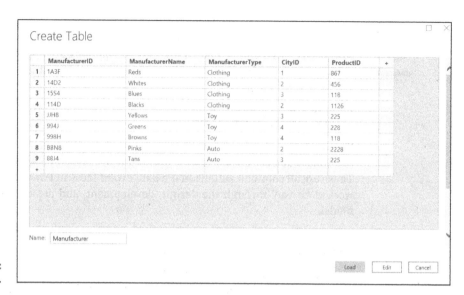

Create Table

	ManufacturerID	ManufacturerName	ManufacturerType	CityID	ProductID	+
1	1A3F	Reds	Clothing	1	867	
2	14D2	Whites	Clothing	2	456	
3	15S4	Blues	Clothing	3	118	
4	114D	Blacks	Clothing	2	1126	
5	JJH8	Yellows	Toy	3	225	
6	994J	Greens	Toy	4	228	
7	998H	Browns	Toy	4	118	
8	BBN8	Pinks	Auto	2	2228	
9	88J4	Tans	Auto	3	225	
+						

Name: Manufacturer

Load   Edit   Cancel

FIGURE 9-12:
Creating a table.

Renaming tables

Renaming a table is a straightforward activity as long as no table already has the same name. With Power BI, every table in a data model must have a unique name. For example, two tables cannot have the name Product. (You can have a table named Product and another named Products, but that would be pretty confusing.) Best practices suggest that you be as descriptive as possible. To rename a table in Power BI Desktop, follow these steps:

1. **In either Data view or Model view, go to the Fields pane.**

2. **Right-click the table name you want to change.**

3. **Choose Rename from the menu that appears, as shown in Figure 9-13.**

4. **Enter a new name for your table in the highlighted field and then press Enter.**

   The table name will refresh within 30 seconds.

Deleting tables

If you want to delete a table from a model, you face a few risks. If relationships are associated with the table, those relationships will break. In addition, if calculated fields are embedded within a report, those too will disappear. That said, removing a table, like moving a column, is a relatively simple process. To remove a table, follow these steps:

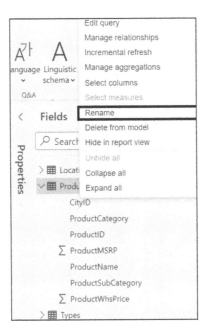

FIGURE 9-13: Updating the table name in Model view.

1. **In either Data view or Model view, go to the Fields pane.**

2. **Right-click a table to remove, and then choose Delete from Model from the menu that appears, as shown in Figure 9-14.**

   A prompt appears, asking whether you're sure you want to delete the table, as shown in Figure 9-15.

3. **Click Delete.**

   The table is deleted from the model.

Renaming and deleting columns

Renaming or deleting a column follows the same practice for renaming or deleting a table. The only caveat is that when dependencies such as key enforcements occur, deleting a column can result in potential broken relationships.

To rename a column, follow these steps:

1. **In either Data view or Model view, go to the Fields pane.**

2. **Right-click the column name you want to rename.**

3. **Rename the column.**

   The column name refreshes automatically.

   If relationship updates require updating, those are revised accordingly.

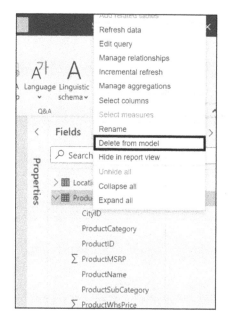

FIGURE 9-14:
Deleting a table
from the model.

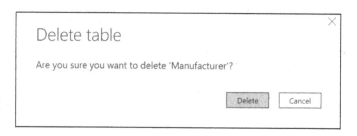

FIGURE 9-15:
Asking whether
you're sure.

When the column is deleted, you'll notice that the link is broken if a relationship exists between two tables. Figure 9-16 shows Before and After views of CityID between Products and Location.

To delete a column, follow these steps:

1. **In either Data view or Model view, go to the Fields pane.**

2. **Right-click the column name, and then choose Delete from Model from the menu that appears.**

   You're alerted that the column is about to be deleted.

3. **Press Delete.**

   The column is deleted, and the model updates automatically.

   If relationships are broken, the links between the tables are updated accordingly.

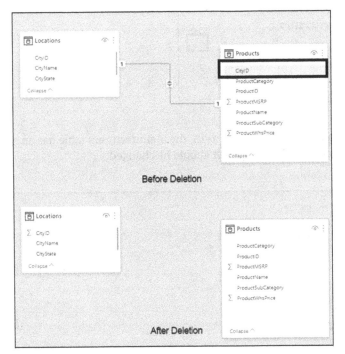

FIGURE 9-16:
Before and After
views for column
removal.

Adding and modifying data in tables

At times, you may want to add or modify data in an existing table. This process is one of the less transparent ones because it requires a user to go into the Power Query Editor to complete the action. If you've created the data within Power BI, the process for adding or modifying is a bit more simplistic than datasets that have been imported using a file or ingested using DataQuery. To add rows or modify cells to rows of tables you've created yourself, follow these steps:

1. **In the Queries area of the Home tab of the Model view's Ribbon, click the Transform Data icon.**

   The Power Query Editor appears onscreen.

2. **Select the dataset you created.**

3. **Go to the source under Applied Steps.**

4. **Click the Gear icon. (See Figure 9-17.)**

   Doing so opens a window that allows you to add or update additional rows or fields.

FIGURE 9-17:
The Gear icon
under Applied
Steps.

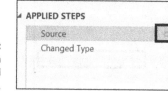

As you can see in Figure 9-18, the Manufacturers table has an empty field, as well as a row indicating that it should be changed.

Create Table

	ManufacturerID	ManufacturerName	CityID	ManufacturerNAIC	POC	ManufacturerType	+
1	123X456	Bluesky Technologies	2	541512	Miles, A.	VAR	
2	123X455	Brownie Catering LLC	2	511611	Brown, M.	VAD	
3	123X451	White Labs Inc.	2	541715	White, E.	REQUIRES CHANGE-->	
4	423X456	Black Out Labs	22	541720	Black, O.	VAR	
5	523X456	Yellow Fin Education LLC	33	611420	Fin, F.	EDU	
6	623X456	Red Rover Cars Inc.	35	541990	Grouch, O.	VAD	
7	173X456	Green Grass Repair Ltd.	11	541690	Green, D.	SI	
8	5594X12	Polkadot Systems	229	611420	Fun, E.		
+	⟳ New Row of Data						

FIGURE 9-18:
The modified
table with
new row and
changed data.

Adding and modifying data to imported, DirectQuery, and composite models

When you import or use DirectQuery and then transform the data in Power BI, your ability to add or change the data can occur only in the native data source. There's an exception, of course: If you create custom columns or calculated columns, those are editable and managed within Power BI.

Assume that you want to make a modification to the Location table in Figure 9-19. The data exists in the Products.xlsx file. You can add an extra three cities or states and change the name of one city or state in Excel directly. As soon as you update the file, click the Refresh icon in the Queries area of the Model view's Home Ribbon. The results are instantaneously updated, as shown in Figure 9-20.

FIGURE 9-19:
Before a
change in the
Products.xlsx file.

1		1	Brooklyn	NY
2		2	Bronx	NY
3		3	Staten Island	NY
4		4	Atlanta	GA
5		5	Marietta	GA
6		6	Boise	ID
7		7	Detroit	MI

FIGURE 9-20:
Seeing the
changes made
in the
Products.xlsx file.

1		1	Brooklyn	NY
2		2	Bronx	NY
3		3	Staten Island	NY
4		4	Atlanta	GA
5		5	Athens	GA
6		6	Boise	ID
7		7	Detroit	MI
8		8	Chicago	IL
9		9	Denver	CO
10		10	Dallas	TX

Managing Relationships

When two tables connect by a common bond, it often signifies that a relationship exists by way of a key. It can be a primary-primary key or a primary-foreign key relationship. In certain circumstances, a table may even be joined together in a single field. That single field can map to another table with a like-kind field, creating a lookup. In this section, I cover the value of relationships in designing and developing the data model.

Creating automatic relationships

Power BI recognizes that, when data is transformed, a relationship exists. For example, if you have two tables with a numeric data type and they're named similarly, they're considered to be in a relationship. Power BI detects these relationships as part of the ETL process. The automatic detection helps reduce the manual work that goes into identifying the relationships yourself. Also, you can reduce the risk of errors from occurring between tables.

To see how Power BI views relationships between datasets, follow these steps:

1. **Go to Model view's Home Ribbon.**

2. **In the Relationships area, click the Manage Relationships icon.**

   Relationships that exist when the datasets are imported are automatically matched.

3. **(Optional) If you want the systems to autodetect the relationships, click the Autodetect button.**

Creating manual relationships

Sometimes the names of primary and foreign keys may not match but you know that the data between them creates a relationship. For example, LocationID and CityID might be one and the same or perhaps StateID and StateAbbreviation. All these are examples where data analysts need to manually map the relationship between two tables even though Power BI should have been able to pick up the pattern. To manually establish relationships between tables and keys, follow these steps:

1. **Go to Model view's Home Ribbon.**

2. **In the Relationships area, click the Manage Relationships icon.**

3. **Click the New button.**

4. **The Create Relationship interface appears, as shown in Figure 9-21.**

5. **Select the two tables that are in a relationship.**

6. **Using the Cardinality and Cross-Filter Direction drop-down menus, choose the settings you want.**

7. **Press OK when you finish.**

Deleting relationships

Deleting relationships occurs in one of three ways. You're either removing the field in one of the two tables that sets up the join between the two tables or using the Manage Relationships interface to disconnect the relationship the same way you created the interface. You'd uncheck the Active box. Then you'd press Delete. A warning appears, showing a break to the relationship. You'd acknowledge the relationship to be broken and then press OK.

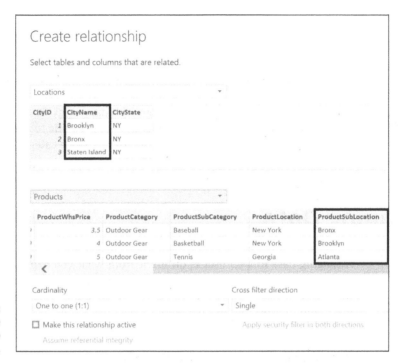

FIGURE 9-21:
The Create
Relationship
interface.

The easiest way to break a relationship is to go to Model view and right-click the link. Choose Delete. You're prompted to acknowledge that the relationship will be broken.

Classifying and codifying data in tables

As you build your data collection in Power BI over time, it is important to add context so that any user who accesses those datasets you've begun to create can put the puzzle pieces together. Whether your descriptive data is tied to a single dataset or to many, it's an ongoing activity for the person responsible for managing the data. A way to help any user who comes across your data better understand exactly what they are reviewing is to add *metadata* — data better describing your data, in other words — within each table or column property.

To add metadata to each table or column, you follow these steps, depending on whether it's a table or a column:

1. **Go to Model view.**

2. **Click to select the table (to describe an entire table) or a column inside the table. (You'll need to select the specific column among tables.)**

3. **In the Properties pane, enter a description in the Description box.**

   This can be an extended sentence regarding the specific item.

4. **Enter synonyms that can also describe the table or column name.**

WARNING

Be careful not to confuse data categories with data types. Data *categories* are a way to group data in a model. whereas data *types* are specific to helping qualify if the data is text, numeric, or mixed. Think of Cities as a data category and the data type as Text.

Arranging Data

Arranging data in a dataset is different from what you experience when data is transformed in visualizing data. Arranging data in Power BI can be classified in a few different ways: Sort By, Group By, and Hide Data. The next few sections drill down into the specifics of each kind.

Sorting by and grouping by

You can easily be confused by Sort By and Group By. Sort By sorts data in ascending order (A–Z) and descending order (Z–A) on a column basis. To ascend or descend the data in a dataset, you need to go to the Power Query Editor to complete any form of sort-by action. You can sort by only one column at a time.

Group By allows a field to be grouped against a mathematical operation (count, sum, and means, for example) and another field. Advanced options allow you to group with one or more fields, as shown in Figure 9-22.

Hiding data

At times, you may want to suppress column data from a table. Perhaps the column may offer little value in the dataset when presenting results, or maybe the data adds too much complexity to the visualization. It might be that the column, when included in the dataset, actually provides inaccurate data. The reasons for hiding data can be many. However, rather than simply delete a column when you may still need the data later, you can hide it temporarily.

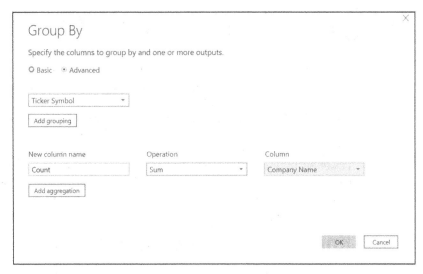

FIGURE 9-22:
Grouping by
capabilities.

To hide a column, as shown in Figure 9-23, follow these steps:

1. **In Model view, go to the table containing the column in question.**

2. **Click to select the field.**

3. **Go to the Properties pane.**

4. **Locate the Is Hidden slider.**

5. **Slide the option from No to Yes.**

   You see an eye with a line through it appear in the field, indicating that it has been hidden.

If at any point you want to unhide the column, simply repeat these steps, but this time slide the Is Hidden slider to No.

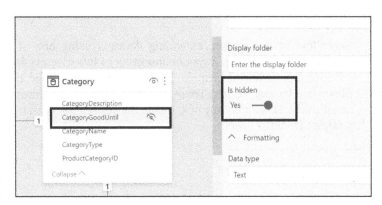

FIGURE 9-23:
Hiding data.

Working with Extended Data Models

Regardless of which import method you use for Power BI Desktop, you face limitations. Not all data models require calculations, but the underlying requirement is that mathematical calculations are needed to help analyze qualitative data at some point. Calculations of percentages and comparing figures are all too common.

DAX (short for Data Analysis eXpression) is the language written for calculation in Power Bi Desktop. This formula-based language consists of over 300 formulas used either alone or in combination to create math-oriented metrics. Many of the formulas found in DAX are identical to ones you'd find in Excel.

Knowing the calculation types

Every time you import data or connect to a data source via DirectQuery to create a visualization, you might be surprised to find out how much easier Power BI makes your life, because you must do little to transform the datasets. There's a catch, though: Suppose that you need to quantify the data you're visualizing. Your goal might be to develop calculations from tables in order to extend your datasets. Power BI Desktop allows for all metric types to be calculated and imported from the source.

These components are important not only to visualization efforts but also to DAX calculations:

>> Components that are used to filter visualization

>> Components that are used in the classification of data

>> Order and rank for datasets

>> Weighting and values to datasets

>> Adding new columns to datasets

Regardless of the reason, extending datasets using one of these techniques arises because importing data or connecting to live datasets doesn't afford users quantitative-ready and formula-rich options. Bear in mind that this list is not exhaustive by any means. There are other reasons to address calculating data quantitively. There's no way of knowing the desired patterns, trends, and needs of a dataset from the onset.

Working with column contents and joins

Though I've tended to talk in this chapter about importing data from only a single source, it's not uncommon for enterprise organizations to import data across multiple sources into a single source. Under these circumstances, organizations must merge the columns from these data sources and connect them into tables and columns.

Let's say you want to create a column having the data on all stock ticker symbols associated with the data for company locations. The data sources are housed in two different sources. What you need to do is create a new column that takes the data from both columns and creates a single entry in one of the tables after being imported and transformed. To do this, you follow these steps:

1. **Open both data sources in Power BI Desktop.**

2. **Go to Report view.**

3. **In the Fields pane, click to select Locations in the Locations table and Ticker Symbol in both tables. (Refer to Figure 9-24.)**

4. **Go to Data view.**

    Doing so creates a joint view of column content that aggregates content based on a common field — the Ticker Symbols field. The difference is that the locations weren't in both tables, as shown in Figure 9-25.

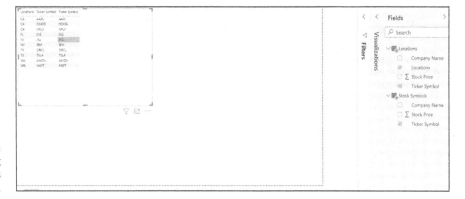

FIGURE 9-24:
Combining content and joins in Report view.

Ticker Symbol	Company Name	Stock Price	Locations
NFLX	Netflix	516.49	CA
JNJ	Johnson and Johnson	171.89	NJ
DIS	Disney	178.74	FL
TSLA	Tesla	657.82	TX
AMZN	Amazon	3699.82	WA
MSFT	Microsoft	289.05	WA
GOOG	Google	2680.7	CA
AAPL	Apple	148.99	CA
ORCL	Oracle	87.86	TX
IBM	IBM	142.96	NY

FIGURE 9-25:
Aggregate of two
data sources
using joins.

Publishing Data Models

When a data model is ready to be published to Power BI Services, the process is as easy as pressing a button — assuming that you've set up your online account with Microsoft's Power BI Services at https://powerbi.microsoft.com. You're asked to supply your username and the email address that logs you in to all Power Platform / Office 365 applications. Depending on the type of license you have, your model's data volume and refresh vary.

To publish your model, go to the Home Tab on the Power BI Desktop and press Publish, as shown in Figure 9-26.

FIGURE 9-26:
The Publish
button for
deploying the
data model and
reports to Power
BI Services.

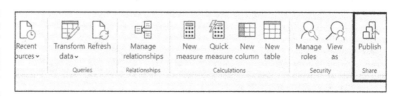

Chapter **10**

Perfecting the Data Model

ere's the dilemma. You have reports that run spectacularly in a test-and-development environment. Why? Because the environment is contained. But when you deploy the data model to production — whether by importing it, using DirectQuery, or using a composite model to production — performance issues immediately crop up. Reports and visualizations take too long to load, for example, or they need more time to update than they should. The result is a bad user experience. Data professionals spend most of their time playing detective by trying to track down data errors and performance concerns. Guess what? Most times, the data model is the culprit. Poorly crafted DAX expressions, or perhaps faulty relationships between tables, can slow a data model tremendously. And, to top it all off, as data grows, so do the problems. That's why you want to address the problems in development so that you can course-correct issues before it's too late. In this chapter, you learn the steps, processes, and concepts necessary to optimize a data model for enterprise-level performance under various conditions.

Matching Queries with Capacity

Depending on the version of Power BI you're using, you're almost certain to experience throughput constraints. When you publish a model to Power BI, the maximum number of concurrent queries that communicate with the underlying data source influence the data environment. In the case of Power BI Desktop, Power BI Pro, Power BI Premium, and even Power Bi Report Server, each has different capacity constraints. Therefore, the capacity influences your querying ability. With capacity, performance varies significantly. That's why pruning away unnecessary elements is one way to improve performance. Limiting the amount of data trying to squeeze through the gap ensures that more data actually makes it through.

Deleting unnecessary columns and rows

Ever heard that having too much of a good thing can be dangerous? You're better off loading only the columns and rows needed for the data model and reporting instances — or at least holding off until you're ready for growth. This means that you should disable the loading of queries that aren't needed to run reports. Also, you should filter the data to only those rows or columns required before loading a model.

Ditching columns

Columns in your data models serve one or more purposes. They're used to support visualizations or calculations or both. Unless the column is being used for a specific purpose — just say no. If the column has a high number of distinct values, consider modifying the model. And if you want a refresher on how to delete columns, flip back to Chapter 9 to see how to remove those extraneous columns.

TECHNICAL STUFF

If you're importing data from a data warehouse, evaluate your dataset and its primary keys for fact tables. Though primary keys are helpful for auditing data, they may create more complexity than you want. Because primary keys have a unique value in every row, the associated fact tables become unnecessarily large at the column level. Do you really want a table that's bloated while also having little value?

Limiting the number of rows from the get-go

Including a filtering criterion is a must-have for a dataset from the onset when building a data model in Power BI. The criteria can be anything from an attribute set to a series of dates. But it's essential to limit the number of rows you have. Suppose that you're concerned only with analyzing a finite dataset. Why not just reduce the number of rows from the onset? It's senseless to include data with little value or parameters that you can add later if it creates extraneous performance concerns with reporting.

Swapping numeric columns with measures and variables

Too many Power BI users despair when it comes to managing columns, yet there's no good reason to get so frustrated. Creating measures and authoring variables in your DAX formulas can provide you with far less complex code and calculation options. It's not uncommon for newcomers to Power BI Desktop to underutilize variables when coming up with data models.

When you put your data modeler hat on, you are often tasked with a tall order of being the code guru, debugging detective, and budding artist for those killer visualizations you produce. But to successfully deliver for each of these roles requires you to come up with some nifty code (and a pull a few tricks from your sleeve now and then), especially when you are crafting DAX calculations. You've already seen a few examples of DAX and know that it takes a dash of compound and complex expressions to create a formula. A compound expression can involve the use of many nested functions, and a whole of lot of expression logic reusability. That's why you'd bring your handy dandy friend, the variable into the mix (which we cover in depth in Chapter 16). A variable is a way to store a DAX calculation efficiently, with the goal of reuse. Variables can help you write more complex calculations', with efficiency and style. Better yet, a variable helps you strengthen your codes performance and reliability, readability, and of course reduce complexity.

You're often forced to use nested functions and reuse logic — the processes that are associated with calculating data, in other words — to come up with effective expressions. And to be successful, the most effective shortcut you can use is by leveraging variables. That means it often takes a long time for expressions to process. And because calculations are often difficult to read, troubleshooting naturally becomes a bit cumbersome. Using measures and DAX variables helps reduce processing time.

Variables in a data model offer the following benefits:

>> **Improves performance:** Reduces the need to evaluate expressions multiple times. The time to query results can be achieved around 50 percent of the processing time.

>> **Enhances readability:** Variables are ideal when you're looking to replace extended expressions. If you need a way to read and understand formulas more readily, variables can help you.

>> **Assists with debugging:** Variables are also a debugging tool. If you need to test formulas or test expressions, variables are the go-to utility for troubleshooting.

An example of transforming a traditional DAX expression to one that includes variables to improve performance, enhance readability, and make it easier to debug includes:

Without variables

SalesGrowth % =
DIVIDE(([ProductSales] - CALCULATE([ProductSales],
PARALLELPERIOD('Date'[Date], -12, MONTH))),
CALCULATE([ProductSales], PARALLELPERIOD('Date'[Date], -12,
MONTH))
)

With variables

SalesGrowth % =
VAR SalesLastYear = CALCULATE([ProductSales],
PARALLELPERIOD('Date'[Date], -12, MONTH))
RETURN
DIVIDE(([Sales] - SalesLastYear), SalesLastYear)

Reducing cardinality

You may not have realized it, but we've talked about cardinality in earlier chapters, in disguise. When looking at the number of elements in a set of data, you are evaluating cardinality. Consider this example: I have lived in many cities but in each of those cities, I could have lived in one or more houses. Cities is represented as many (M) and the places I've lived within each city could be one or many (1 or M). The cardinality or relationship described in a data model would likely be notated as a many-to-many (M:M) relationship, although some may argue the relationship is many-to-one (M:1).

As you are looking to clean up your update, part of the process is reducing cardinality to create the most reliable, tightly coupled dataset possible. When you try to perfect model performance, you probably never consider that cardinality may create performance delays — though it can definitely play a role. One piece of evidence that makes this point crystal-clear is that when you're using Power Query Editor to conduct data analysis of entities (tables) and attributes (fields), you're offered column distribution options that provide you with statistics on how many distinct and unique items are available on a per column basis.

Distinct values represent the various values found in columns. In contrast, *unique* values are those that appear just once in a column.

When you have columns with lots of values, especially when the values are repetitious, there is a strong likelihood that the cardinality level is insignificant. Columns containing many unique values have a high level of cardinality. That's why you want to *lower* cardinality — it optimizes model performance. In other words, you want to reduce the number of columns as much as possible to just those values that are meaningful.

Depending on how relationships are created or edited, column configuration varies — and impacts cardinality accordingly. With cardinality, the direction of the relationship and the model of said relationship are defined by the relationship type. Table 10-1 illustrates the four cardinality types and the impact of cardinality reduction.

TABLE 10-1 **Cardinality and Direction**

Cardinality	Description
One-to-one (1:1)	Both tables have only a single instance of a particular value.
Many-to-one (M:1)	The most common cardinality and thus the default type. The column in one table can have many instances of a value. The other related table is often a lookup table with only one instance.
One-to-many (1:M)	When a column in one table has a single instance of a particular value. The related table has one or more values.
Many-to-many (M: M)	Appropriate for composite models and can be used as many-to-many between tables. There is no specific requirement for unique values. There is also no need to establish new tables for relationships.

During data model development, creating and editing relationships is par for the course. No matter the relationship (or the cardinality selected) in your model, the data type enforced is consistent. Remember, though, that relationships fail if two columns have a data type mismatch.

Power BI Desktop offers different techniques to help reduce the amount of data loaded into data models — summarization, for example. Reducing the data that's loaded into your model improves the relationship cardinality. That's why you want your models to be as small as possible, especially if you know they will grow over time.

Reducing queries

Under Power BI Desktop's Options and Settings (found under the File menu) you find an entire Query Reductions page. (See Figure 10-1.) A few options exist under this menu choice, categorized under three major headings: reduce number of queries sent by, slicers, and filters. The purpose of each of these options is as follows:

>> **Reduce number of queries sent by:** Allows you to disable cross-highlighting on reports. You also ensure that back-end queries are reduced, supplying a more efficient navigational experience. Unless you want queries reduced, do not select disabling cross-highlighting/filtering by default.

>> **Slicers:** Allows you to have an Apply button appear only under specific conditions, specifically when one of two conditions are met. Either instantly apply slicer changes or add an Apply button to each slicer to apply changes when you're ready. You generally want to use the Instantly Apply Slicer Changes option unless there is a multi-step process involved in evaluating a query.

>> **Filters:** Allows an Apply button to appear when one of the options is selected. You can choose from instantly applying basic filter changes, adding an Apply button to all basic filters to apply changes when you're ready, or add a single Apply button to the Filter pane to apply changes at once. You'll generally want to select the Instantly Apply Basic Filter Changes option unless the filter is needed to support more complex query types.

When you are looking to send fewer queries to a report or want to disable certain interactions that result in a poor performance experience (assuming the queries take a tad longer than you'd like), applying a query reduction option is highly recommended. To enable query reduction options, go to Power BI Desktop and follow these steps:

1. **Choose File ⇨ Options and Settings from the main menu and then choose Options from the menu that appears.**

2. **Under the Current File heading in the listing that runs down the left side of the screen, select Query Reduction under Current File.**

3. **The main window refreshes to show your query reduction options, as shown in Figure 10-1.**

Converting to a composite model

Sometimes, direct import and DirectQuery results should be combined into a single model to better support storage configuration. The table storage model can be dual, having both direct import and DirectQuery support. When both model types are available, you ultimately create a composite model. As a refresher, a composite model allows you to combine two or more data connections from different source types. You may have one or more DirectQuery connections as well as a direct import connection, or perhaps you could have several DirectQuery connections. There is also a possibility for a combination of all the above options.

So why would you want to convert your connections from one specific model type to a composite model? The key is performance. You'll find that the functional and performance experience are significantly improved for both DirectQuery and direct import options because you can integrate more than one DirectQuery or import model into a composite model, which then supports aggregation. When dealing with a composite model derived from aggregated sources, you are lessening the query load, which yields better results much faster.

WARNING

Don't be so quick to jump into developing a composite model — your first choice should always be to create a direct import model. It gives you the most control, the most significant design flexibility, and the best performance options. Of course, there are exceptions to the rule. Large data volumes and reporting in real time cannot be resolved with direct import models alone. DirectQuery is a good second choice if you know that your data will be stored in a single data model.

Here are the times when it is wise to ignore the general rule and consider composite modeling:

>> You need to boost performance by consolidating many sources into a single source of truth, hence the focus on data aggregation.

>> You want to combine DirectQuery models with additional datasets that must be imported into a new model.

>> You need to combine two or more DirectQuery data sources into a single model.

REMEMBER

The DirectQuery method involves connecting directly to data in its source repository from within Power BI Desktop. As such, it's an alternative to importing data into Power BI Desktop. The trouble is, when you use the DirectQuery method, the overall user experience depends heavily on the performance of the underlying data source. Problems run the gamut from time-out issues to the number of concurrent users accessing the source, affecting the load and data source.

Unfortunately, the performance of your Power BI model won't be affected only by the performance of the underlying data source but also by other uncontrollable factors, including network latency and server performance. Both factors are well beyond a user's control. Therefore, using DirectQuery poses a risk to model quality if performance optimization is the main goal. If you have limited control over the source files or database, DirectQuery has limited effectiveness.

Creating and managing aggregations

A major theme of this chapter deals with the fact that too much data can create performance issues. Therefore, summarizing the data and presenting it at a higher level may be beneficial. For example, it may be possible to *aggregate* all data regarding vendors, sales, products, and agencies — taking the raw data and summarizing it, in other words. By aggregating data, you reduce the table sizes in a data model. Instead of having many tables, you just have a few to focus on, helping to improve querying.

Your organization might decide to use aggregations in its data models, for the following reasons:

>> **Handling big data**: Aggregation is a better alternative for query performance when dealing with big data. You can analyze and evaluate insights for large

datasets quickly, especially when they're cached. Because a smaller number of resources is required in order to operate, you're likely to shift more data model resources to this design alternative.

>> **Optimizing data refreshes:** Aggregation can help reduce the speed of the refresh process. Because you're reducing the cache size with a small data model, the refresh time is reduced. Users gain access to data faster. The dataset is often compressed from a large set of records.

>> **Managing model size:** Some models are robust. If you consolidate tables by way of aggregation, you're helping to ensure the data model doesn't get out of control as the dataset grows.

>> **Keeping the model relevant:** Aggregating is a proactive method for ensuring that the data model doesn't experience potential performance hiccups. When you experience refresh and query problems caused by data volume concerns, a way to circumvent issues is to aggregate the data model.

The creating part

Aggregation isn't an activity to be taken lightly. You need to do the hard work of deciding the level at which you want to aggregate the dataset. Take, for example, my Award dataset. Should I aggregate the data at the Agency level, at the NAICS Code level, or at another grain? I'd argue for aggregating the data at the Agency level because you want to choose the data grouping where you'll find the greatest number of possible synergies that may also have attributes associated at a lower level. In the Award dataset, you can have ten agencies that each support one or more NAICS codes. (Many can overlap.) You are likely to also have one or more awards associated with the agency and NAICS code. The common thread that will yield the best insight across the dataset is the agency as it offers the most precision across the data.

Once you decide on the grain, you need to figure out how you want to create the aggregation. Though there are many methods for aggregations, the results for each method are essentially the same.

With the Direct Import method, you can create a table with the necessary aggregation if you have access to the database directly. This means you need to add another table to the database with those fields you want to combine into a single table. When the table is complete, you can then import the dataset directly into Power BI Desktop. The reality is though, you may not have access to the source database; therefore, consider plan B which is directly in Power BI Desktop.

Suppose that you prefer doing the work in Power BI Desktop. In that case, it might be easier and more efficient to use the Power Query Editor to create the aggregation. Figure 10-2 lets you take a peek at the process. The idea is to open the query in Power Query Editor and aggregate the data in three of the Award List table's columns: the AgencyID column, the VendorID column, and the NAICSID column. To access the table, follow these steps:

1. **Go to the Power Query Editor.**

2. **In the Queries pane, select the Awards List table.**

3. **Click the Choose Columns button in the Manage Columns area of the Ribbon's Home tab.**

4. **Choose Columns. (Figure 10-2).**

   By selecting the Awards List table, all the fields available from that table will appear in the Choose Columns screen.

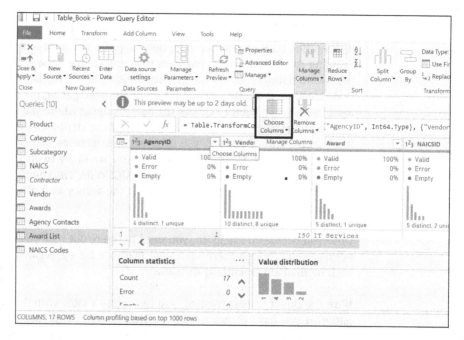

FIGURE 10-2:
The Choose
Columns icon on
the Ribbon's
Home tab.

5. **Select AgencyID, VendorID, and NAICSID in the Choose Columns screen. (See Figure 10-3.)**

   Selecting these three columns will be the first step in creating an aggregation entry.

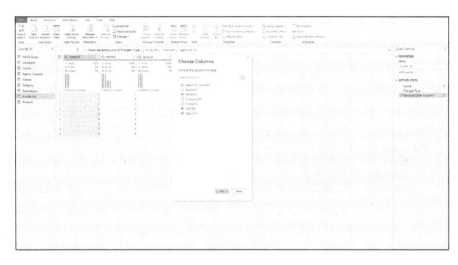

FIGURE 10-3:
Selecting columns to aggregate.

6. Press OK.

You've now removed all but three columns. As noted in the Query Settings pane, you can see that the Power Query Editor acknowledges the columns being removed (Remove Other Columns). On the screen, you'll find just those three columns within the Power Query Editor. (Figure 10-4)

FIGURE 10-4:
Aggregated columns in Power Query Editor.

7. After the three columns are displayed in the Power Query Editor, click the Group By icon in the Transform area of the Ribbon's Home tab. (See Figure 10-5.)

8. In the Group By window that appears, choose the item you want to group by.

In this case, I choose AgencyID.

You should create a name for the new column. The name I have created is AgencyAwardedByVendor. In this case, I've created a new column name, selected Sum Column as the aggregation action, and chosen VendorID to be the item aggregated when grouping by Agency ID, as shown in Figure 10-6.

Group By

FIGURE 10-5:
The Group By
icon on the
Ribbon's
Home tab.

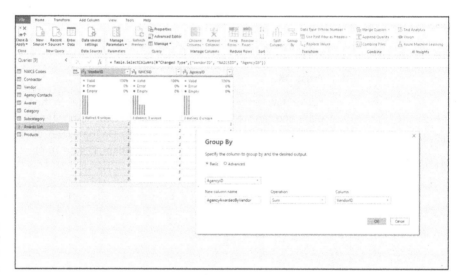

FIGURE 10-6:
Adding a new
sum column
using Group By.

The result is the sum of values grouped by AgencyID so that instead of having multiple columns, you now only have one aggregate column with each AgencyID. You've combined several columns into one, which supports better performance. The aggregated result can be found in Figure 10-7.

9. **Click the Close & Apply button on the Ribbon's Home tab to close the Power Query Editor.**

You are now closing the Power Query Editor and going back to the Data Model View tab. This action saves all changes to the data model. The data model automatically refreshes, resulting in a significantly smaller data model because you've just pared down the criteria using the aggregation conditions. You'll see in Figure 10-8 that all the tables that were linked are now separate, which means they are to be used only as lookups when necessary. The only two tables in the model where significant activity now materializes is the Agency Contacts table and the Awards List table.

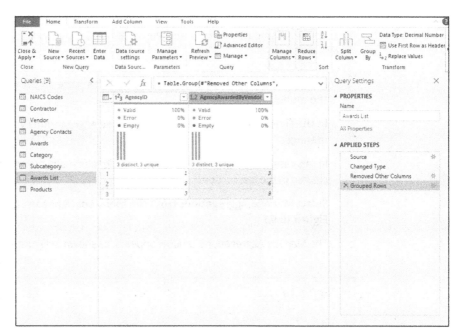

FIGURE 10-7:
The Aggregated
column.

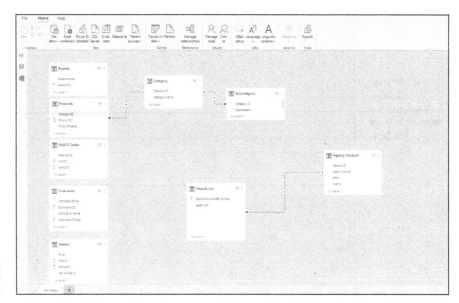

FIGURE 10-8:
The updated data
model view.

The managing part

It should come as no surprise to you that you have to manage the aggregations in
the Power BI Desktop environment after creating them — which includes managing their behavior.

To manage aggregations from any Power BI Desktop environment, follow these steps:

1. **In the data model view, navigate to the Fields pane on the right side of the model.**

2. **In the Fields pane, right-click a table whose aggregations you want to manage.**

   In this case, I've selected the Awards List table to manage the aggregation created in the last section.

3. **Select Manage Aggregations from the menu that appears. (See Figure 10-9.)**

   The Manage Aggregations window appears, as shown in Figure 10-10.

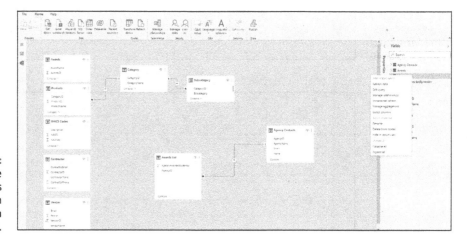

FIGURE 10-9:
Manage aggregations accessible from the Data View tab.

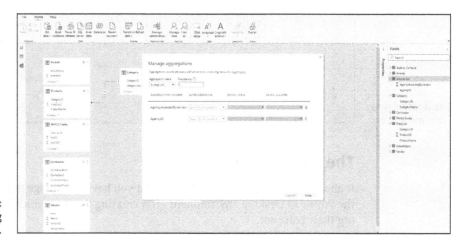

FIGURE 10-10:
Managing aggregations.

4. **For each aggregation you've created, you can then select a choice from the Summarization drop-down list.**

   You can change the table and columns based on predefined conditions decided by Power BI Desktop for each summarization type selected.

5. **When done, click the Apply All button. (Again, see Figure 10-10.)**

   You've now changed the original model aggregation based on updated conditions you've just specified.

Chapter **11**

Visualizing Data

The adage "A picture speaks a thousand words" is one of the reasons so many people use Power BI. You've imported the data, perhaps millions of records, and now you want to understand what the data says. A visualization is likely a bit easier for you or your organization to use than a large, complex dataset or a single-page report. And, of course, depending on the number of variables involved or the type of data you want to explore, having a specific type of visualization can only enhance the readability and fluency of your data experience. In this chapter, you can see how to access the visualizations, select a proper choice, and configure your visualization for report creation.

Looking at Report Fundamentals and Visualizations

There's a simple division of labor to Power BI: You use the Desktop version to create the data model and visualizations, and Services is there for you to deploy datasets, reports, and dashboards to the web. In other words, if you want to share your data, you must become familiar with Power BI Desktop as well as with the variations in Services options. That doesn't mean you can't manipulate visualizations or update them from within Services. You can, in fact, collaborate or make edits on your own to your reports. Nevertheless, the majority of your visualization manipulation occurs in Power BI Desktop, not in Power BI Services.

Creating visualizations

Assume that you have a dataset stored in Power BI Desktop and you want to share it as a visualization. Start heading over to the Report tab (see Figure 11-1) by clicking the Report View tab on the left-side navigation.

FIGURE 11-1:
The Report
View icon.

At this point, you're introduced to the visualization interface, where you have the choice to drag-and-drop a visualization type from the Visualizations pane on the right side to the Visualization canvas. Figure 11-2 presents an example of Report view in Power BI Desktop, where visualization occurs.

FIGURE 11-2:
Overview of
Report view in
Power BI.

In Report view, you can complete a number of activities associated with visualization, such as

>> Selecting a visual icon from the Visualizations pane

>> Selecting the fields to be used in the visualization

>> Dragging fields from the Fields pane to the canvas for visualization creation

>> Utilizing the Ribbon to create and manage the visuals

>> Interpreting the results of the visuals using the Q&A editor

To enhance one's comprehension of a report, a user can integrate text boxes, custom shapes, and images. For those looking to create multipage reports using visualizations, you have the choice to add buttons, bookmarks, and page navigation on each visualization.

Choosing a visualization

The Visualizations pane of Power BI Desktop's Report view hosts more than 20 visualization options that you can drag to the Visualization canvas. Each visualization requires a user to select one or more fields from the Fields pane after dragging the visual to the canvas. A user must select the check box to include the field from the Fields pane for a visual. Figure 11-3 provides you with an example of the Visualizations pane, and Figure 11-4 illustrates the associated Fields pane.

TIP

Limit the number of check boxes you select, or else you may create a poor visualization. Select only those variables from the Fields pane that are relevant. Use those fields that contribute to the report's specificity. Keep in mind that "The more, the merrier" isn't necessarily always the best-case scenario.

Filtering data

You will often meet the need to filter data while crafting a visualization. Every time you select a new field to incorporate into the visualization, the field appears as another value that can be filtered. Depending on the size of your dataset for a specific value, you may want to narrow the focus. For example, you've selected a value named Award as a choice. Under Award, you have five options to filter from, including Select All. Under conditions where the data is based on a category or qualitative measure, you have the choice to select which fields you prefer. (That is the case with Figure 11-5.) You'll run into instances where reducing a dataset based on a value found is always necessary. For example, if you're looking for any award data where the value is over $100,000, you'd use that as a filtering condition, as shown in Figure 11-6.

FIGURE 11-3:
The Visualizations
pane.

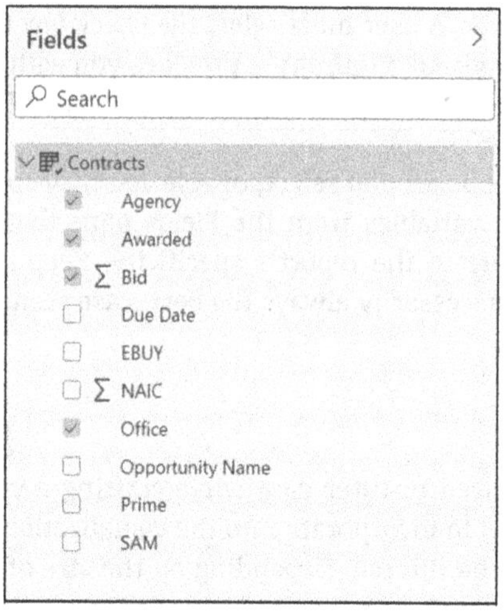

FIGURE 11-4:
The Fields pane.

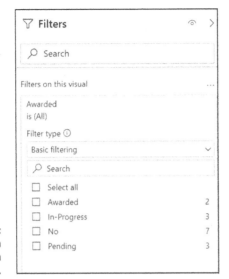

FIGURE 11-5:
Filtering data based on a category.

FIGURE 11-6:
Setting up filtering conditions with quantitative data.

TIP

Users can filter the data on just the specific visualization or across all visualizations by using the Filter on This Page or Filter on All Pages options within the Filter pane, as shown in Figure 11-7.

FIGURE 11-7:
The Filter on This Page and Filter on All Page options.

Working with Bar charts and Column charts

Power BI offers several varieties of the Bar chart and Column chart. Each one allows you to summarize and compare two or more values within a focused data category. You would use a Bar chart or Column chart for comparisons because they offer a snapshot of a dataset.

Stacked Bar charts and Stacked Column charts

The Stacked Bar charts and Stacked Column charts are best used when trying to compare categories against a standard quantitative variable. The bars are proportionally displayed based on the values displayed — horizontally for Stacked Bar charts, and a vertical alignment for Stacked Column charts. One axis of a chart presents a category for comparison, and the other is the focused value.

TIP

You usually begin comparing just two variables, but should you have more, Power BI supports the breakout of datasets into finer-grained details. For example, in Figure 11-8, you see a Stacked Bar chart with a single data category, Bid. A bid is then broken into segments with the value assigned to the different Award categories (No, Awarded, Pending, and In-Progress). The proportionality of the bars is the No, Awarded, Pending, and In-Progress ratio for the total bid amount (sum).

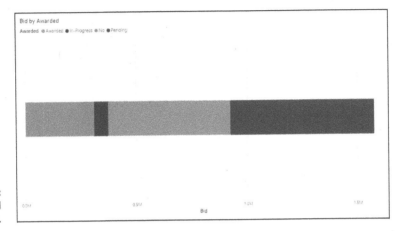

FIGURE 11-8:
A Stacked
Bar chart.

If you add a second dimension, Agency, you can see that the Stacked Bar charts are broken out even further. (See Figure 11-9.) There may be only one status with some stacked bars, and several in others.

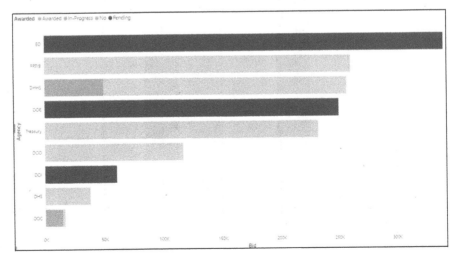

FIGURE 11-9:
Using multiple
dimensions
in a Stacked
Bar chart.

A Stacked Column chart changes the direction of the data from horizontal to vertical. There is no actual difference in the summarization of data — only the visualization of the dataset. Figure 11-10 shows the same data as shown in Figure 11-8, but this time displayed vertically. The same is true for the multiple dimensions shown in Figure 11-11.

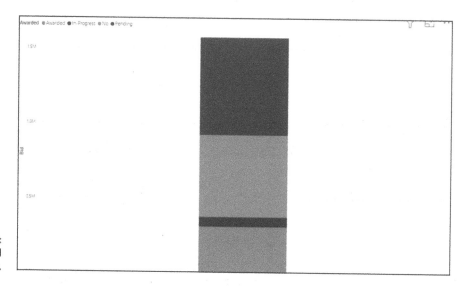

FIGURE 11-10:
A Stacked
Column chart.

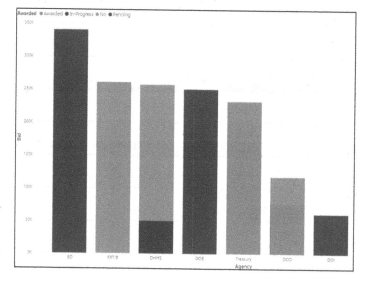

FIGURE 11-11:
Using multiple
dimensions in a
Stacked Column
chart.

Clustered Bar charts and Clustered Column charts

Unlike Stacked Bar charts and Stacked Column charts, where the data is compressed into a single bar or column per category, the data is broken out more discretely in Clustered Bar charts and Clustered Column charts. It's easier to discern values as larger or smaller when the values are broken out in a cluster. For example, the Bid by Awarded scenario is presented in Figure 11-12 using a Clustered Bar chart, and in Figure 11-13 using a Clustered Column chart. As noted by In-Progress, you notice that few opportunities are being worked on, whereas Pending has the most significant dollar volume.

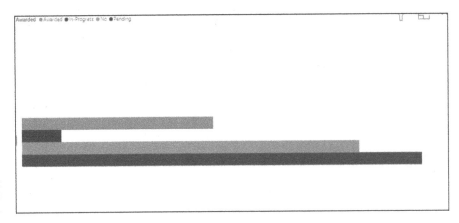

FIGURE 11-12:
A Clustered Bar chart.

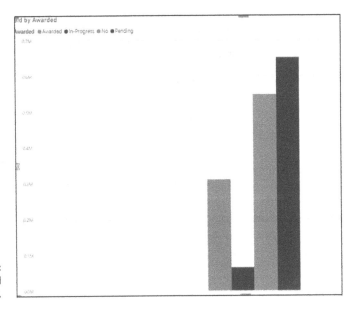

FIGURE 11-13:
A Clustered Column chart.

Your data drives your visualization choice. Sometimes you may want to show how the data within a category is consistent. At other times, you may want to show extremes. Your business use case, the number of data categories and fields, and the impact you hope to achieve must dictate your visualization choices.

100% Stacked Bar charts and 100% Stacked Column charts

When you compare multiple data series in a Stacked Bar chart, you use a 100% Stacked Bar chart or 100% Stacked Column chart. For this type of visualization, the total of each stacked bar or column always equals 100 percent. The goal of this visualization is to show how one part stands in relationship to the whole. In Figures 11-14 and 11-15, two series are being compared: Bid Role (Prime or Sub-Contractor) and Awarded Status. The left is all categories tied to being the Prime, and the right is all Sub-Contractor-related statuses.

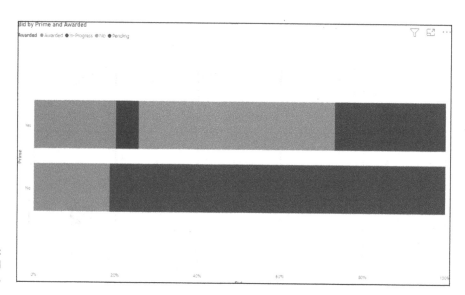

FIGURE 11-14:
A 100% Stacked Bar chart.

Think twice before you use the 100% Stacked Bar chart and 100% Stacked Column chart as your go-to first option. The output can be problematic because it lacks the necessary precision. If the data is insufficient, you won't achieve the level of precision you want. The counter to this is that such charts can be beneficial when you show the sum of values. The catch: It works only if summarizing data is your only goal.

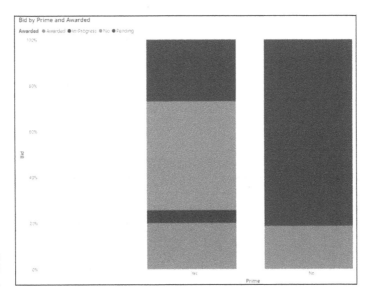

FIGURE 11-15:
A 100% Stacked
Column chart.

Using basic Line charts and Area charts

When trend analysis over a period is your goal, consider using a Line chart or an Area chart. For both chart types, you assign the x-axis a numerical value while the y-axis acts as a key measure. A Line chart connects specific data points by using a straight-line segment. The Area chart is more proper when you're looking for changes among a dataset. Though both adhere to a trend, the Area chart is filled with a particular color or texture to show data variation.

In the examples shown in Figure 11-16 (Line chart) and in 11-17 (Area chart), you see a snapshot of Awards Lost during a specific period as well as the figures for Amount Bid. You can see that the highest bid was $261,000; and the lowest bid, $2,000. The goal is to see the exact bid amount and the loss rate across agencies, not necessarily just the agency who awarded a bid to specific contractors.

Combining Line charts and Bar charts

There might be times when you're trying to complete an analysis for multiple trends. When the dataset is significant, and you want to put as much information as possible into a single visualization, combining chart types is a possibility. Two choices to consider are the Line and Stacked Column chart and the Line and Clustered Column chart.

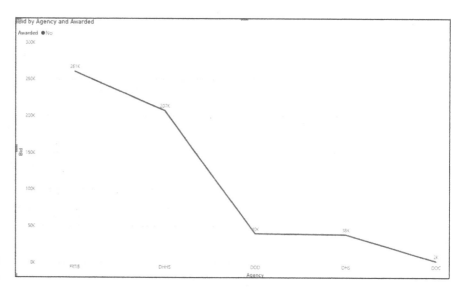

FIGURE 11-16:
A Line chart.

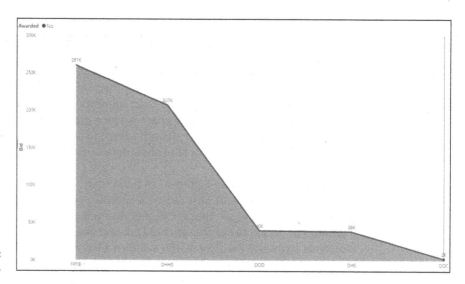

FIGURE 11-17:
An Area chart.

Take the example presented in Figure 11-18, which depicts a specific evaluation of the largest number of dollars obligated in three different states. That's one comparison measure. The second comparison measure is how many unique NAICS codes are associated with the dataset. Two states are associated with four NAICS codes, and one state is associated with only three. The volume of award activity, the dollar amount of that activity at the maximum obligation, and the number of distinct NAICS codes tell you that more awards were issued for the state of Maryland than for the state of Georgia.

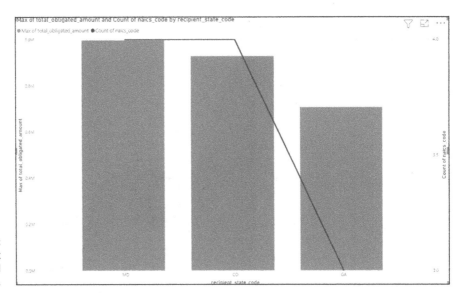

Max of total_obligated_amount and Count of naics_code by recipient_state_code

● Max of total_obligated_amount ● Count of naics_code

FIGURE 11-18:
A Line chart and a Stacked Column chart.

REMEMBER

When you're trying to create comparisons for joint charts, make sure they're relevant to one another. The data comparison shouldn't be too ambiguous, because you don't want to dilute the value of your report. Also, be sure not to add too many comparison layers.

Working with Ribbon charts

Should you want to see the values in the order in which they appear as items in a legend, your best choice is to consider the Ribbon chart. A *Ribbon chart* orders items based on which item has most of its measures in a particular axis. When a category has multiple values being evaluated, each category type is represented differently.

In Figure 11-19, notice that the state that has received the highest number of obligated dollars is Virginia. In contrast, the District of Columbia has the smallest allocation. In proportion, the number of procurements associated with a given NAICS code is also visible and differentiated by different colors.

Going with the flow with Waterfall charts

When comparing the strength or weakness of a given value from its start and understanding how the value transforms based on one or more other conditions, consider using a Waterfall chart. A classic use case for a Waterfall chart is a cost analysis or checking account balance. You have intermediate actions displayed in the chart that shows positives and negatives.

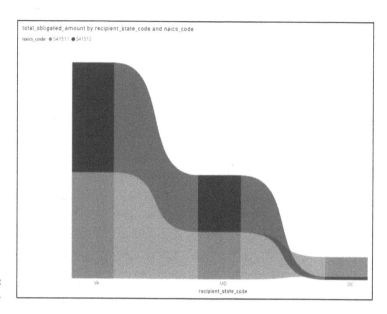

FIGURE 11-19:
A Ribbon chart.

In the example shown in Figure 11-20, notice that the most significant total financial obligation is attached to the state of Virginia. The difference between the two NAICS codes, 541511 and 541512, creates the gap between financial obligations to the second highest-funded state (beyond Maryland). In this case, the answer is Virginia. The negative represented shows you the difference (or it could be the *added*) funds assigned to a given NAICS code between states.

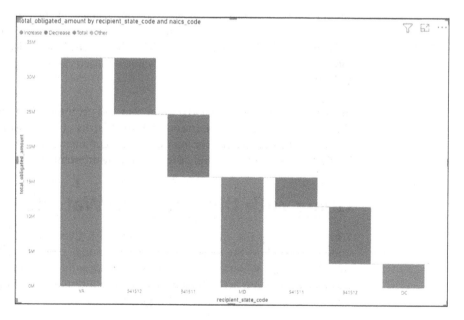

FIGURE 11-20:
A Waterfall chart.

Funneling with Funnel charts

When you're looking for a way to understand linear processes, visualize sequential stages, or rationalize the weight of critical items in a dataset, a Funnel chart is the way to go. Using the Sales Funnel modeling analogy, if the pipeline included bids of various amounts, you could better understand where the bulk of the focus is placed.

In Figure 11-21, the most significant bid opportunity is, hypothetically, the Department of Education, with a $340,000 bid. The smallest bid was sent to the Department of Commerce, for about $16,800. The smallest amount is 4.9 percent of the overall bid forecast. In contrast, the $340,000 is the most significant bid, as represented by 100% in the funnel.

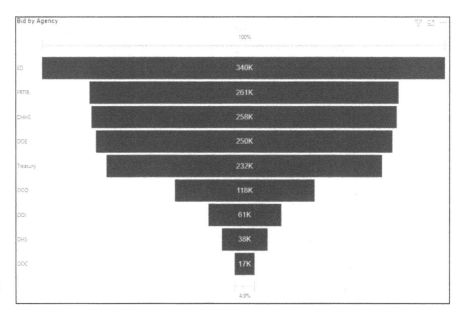

FIGURE 11-21:
A Funnel chart.

TECHNICAL STUFF

You've probably noticed that some of the reports described in this chapter become specific when it comes to filtering. Much of the specificity correlates to field association in the Visualizations pane. Regardless of the visualization, you may need to tailor the following areas under Formatting in the Visualizations pane:

» **Categories:** Represent the columns placed within the horizontal axis. You can add more than one category and drill down.

» **Breakdown:** Allows for you to show changes between categories.

>> **Values:** Designates the key numerical field that will be plotted.

>> **Tooltip:** Adds field descriptions automatically as a user hovers the mouse cursor over a bar or column in a visualization.

Scattering with Scatter charts

Suppose that you have an extensive dataset where you want to find the relationship between one variable found among two axes and then decide the *correlation* — the similarity or lack thereof. In that case, a Scatter chart is a decisive choice to consider. When more cases correlate to a specific behavior, the points are tighter and more aligned, as is the case in Figure 11-22, where you can see the extreme outliers of CA, MD, and VA as well as slight outliers of OH, DC, and CO. Each of these states had a more significant proportion of funds given to IT-related services (NAICS 54151 Series) than the remaining 44 states clustered together in the lower left quadrant of the screen.

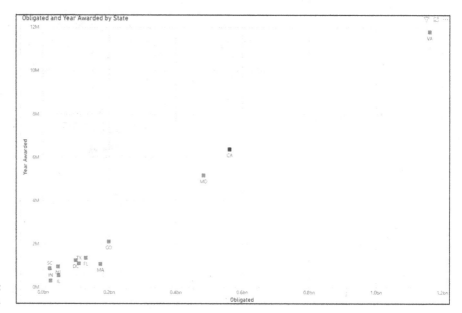

FIGURE 11-22: Scatterplot.

Salivating with Pie charts and Donut charts

Pie charts are circular graphics that break the values from an individual category into slices (or percentages). The whole piece adds up to 100 percent. The *Donut chart* is an extension of the Pie chart in that it displays categories as arcs with a big hole in the center. The values are precisely the same — it's more about aesthetic design.

In Figure 11-23 (Pie chart) and Figure 11-24 (Donut chart), you see a breakdown of the bid statuses totaling 100 percentage distributed to the various award categories based on current awarded standing.

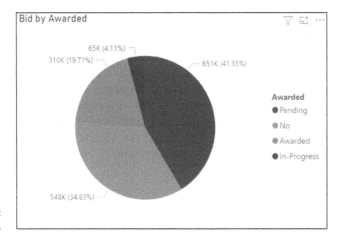

FIGURE 11-23:
A Pie chart.

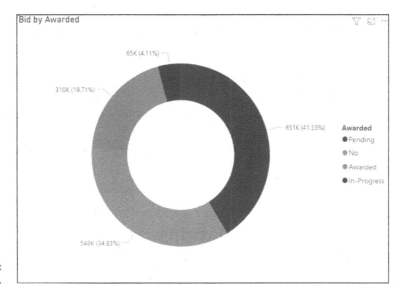

FIGURE 11-24:
A Donut chart.

Branching out with treemaps

Weight and proportionality require that a user have a better understanding of data from a hierarchical perspective. The treemap, with its series of nested rectangles of various sizes, offers such a perspective. Corresponding to the summarization of values or frequency, more prominent representations show more activity. In contrast, smaller rectangles represent a smaller subset of data within a branch. The data volume on the left side of a treemap is always proportionally greater than that on the right, as though you're reading a book by its cover from left to right to tell a story.

In the example shown in Figure 11-25, all states where the US government supplied COVID-19-related funding for an IT project are accounted for in this diagram. The more businesses within a given state that benefited from this special allocation, the larger the square in the treemap. Using the treemap, the state of Maryland had the most IT-related COVID-19 acquisitions, followed by the state of Virginia. Four other states (CA, DC, OH, CO) had a disproportionally higher number of added IT purchases. The rest of the US states often had only one or two COVID-19-related emergency procurements.

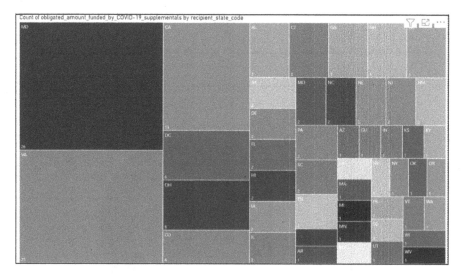

FIGURE 11-25:
A treemap.

Mapping with maps

If you thought Power BI didn't include geospatial analytics, think again. You're quite able to conduct various analytics evaluations using Power BI, based on location, latitude, and longitude as field parameters.

You would use this kind of mapping feature when looking to understand the impact of spatial data compared to geographical distribution. Power BI can automatically zoom in to show the most proper geographical distribution for a visual. To ensure that users have an optimized user experience, they can choose between the Maps and Filled Maps options. Figure 11-26 shows the distribution of funding provided across the United States for obligated COVID-19-related IT emergency expenditures, using geographical distribution as the primary consideration.

Granularity is vital when it comes to mapping. In this particular case of geospatial specificity, I've added a filter to my Maps example. The parameter set is all obligations that are greater than $500,000 but less than $10 million. The Filled map in Figure 11-27 offers a precise answer to only those states given allocations within that range across the geospatial distribution.

Mapping requires precision and accuracy. You'll want to geocode as many fields as possible by selecting in the Fields pane the data category that can provide as much laser focus as possible.

TIP

Indicating with indicators

Whenever you're trying to measure the effectiveness of a business goal, you want to compare one or more like-kind measures. Indicators available in Power BI allow a user to be focused on measuring the value their business provides against one or more variables. Several types of critical performance indicator visualizations are available.

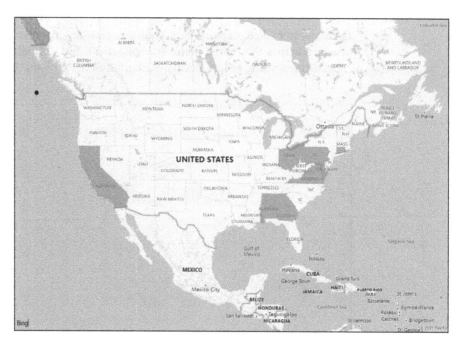

FIGURE 11-27:
A Filled Map
example.

Gauges

When you think of key performance indicators (KPI), a gauge is often used as a quick way to display a data point comparing a value to a target range. For example, you're tracking budget financials. If you want to be assured that they're in line with your range, you can use a *gauge* — a pictorial representation of how close you are to meeting your target. In Figure 11-28, the total fiscal year 2021 Budget for Small Businesses with awards under a million dollars distributed was $784.81M. Of that amount, $741.07M was already distributed. The gray area shows that the overall fiscal picture is on track, because the gauge doesn't show an overage.

Cards and multi-cards

Suppose that you're looking for a single number to help you address a specific statistic. In that case, the Card indicator can help you track your data. Examples of card uses are total sales, market share, or, as shown in Figure 11-29, the number of contracts awarded. When assessing multiple indicators in a single card, you need to add each of those values to the visualization, creating a multi-card indicator. Each field is a new indicator within a card. In Figure 11-30, three indicators are listed as an example of fiscal year spending. The first indicator is the state, the second indicator is obligated amount, and the third is the total obligated.

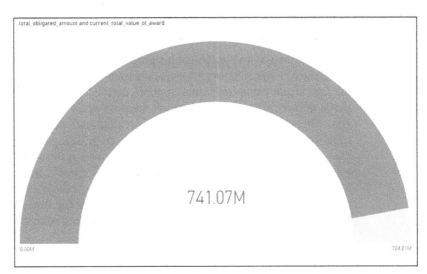

total_obligated_amount and current_total_value_of_award

741.07M

0.00M   784.81M

FIGURE 11-28:
Using a gauge.

5317

Count of Small Disadvantaged Business

FIGURE 11-29:
A Card example.

VA
1.160.950.789.10   3.307.959.447.32
Obligated   Total Value

CA
561.921.668.21   603.294.692.94
Obligated   Total Value

MD
484.031.557.03   534.245.543.22
Obligated   Total Value

FIGURE 11-30:
A Multi-card
example.

Key performance indicators (KPI)

Supplying textual and graphical insights tells a story with true impact. Consider using the KPI visualization: The visualization looks at a single measure, evaluating the current value and status against a defined target. You need a base measure that's numerical in nature — a target measure or a value — as well as a threshold goal. The output for a KPI can be both textual and visual, based on the type of trend you're looking to output. With Figure 11-31, using a subset of data in Fiscal Year 2021 that has been filtered, I'm able to show that the average highly compensated individuals doing business who have won at least one contract with the US federal government during FY21 earned an average of $1.382 million. The compensation trend is visible in the background from many firms paying their executives around $100,000 with fewer paying $1.5+ million compensation packages on the right side.

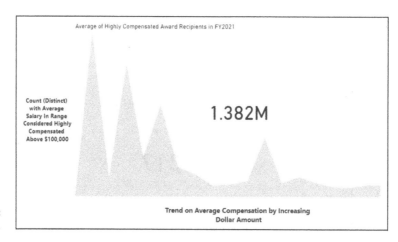

Average of Highly Compensated Award Recipients in FY2021

Count (Distinct)
with Average
Salary In Range
Considered Highly
Compensated
Above $100,000

1.382M

Trend on Average Compensation by Increasing
Dollar Amount

FIGURE 11-31:
A KPI example.

TECHNICAL STUFF

With many indicators, you can only assign a single value. You need to adjust the data category parameters to precisely calculate the output, whether you're looking for average, sum, distinct (single instances), or another measure.

TIP

Use the Card visual only if there's a single value to display. If you need to compare a value against more than one target, use the KPI visual — it offers users the ability to add trends in the background. Though it has limited information, the data is nonetheless focused. The multi-card choice can fulfill the business requirement for those looking to put together unrelated metrics on a single page.

Dealing with Table-Based and Complex Visualizations

Sometimes you need a bit more insight than a single graphical representation to tell your story. You may even want to manipulate the dataset or perform sorting activity on a subset of data based on a defined condition. What you want are table-based visualizations, and Power BI is ready to help, with visualization options ranging from slicers to tables to matrices. At other times, you may want to drill down into a many-layered dataset using decomposition trees or key influencers. With each choice, you can manipulate an extensive dataset with the help of Power BI's filtering features.

Slicing with slicers

Suppose that you want to create a visual drill-down filter on a canvas so that the user can sort and filter a report full of data relevant to their needs. In that case, a slicer — a dashboard-style tool integrated directly into the report, letting users select values as they analyze the data — may be just what you need. An example of a slicer can be found in Figure 11-32.

FIGURE 11-32:
A slicer example.

Tabling with table visualizations

You might scratch your head and wonder why you shouldn't just go to the dataset if you want to look at data in a table format. The reason you might want to use a table visualization versus a plain view of the table has to do with sorting and searching. Visualizations can give you a glimpse of the world. Still, a table is handy for displaying precise numerical data and summarized information found in rows and columns. When a table is enabled for sorting and filtering, the end user can better understand what the values behind the graphics mean. Check out Figure 11-33, which uses sorting and filtering to show which unique company entities (DUNS) were awarded contracts under $1 million for three NAICS codes (541511, 541512, 541519).

FIGURE 11-33:
Table
visualization.

State	Count of DUNS Number
VA	223
MD	117
CA	68
FL	37
CO	25
TX	25
NY	23
PA	20
DC	19
GA	18
MA	18
OH	18
NJ	17
IL	15
WA	15
MO	14
NC	14
AZ	12
AL	9
MI	9
OR	9
CT	8
AK	7
NM	7
KS	6
WI	6
HI	5
IN	5
MN	5
OK	5
Total	817

Combing through data with matrices

Assume for a moment that you're looking to aggregate data across one or more datasets. Perhaps you need to drill down into the data cross-section to find the needle in the haystack. Your best choice for mixing and matching aggregate data to cross-highlight elements that require attention is using the Matrix visual. You can select many rows and columns and even drop down to the cellular level to highlight data. In Figure 11-34, you see a cross-section of the contract award status for the fictitious company Data Power, highlighting awarded amounts, pending amounts, in-progress amounts, and lost awards across several federal agencies.

FIGURE 11-34:
A Matrix example.

Awarded	DHHS	DHS	DOC	DOD	DOE	DOI	ED	Treasury	Total
Awarded				78,000.00				232,254.00	310,254.00
In-Progress	50,000.00		14,683.20	0.00					64,683.20
No	207,252.45	38,248.10	2,110.24	39,567.00					287,177.79
Pending					250,000.00	60,898.25	340,000.00		650,898.25
Total	257,252.45	38,248.10	16,793.44	117,567.00	250,000.00	60,898.25	340,000.00	232,254.00	1,313,013.24

Decomposing with decomposition trees

When you think of an organization chart, you likely envision a chart that displays leadership to the worker bee. A *decomposition tree* is a type of chart that allows you to visualize data across multiple dimensions. Looking at the top value as an aggregate, you can then drill down into a dataset to a more finite scope. As is the case with Figure 11-35, the decomposition tree shows total obligations for all small businesses awarded contracts under $1 million in a fiscal year (total obligation). The decomposition is the amount distributed per state (aggregate) across all contracts awarded.

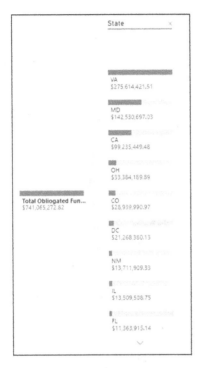

FIGURE 11-35:
A decomposition tree.

Zooming in on key influencers

Ever wonder what the data driver is within a graphic? Or perhaps you're looking to measure performance respective of one or more measures in use based on some form of rank system. Now, it's realistic to understand that not everything ranks as triggering an explicit condition. At other times, you see clear visuals pointing to a scenario where you should pay close attention. Examples of datasets that act as red flags are signs of unusual drops in sales volume or a significant reduction in another specific metric. Another extreme is an outlier that stands out like a sore thumb. Key influencers use the Microsoft AI engine, supported by Azure, to illustrate impacting metrics at speed and scale. If an influencer is designated an identifier, the user can complete various forms of analysis, including segment analysis. As shown in Figure 11-36, a few US states have a huge government contracting presence based on award volume and dollars obligated relative to others.

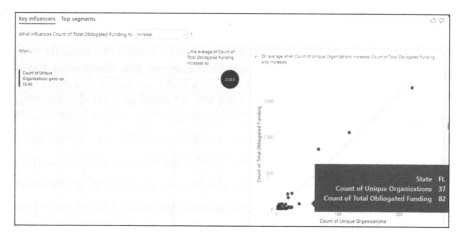

FIGURE 11-36:
Working with key
influencers.

All the datasets found in this chapter, including the DataPower.xls and Small-
BusinessAwards.xls, can be found in the Zip file, downloadable at www.dummies.
com/go/microsoftpowerBIfd.

Dabbling in Data Science

Microsoft Power BI includes the use of a Python scripting editor and R scripting
editor. Python and R are two data-science oriented, calculation-based programming languages. When combined with Power BI, these two languages help to
expand upon the analysis of datasets that may be in the millions to tens of millions
of records at speed and scale using a structured approach to analysis. Both editors
are accessible from the Visualizations pane. (See Figure 11-37.). A user can run
either script type directly in Power BI Desktop. Alternatively, they can import the
resulting dataset from an R or Python editor into a Power BI data model.

Regardless of the editor you end up using, you're prompted to enable script visuals in order to execute code coming from one of the data-science-based code
editors. (See Figure 11-38.) A placeholder visual appears, as shown in Figure 11-39.
To start building a Python or R script, drag fields from the Fields pane over to the
Visualizations pane under Values. If you need to change the settings, click the Settings icon (the small cog) in the lower right corner of the scripting interface to
access your options.

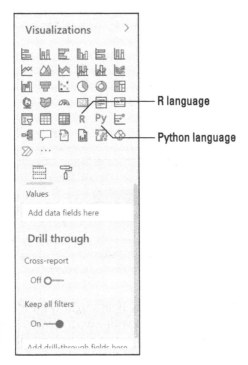

R language

Python language

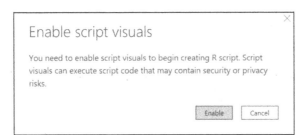

Enable script visuals

You need to enable script visuals to begin creating R script. Script visuals can execute script code that may contain security or privacy risks.

Enable   Cancel

TIP

Python and R code requires an image to produce a visual. Unless you follow this process, no other forms of output, including data frames, will work. Also, data-science-based outputs don't allow for cross-filtering. Though you can't cross-filter an R or Python visual with another visual, you can select elements from multiple visuals to comingle.

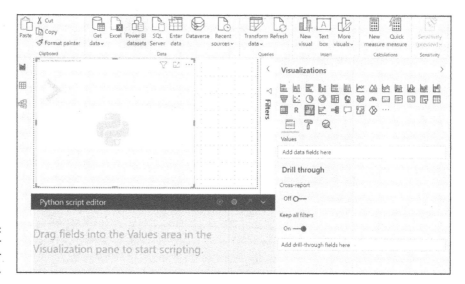

WARNING

The data-science editor in Power BI is lightweight. And Microsoft knows it! That's why it allows for the integration with external editors to quickly craft R and Python code. Though Microsoft makes you believe that all data-science editors will work with both the Desktop and Services versions of Power BI, guess again: Power BI Services has technical limitations with the editors supported. Therefore, to see whether the editor you want to use is supported for Python or R, check out either of these Microsoft documentation pages for the latest compatibility reports:

```
https://docs.microsoft.com/en-us/power-bi/connect-data/service-r-packages-support
```

```
https://docs.microsoft.com/en-us/power-bi/connect-data/service-python-packages-support
```

Questions and Answers

It should come as no surprise that Microsoft has integrated its powerful artificial intelligence and machine learning tools inside of Power BI to help users ask questions and provide answers about their data. Microsoft's artificial intelligence engine decides questions for the Q&A feature based on data volume, quality, and attribution. Looking for trends and relationships, Power BI offers users two options: Access prebuilt what-if question scenarios already conceived by the application, or ask the application pointed questions. In Figure 11-40, you can see potential questions crafted based on the finite number of fields associated with a given report. Or, you can come up with your own question, as shown in Figure 11-41.

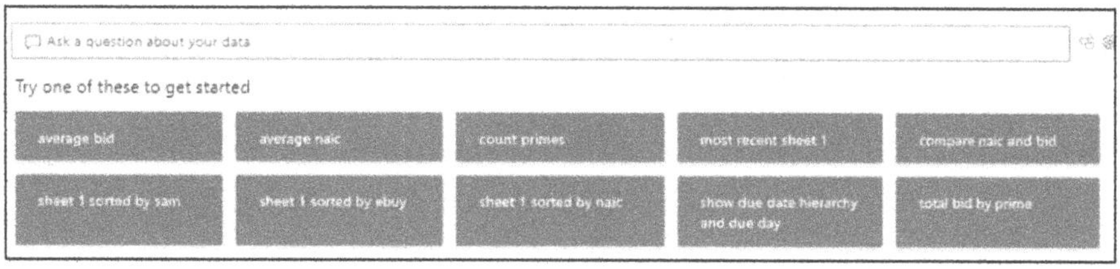

FIGURE 11-40: Prescribed questions and answers.

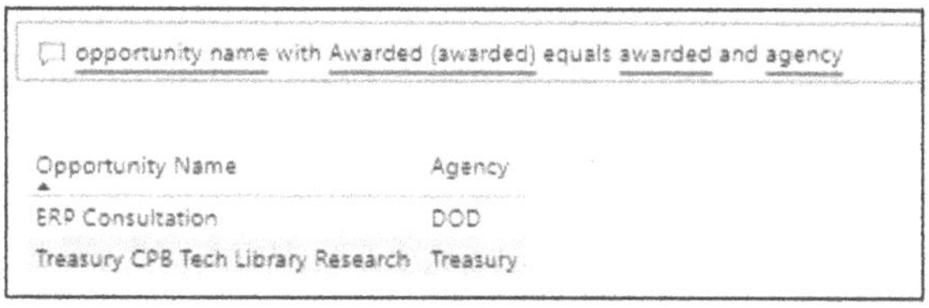

FIGURE 11-41: Self-created questions and answers.

ADDITIONAL VISUALIZATION OPTIONS

If you've ever used the Internet (and who hasn't?), you might have guessed that other vendors have created or integrated other visualization types for their own business intelligence solutions. Most vendors also have app stores or third-party websites where you can download additional templates and models. Microsoft is no different.

What I cover in this book are the core out-of-the-box visualizations for Power BI Desktop. Microsoft offers an added set of Power BI visualizations via the AppSource marketplace. To access the added visualization choices, go to the option that has the ellipsis (three dots) found on the Visualizations pane. (See the figure below). From there, select Get More Visuals from the menu that appears. (See the second figure below.) You can then select from hundreds of other templates, including advanced analytics models, KPIs, gauges, and a cadre of other visualization alternatives, as shown in the sidebar figure. If you want to try your hand at creating your own template or importing one

(continued)

(continued)

from a source outside of the Microsoft AppSource platform, that, too, is possible. Go to the ellipsis and choose the option, Import a Visual from a File.

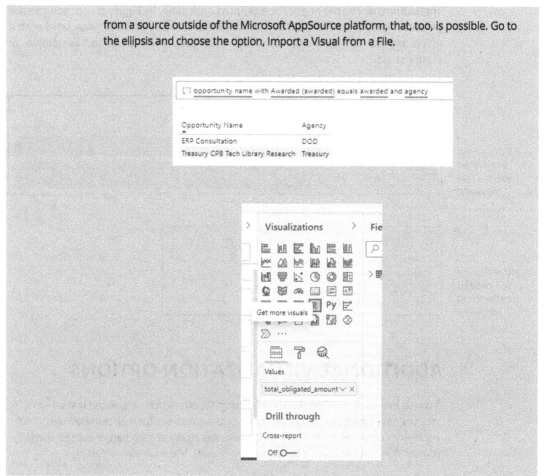

Chapter **12**

Pumping Out Reports

Think of each visualization you can create using Power BI as offering a different set of insights for a dataset. Visualizations can also be stand-alone or combined with many other visuals. Either way, the output of a visualization is an end-state deliverable: a report. Though it's not uncommon for a report to include a single visualization, having many visualizations can offer tremendous perspective to an organization. Depending on the user's role, the report can also take on many different lives. Some users may be the report's designer, and others may be the consumer of report data. This chapter uncovers how to configure visuals and report settings for end user consumption using Power BI Desktop and Power BI Services.

Formatting and Configuring Report Visualizations

All visuals in Power BI are configurable in some shape or form. Though some visualizations have report-specific configurations based on their predefined criteria, many items can be considered standard across all visualizations. No matter what, you can format a visual by selecting the item and clicking the Visualization pane's handy Paint Roller icon (see Figure 12-1) to access the formatting tools.

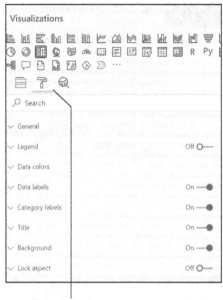

FIGURE 12-1:
Formatting
features
found in the
Visualizations
pane.

Paint Roller icon

Here's a description of some common formatting choices:

>> **General formatting:** Here's where you can select the *x*-position, *y*-position, width, height, and *alt text* — the description used for accessibility options.

>> **Title:** Format the title text, text and word wrapping, color (font and background), and text features (alignment, font size, and font face).

>> **Background:** Set the page and visualization background.

>> **Lock aspect:** Lock a visual element based on the proportion of the specific object on the canvas.

>> **Borders:** Format the border colors and radii of your visuals.

>> **Shadow:** Set the shadow color and position.

>> **Tooltips:** Format any default or report-specific tooltips (descriptors).

>> **Headers:** Hide or show headers based on conditions.

REMEMBER

Many other options are available, depending on the visualization. The list I came up with here covers only the ones you see across all visualizations.

Working with basic visualization configurations

Don't confuse *visualization* configurations and *report* configurations. The difference is that each time you include a visualization in a report, you're free to configure that particular visualization with specific settings. A *report* configuration is for the layout and design of all your visualizations on a single page.

REMEMBER

You need to have one or more visualizations on a page in order to generate a report. Each time you want to configure the visualization, you select the particular visualization in the Canvas window and click the Visualization pane's Paint Roller icon. That action brings up the visualization formatting settings.

When trying to configure the position and size of a visualization, go to the General section (see Figure 12-2) and choose from the following:

» **Responsive:** This allows for the visualization to be adjustable based on the canvas size. It automatically adjusts on your behalf.

» **X-Position:** The visual will be flush left starting at this position on the canvas.

» **Y-Position:** The visual will be flush top starting at this position on the canvas.

» **Width:** This is the default size horizontally for the visualization.

» **Height:** This is the default size vertically for the visualization.

» **Maintain layer order:** Selecting this option automatically brings the visualization to the front, above other overlapping visuals. Deselecting pushes the visualization backward.

» **Alt-Text:** The ability to textually describe the visualization for those requiring help using adaptive technologies.

You might have added a legend to help differentiate the boxes, lines, or plot points, depending on the visualization. You can position the legend in several regions of a page as well as custom-format the presentation of the legend, based on the location on the page, as shown in Figure 12-3.

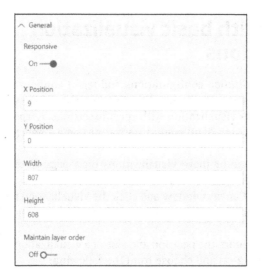

FIGURE 12-2:
The General
settings for
formatting a
visualization.

FIGURE 12-2:
The General
settings for
formatting a
visualization.

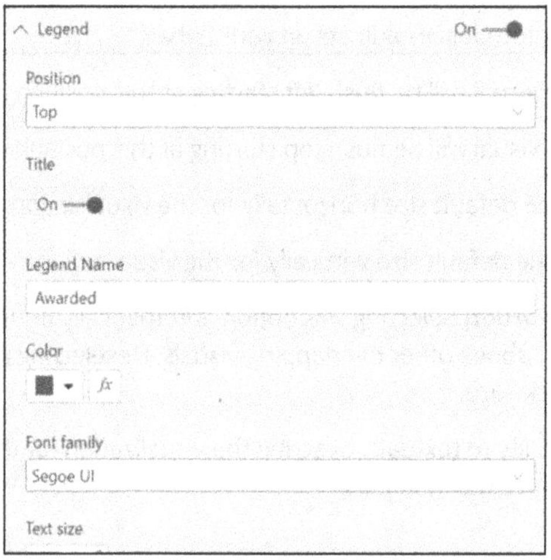

FIGURE 12-3:
Configuring
the legend.

The Data Colors, Data Labels, and Total Labels options vary from visualization to visualization. For example, if you have a Bar chart, you can change the colors of each bar beyond the Microsoft suggestion for the default. Similarly, you can change the text color for any data labels, as shown in Figure 12-4. An excellent example of when you need to do this is when you're using a lot of dark colors as background. You'll likely want to change the data labels to a light color, such as white or yellow, for readability.

FIGURE 12-4:
The Data Colors
and Data Labels
options.

Visualizations have a title separate from a report header title. Therefore, you can update the title text if you want to change what Microsoft titles a visualization. Additionally, you change the font size using the Title Heading option. If positioning, color, alignment, and even title background color mean much to you, you can make these adjustments as well. These features are shown in Figure 12-5.

FIGURE 12-5:
The title settings.

Should you want to make the background color of a visualization stand out, you can opt to change the color and offer transparency for other objects on the page, as shown in Figure 12-6. Examples of items that may require transparency are the legend, header, and x- and y-axis text.

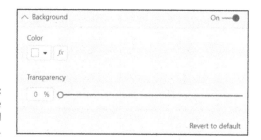

FIGURE 12-6:
Setting the background color.

Here are some other formatting features that can be configured on a case-by-case basis:

>> **Lock aspect:** Visualizations can scale based on size and position.

>> **Border:** A visualization border can be configured based on thickness and color.

>> **Shadow:** A visualization border shadow can be configured based on color, direction, and position.

Figure 12-7 shows these options.

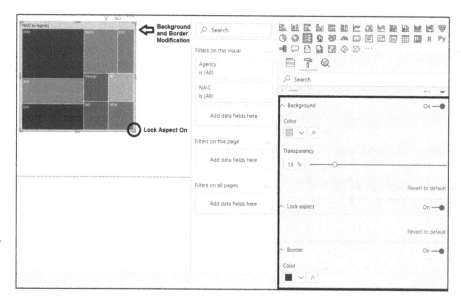

FIGURE 12-7:
Integration of lock aspect, background and border.

One last configuration to consider changing on a previsualization basis concerns the Visual Header settings, as shown in Figure 12-8. Every visualization allows for a user to transform the visual experience via action-based controls. You have the option to hide or show the header of each visual in a report. You can turn the visual header on or off as you design your visualizations and configure the aesthetics, including the filter functionality. Visual indicators include the Visual Warning icon, Visual Error icon, and 10+ drilling options. For each option, you can turn them on or off.

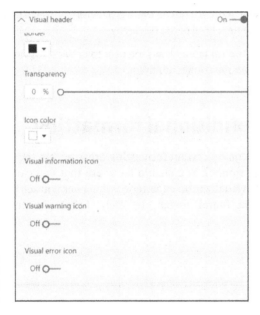

FIGURE 12-8:
Visual Header
configuration
options.

Here are some other icons included in the Visual Headers field:

>> **Drill on icon:** Review specific data points within a report.

>> **Drill Up icon:** Provides a higher-level perspective of a current view.

>> **Drill Down icon:** Provides a more granular view of a current view.

>> **Expand to Next Level icon:** Adds an additional hierarchy level to the current view.

- » **Filter icon:** Provides a user the ability to filter the data assuming there are fields configured for filtering.

- » **Focus Mode icon:** Allows a user to see the report data exclusively.

- » **More Options icon:** Gives a user access to additional options.

- » **Pin icon:** Allows you to pin an item to a canvas.

- » **See Data Layout icon:** Lets you review the data in a tabular format, if available.

- » **Show Next Level icon:** Assuming there is a hierarchy, the user can use this icon to show the next level of the hierarchy.

- » **Visual Header Tooltip icon:** Allows the user to provide custom tooltips to the user, assuming you've configured them.

Applying conditional formatting

You may notice an icon on certain formatting areas within the Visualization pane that includes the *fx* symbol. You should be aware that you can customize one or more aspects of the visualization experience whenever you see this. An example of this button can be found under the Data Labels heading, as shown in Figure 12-9.

FIGURE 12-9:
The Conditional
Formatting
button.

A configuration screen appears whenever you press the *fx* symbol, allowing users to configure one or more sides of the user experience under certain conditions. (See Figure 12-10.) For example, for Data Labels, a user can format by color scale, rules, or field value. Upon selecting the preferred choice, you have the option to select the condition based on options including Field, Summarization, Minimum, and Maximum. Of course, there is a Default formatting parameter that is considered the user baseline.

FIGURE 12-10:
The Conditional
Formatting
interface.

Filtering and Sorting

You can filter data based on the visual element itself, across an entire page, or across all pages for every visualization. Most users filter based on a visual because a report with multiple visuals often has different behaviors.

TIP

Don't be too quick to create an all-encompassing filtering-and-sorting routine for an entire report. You'll likely find at least one visual where the behavior for a field is slightly different even though it appears at first that all fields are equal.

Regardless of the filtering-and-sorting option you choose, you need to select Filter on This Visual, Filter on This Page, or Filter on All Pages. In Figure 12-11, you can see that I've selected and placed particular fields into the area-specific visuals under Filters on this Visual heading.

Here's how you'd manage it:

1. **In the Reports View, drag one or more fields from the Fields pane to one of the Add Data Fields text boxes in the Filter pane.**

2. **Expand (or collapse) the fields you just brought over from the Fields pane.**

   Each field creates an object called a *filter card* — a way to filter the dataset visually.

FIGURE 12-11:
Configuring fields
for a specific
visuals example.

3. **Configure the filter based on the condition needed.**

    Text-based conditions are different from numerical conditions.

REMEMBER A user can choose between Basic Filtering, Advanced Filtering, and Top N Filtering — Figure 12-12 shows an example of advanced filtering:

>> **Basic filtering** limits the user to those fields in the dataset.

>> **Advanced filtering** integrates the use of Boolean conditions such as AND, OR, or NOT in addition to the value meeting a particular condition.

>> **Top N filtering** is associated with the rank order of items.

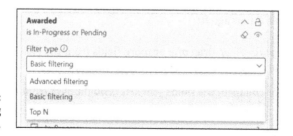

FIGURE 12-12:
Your Filtering
menu options.

REMEMBER

Over filtering can be a problem for some reports, so be sure not to add too many fields; the more complex your report becomes, the more you end up adding. If you decide to filter across multiple fields, be sure not to add too many conditions unless your report requires a specific level of granularity. The Search box at the top of the Filter pane is a way to find those fields and their values a bit easier, should you need a bit of help.

WARNING

If you look at each field, you notice a Lock option as well as a Hiding option at the field level. (Refer to Figure 12-12.)These features work only when using the Power BI Services, not in Power BI Desktop.

Configuring the Report Page

Formatting a report page isn't much different from formatting a visual element except that a report may have multiple visuals. To handle, go straight to the Visualizations panel. Once there, click the Paint Roller icon. On the screen that appears, you see many options to change the layout and design of your report page, as shown in Figure 12-13. Most of your options focus on positioning, alignment, and color of the overall report experience.

FIGURE 12-13: Configuring a report page.

A user can format the following page-related features:

>> **Page information:** Modify the report's name, turn tooltips on and off, and enable Q&A across an entire page, not just a specific visual.

>> **Page size:** Pick the size factor and/or paper type. Depending on how you want to deploy the report, paper sizes and interface options are available.

>> **Page background:** Configure the background color of the report page.

>> **Page alignment:** Decide whether to make the content of their reports flush-left top or flush-left center on a page.

>> **Wallpaper:** Brand a report with specific colors or perhaps a logo to take advantage of the Wallpaper option.

>> **Filter pane:** To change the Filter pane, an integral part of online-based report viewing, a user can configure the user experience to match the paper-style interface with color, transparency, borders, and specific text.

>> **Filter cards:** Like the Filter pane, Filter cards are specific to a given field (a column found in a table, for example). They let a user highlight one or more objects in a report using various aesthetic tools.

REMEMBER

The best way to ensure consistency when it comes to report formatting is to create a page once and duplicate the page configuration multiple times. That saves you the wasted effort of re-creating the wheel several times over.

Refreshing Data

Power BI offers you several ways to import data. Though some methods require constant updating by the users (Import, for example), others can automatically refresh. If you're using DirectQuery to import data, for example, you definitely want to have your data automatically refresh, especially when trying to check data in real time.

You have the choice to set the automatic page refresh by enabling the Page Refresh button in the Visualizations pane of a report page. You need to toggle to the Page Refresh section and set the option to On. Once activated, Power BI refreshes all visuals on a page at a given interval that you select: fixed interval or change detection.

Though a fixed interval is available in all Power BI Service editions, change detection is available only in Premium. Change detection updates the Power BI dataset as soon as it detects (ok, not the very second, but usually a short while after) it's being on a host server with fresh data.

You can use Page Refresh only in Power BI Services. Also, if you chose to support automatic page refresh, it must be enabled by an administrator.

Working with reports

It may seem that there's *so* much to get done using Power BI Desktop for a report to be shared with the masses, but the truth is that I have described only a fraction of what can be done. Your hard work in preparing a report aesthetically for distribution over the Internet using Power BI Desktop will save you time later.

If your business goal is to create reports at the Desktop client and distribute PDF versions of your outputs, you likely don't need to use Power BI Services. The catch: Your audience can't interactively manipulate or view data in real time. A piece of paper is only a snapshot in time.

The very moment that you decide more than one user must manipulate your data, even if it's basic filtering or sorting on the Internet, you need to publish your datasets and visualizations to the Internet. If the scope of your sharing is limited to view-only on a platform such as SharePoint, Power BI Services Free is adequate. If, however, you want users to have the opportunity to collaborate with your Workspace, either the Pro or Premium version of Power BI Services is necessary.

Everything you read about in this chapter can be done online rather than on a desktop, but the level of effort to configure the entire experience is highly dependent on an Internet connection. That's why you want to start on your desktop first and then push the visualizations and report to the Services site.

To publish a report, follow these steps:

1. **Go to the Home tab on the Power BI Desktop Ribbon.**

2. **Click the Publish button, found on the right end of the Ribbon.**

   You're prompted to save all your desktop work.

3. **Save your work by clicking Save.**

4. **In the new dialog box that appears, select the location where you want your dataset and visualizations housed.**

   The assumption is that you've created one or more workspaces on the Services site. If you haven't, you're prompted to create a workspace or save it to My Workspace. (See Figure 12-14.)

FIGURE 12-14:
Saving dataset and visualizations in the report to a workspace.

5. **After choosing a workspace as your Save location, click Select.**

6. **If this is the first time you've saved it to the workspace, click Save. If you've already saved an item to the workspace, you're asked to replace the item because it already exists, as shown in Figure 12-15.**

Finding migrated data

You have two ways to gain access to the data you have just published to Power BI Services. First, you can find all your data by clicking the Recent button on the left-side navigation bar. There, you'll find all your most recent items in chronological order. (See Figure 12-16.) After you find the file you imported, double-click to continue making modifications over the Internet.

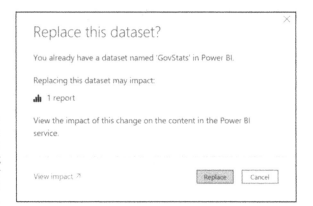

FIGURE 12-15:
Creating an
updated version
of a reporting
package for
Power BI
Services.

Recent

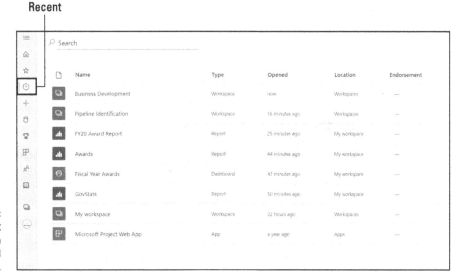

FIGURE 12-16:
The Recent
menu in
Power BI
Services.

The second possibility is to go directly to the Workspace section of Power BI Ser-vices where you've imported the data after initiating the publishing process. Once there, select the imported items in the list you want to review, as shown in Figure 12-17.

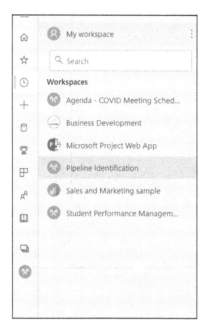

FIGURE 12-17:
Selecting an
item from the
My Workspace
menu in Power BI
Services.

Exporting reports

Suppose that you don't want to save the report you've created to Power BI Services. Your singular aim is to print a snapshot in time, thereby saving the data to a PDF file. That is entirely possible using Power BI Desktop. To export a report without saving to Power BI Services, follow these steps:

1. **Choose File ⇨ Export from the main menu.**

2. **Choose Export from the menu that appears.**

3. **Save the file either as a Power BI template by providing a description and pressing OK or selecting PDF file which automatically generates an Adobe Acrobat PDF to your Web browser, as shown in Figure 12-18.**

   The export is saved to the desktop.

A user who selects the Power BI template option gets the equivalent of a Zip file. A Power BI template is based on an existing desktop report template. It has report layout, report pages and visuals, schema, relationships, measures, datasets, and prebuilt data models. Also, part of a definition file may include queries and query parameters. The PDF file, on the other hand, has only static copies of the visualizations accumulated across all tabs.

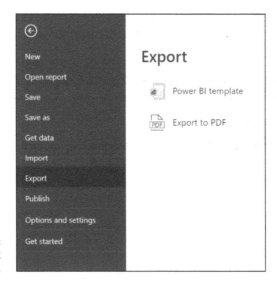

FIGURE 12-18:
Your export
choices.

Perfecting reports for distribution

Yes, you can create a report in Power BI Desktop and save it in PDF format or even print it. But, generally, the real purpose of reporting is to share the data online using either the Power BI service or a mobile app. Microsoft has made it relatively easy for a designer to create rich reports that can fit on either a computer screen or a mobile device. The company has recognized that not everything can fit on one page either — hence, the use of tab management.

Sometimes it makes complete sense to keep any reporting local to the desktop. An example is sales performance forecasting or human resource management distribution. Suppose that your goal is to distribute by print or deliver a digital document without an Internet connection. In that case, you should consider creating a paginated report.

TIP

Exporting report visuals to a PDF just doesn't cut it sometimes! That's why you want to use the Power BI Report Builder, an extension found at www.microsoft. com/en-us/download/details.aspx?id=58158.

You can use almost any data source you'd expect to find with Power BI Reports on your desktop. In fact, you can even use Power BI Services data if you decide to create one in the application.

Follow these steps to create a Power BI data-based paginated report using Power BI Services:

1. **Go to My Workspace and then find the workspace containing the data you'd like to use for a paginated report.**

2. **Open the workspace.**

3. **Click the workspace's New button and choose Paginated Report from the menu that appears, as shown in Figure 12-19.**

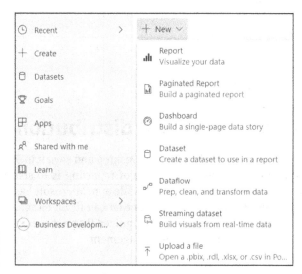

FIGURE 12-19:
The Paginated
Report menu.

If this is your first time using Power BI Report Builder, you're asked to download the application. Otherwise, the application launches Power BI Desktop along with the Report Builder.

After the Report Builder launches, you're prompted to create a report using the wizard or a blank report, as shown in Figure 12-20.

4. **Choose Blank Report.**

5. **Using the pane on the left, connect your data sources to the Report Builder so that you can begin to create a paginated report.**

Notice the blank canvas with some typed-in text, as shown in Figure 12-21.

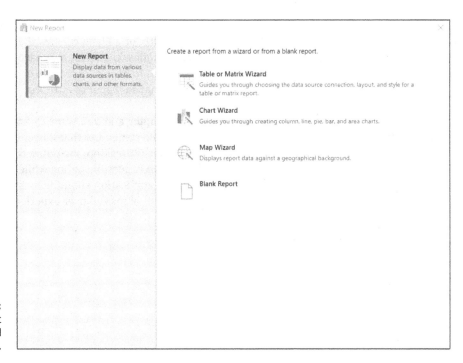

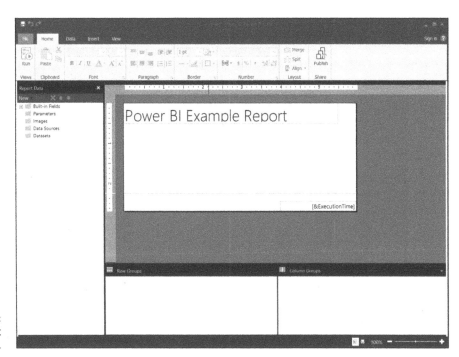

You can paginate a report in many ways, depending on the choice you select using the wizard. Whether you select a matrix or a blank canvas, the steps to configure a paginated report are extensive. To follow the latest approaches as suggested by Microsoft and its solution offering, go to `https://docs.microsoft.com/en-us/power-bi/paginated-reports/paginated-reports-quickstart-aw`.

If you've come to the end of this chapter and you want to know how to format visualizations for reporting, you should remember that Power BI Services offers a virtually identical experience to Power BI Desktop, including the user experience. The big difference is that collaboration is possible online while using the Desktop client; only one user can manage the application simultaneously. What you know about configuring a report is consistent across all user experiences.

Chapter **13**

Diving into Dashboarding

Picture this: a mixture of pictures and text neatly organized like a beautiful canvas. It tells you that everything in your organization is running smoothly, but then one of the visuals changes. Alarm bells go off — figurative ones, at least — causing many phones to ring and SMS messages to be sent. And the person responding to the emergency doesn't have to dig too deep, either. Why, might you wonder? Because the organization has collected a series of datasets, available in the form of a single user experience, not a collection of ad hoc reports. The datasets on a single canvas all give real-time access to the current state of operations. The dashboard may appear to be a big mush of data, but it's meaningful data presented in a way that those who have mastered the intricacies of the dashboard can immediately see what's wrong. In this chapter, I introduce you to the mysteries of dashboarding using Power BI Services.

Before your initiation into the mysteries, here are a few critical principles regarding dashboarding with Power BI:

» **You can only create a dashboard using Power BI Services.** In fact, to truly experience the full breadth of dashboarding, you need to have a Pro or Premium license.

>> **A dashboard is meant to fill a business void.** A report can contain only a single dataset. Though it's perfectly okay to use just one dataset in a dashboard, using dashboards as a way to present multiple datasets are far more common.

>> **A dashboard is a compilation of many objects.** It manages that compilation by limiting itself to only one screen.

>> **Each visual in a dashboard is referred to as a *tile*.** In reports, visuals are referred to as *outputs*.

>> **Power BI Services is web-based service.** Power BI Desktop doesn't require an Internet connection. Data alerts are only available using Power BI Services.

Configuring Dashboards

A *dashboard*, in its simplest form, is merely a collage of many data objects that can be pinned to a single page. Most times, the items are visual; at other times, the content contained in the dashboard may have text, video, audio, or navigation to other dashboards and data sources. Dashboards can integrate resources using reports, Excel workbooks, insights, Q&A results, and multimedia across content providers.

Creating a New Dashboard

If you're logged into Power BI Services, you should ensure that you have a dataset and some visuals that can be placed on a dashboard. If you've never created a dashboard, follow these steps:

1. **In Power BI Services, go to My Workspaces.**

2. **Click New at the top of My Workspaces.**

3. **Choose Dashboard from the menu that appears, as shown in Figure 13-1.**

4. **Enter the name of the new dashboard (see Figure 13-2) and then click Create.**

    A blank canvas is set up for you, as shown in Figure 13-3.

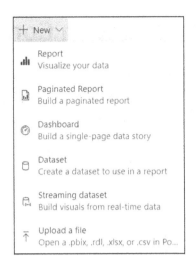

FIGURE 13-1:
Creating a
dashboard.

FIGURE 13-2:
Naming a new
dashboard.

FIGURE 13-3:
A blank
Dashboard
canvas.

Enriching Your Dashboard with Content

You need to keep a couple of points in mind when trying to integrate an object on your Dashboard canvas. The first thing to consider is what type of objects are needed to accentuate a planned report compilation on a dashboard. The second has to do with the layout and number of objects you intend to pin to the canvas.

At this point, you can add a few different items beyond the reports proper:

» **Web content:** HTML-based web content

» **Images:** Publicly accessible images exclusively

» **Text boxes:** Static text that can be formatted

» **Video:** Videos that can be embedded either on YouTube or Vimeo

» **Custom streaming data:** Real-time data coming from an API, Azure Stream, or PubNub source

TECHNICAL
STUFF

You are probably familiar with most of the content sources listed above, but if you are interested in extremely large datasets being presented in a dashboard, consider using Azure Streams or PubNub. Azure Stream is the abbreviated name for Azure Stream Analytics, a real-time analytics and complex event-processing engine designed to analyze and process high volumes of (usually live) data from multiple sources simultaneously. PubNub, like Azure Streams, is another real-time analytics streaming service focused on delivering content using a real-time publish/subscribe messaging process, primarily for Internet of Things (IoT) devices.

To add content-based objects to the canvas — *tiles*, in Power BI-speak — follow these steps:

1. **On the Dashboard canvas, go to the Edit menu.**

2. **Choose Add a Tile, as shown in Figure 13-4.**

FIGURE 13-4:
Accessing the
Add a Tile menu.

3. **From the new menu that appears, choose one of the listed object types. (See Figure 13-5.)**

Notice that the menu has no Report option.

All the content you place on a dashboard must be publicly accessible. Even if authentication or uploading is necessary for a user to view the data, Power BI doesn't presently support such features.

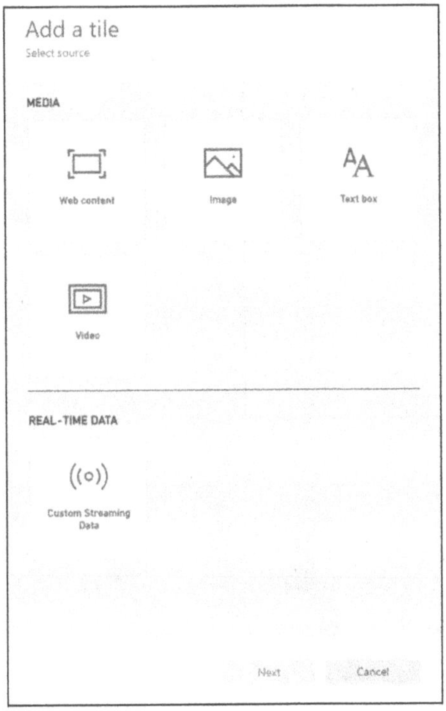

Add a tile

Select source

MEDIA

Web content   Image   Text box

Video

REAL-TIME DATA

Custom Streaming
Data

Next   Cancel

FIGURE 13-5: Selecting a tile type.

4. **After choosing an option, use the option's customizing features to place your content the way you want it.**

For example, if you were to choose the Text Box option, a new screen would appear (see Figure 13-6) where you could add titles, subtitles, and text. You could even tweak whatever you've added, by using any of the displayed formatting commands. When you finish, click Apply. Any changes you've made show up on your dashboard, as shown in Figure 13-7.

Once the tile is on the Dashboard canvas, you can move it anywhere you want. By default, it sits flush-left top unless other tiles are in the region. In the earlier example, I moved the tile to the upper right corner so that I can add other tiles later.

FIGURE 13-6:
Configuring a tile.

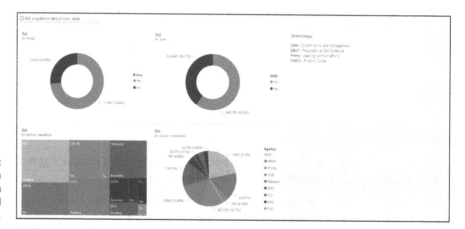

FIGURE 13-7:
Customizing a
content tile on
the Dashboard
canvas.

Pinning Reports

Because you create visualization reports inside Power BI, creating a report Visualization tile is a slightly different process from other content additions. Basically, you pin the existing report visualization to the dashboard rather than create a new tile — the asset is already stored in Power BI, so you don't have to "create" anything. To pin a report visualization, follow these steps:

1. **Go to a workspace that contains a report, including one or more visualizations you'd like to include in a dashboard.**

2. **Locate the Pin icon in the Visual header. (See Figure 13-8.)**

FIGURE 13-8:
The Pin icon.

3. **On the new screen that appears, click a radio button to specify whether the visualization will be part of a new dashboard or added to an existing dashboard. (See Figure 13-9.)**

   You'll add the visualization to an existing dashboard, so you should choose that option. You then use the drop-down menu to select the dashboard you want.

4. **After making your selections, click Pin.**

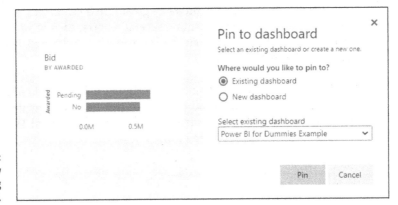

FIGURE 13-9:
Opting for a new
or existing
dashboard.

Repeat Steps 1–4 for as many visualizations as you want to include on your dashboard. The result is a dashboard like the one you see in Figure 13-10.

REMEMBER

Pinned visualizations aren't interactive. Updates are visible only after you refresh the dataset from which the visualization was derived. If you're looking for real-time data, you use the Custom Streaming Data tile.

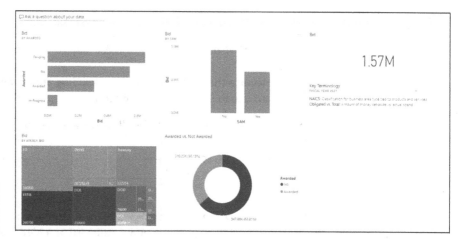

FIGURE 13-10:
A finished
dashboard
with tiles.

Customizing with Themes

Users who like a unified look often add a theme to a Power BI visualization. It turns out that you can do the very same thing to a dashboard. In fact, the need for an overarching theme is probably greater in a dashboard. Just think about it: Suppose that you have to integrate several reports, each of which has a different look and feel, into one dashboard? By developing a dashboard theme, you keep the user experience consistent.

Configuring a dashboard theme is like adding a tile. To add a theme to a dashboard, go to the dashboard you want to add the theme to. Just above the dashboard in the menu, select the Edit menu. Then, choose Dashboard Theme from the list of options, as shown in Figure 13-11.

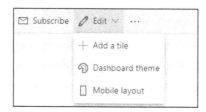

FIGURE 13-11:
Choosing the
Dashboard
Theme option.

A user can use a prebuilt theme on the Dashboard Theme screen, as shown in Figure 13-12, or develop their own, custom theme. When you choose Custom from the drop-down menu, you have complete control over the images, color, font color, and tile background. Figure 13-13 shows you your Custom Theme menu choices.

FIGURE 13-12:
Choosing a
prebuilt theme.

FIGURE 13-13:
Customizing
a theme.

**TECHNICAL
STUFF**

You might have noticed a choice labeled Upload JSON theme. If you want to add more complex theme designs, you can add these scripts by selecting this option. To download additional themes created by Microsoft that apply the JSON theme schema, go to `https://community.powerbi.com/t5/Themes-Gallery/bd-p/ThemesGallery`.

Working with Dashboard Layouts

Like Power BI reports, dashboards also have different layout options to cater to various device form factors. For dashboards, a web view and mobile view are available — a web layout occupies far greater screen real estate than a mobile layout. Figure 13-14 shows an example of a web layout.

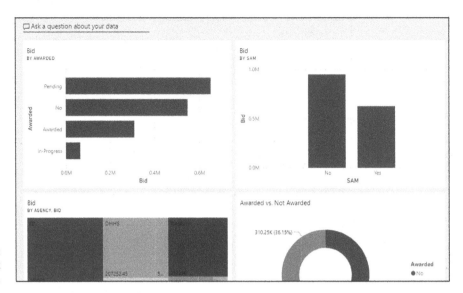

FIGURE 13-14:
The web layout
for a dashboard.

The mobile layout organizes each visual as a stacked asset. There's only one pinned visual horizontally, by default. A user can change the layout of a dashboard for mobile consumption by choosing Edit ⇨ Mobile Layout from the dashboard navigation menu. A user who wants more than one dashboard tile horizontally can resize each tile. Figure 13-15 shows an example of a mobile layout.

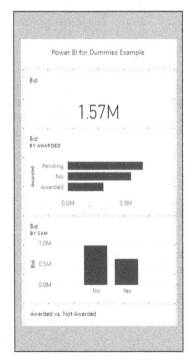

FIGURE 13-15:
A dashboard's
mobile layout.

Integrating Q&A

As I discuss in Chapter 11, the Q&A feature is a powerful capability, based on machine learning, that's incorporated into the Power BI Desktop and Services application. A user can ask a question about one or more datasets by using natural language queries. Q&A is not only available for reports but for dashboards as well.

You can start using the feature immediately, because no configuration is required. To start using the Q&A on a web layout dashboard, select Ask a Question About Your Data at the top of a dashboard by filling in a question using the query box. (See Figure 13-16.)

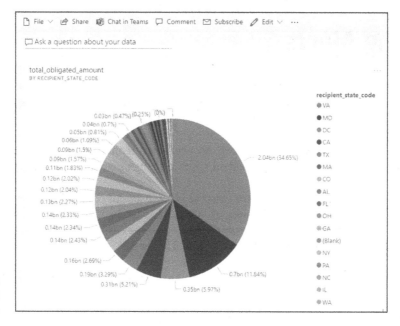

FIGURE 13-16:
Posing a question.

For the example shown in Figure 13-17, I added a report for all state awards to my dashboard by using the Awards.xlsx data source. I then created a query to determine all cities in Alaska (AK) where a contract was awarded. Using natural language code, which autofills as you type, a set of results was produced and refined in seconds.

| recipient state name, sorted by recipient city, state in which recipient state code is AK |

Showing results for *Recipient state name that contracts prime award summaries 2021 02 13 H19M21S17 1 are in with r*

recipient_state_name	recipient_state_code	recipient_city_name
ALASKA	AK	ALLAKAKET
ALASKA	AK	ANCHORAGE
ALASKA	AK	EAGLE RIVER
ALASKA	AK	FAIRBANKS
ALASKA	AK	JUNEAU
ALASKA	AK	KAKE
ALASKA	AK	NOME
ALASKA	AK	SKAGWAY

FIGURE 13-17:
A Q&A example.

Setting Alerts

At the beginning of this chapter, I describe a worst-case scenario: Everything is running smoothly and then sudden chaos erupts. Emails start pouring in at unsustainable levels, as do SMS messages.

In business, this is an all-too-common reality. With Power BI, though, you can create data alerts based on specific business conditions that trigger notifications.

Power BI's Dashboard features allow users to create alerts based on data-driven conditions found using visuals such as cards, KPI indicators, and gauges. If you have one or more of these visuals on your dashboard, you can configure an alert. To configure a data alert, follow these steps:

1. **Click the ellipses in the tile you want to create a notification for in your selected dashboard.**

   Your options are limited to three visualization types: cards, KPI indicators and gauges.

REMEMBER

2. **On the menu that appears, choose More Options ⇨ Manage Alerts, as shown in Figure 13-18.**

3. **On the Alert panel that appears, select Add Alert Rule.**

4. **Fill in the form with your defined criteria, as shown in Figure 13-19.**

   In this case, an alert is triggered every hour when the bid amount exceeds $2 million in total pending submissions.

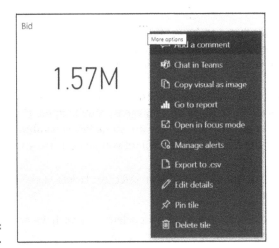

FIGURE 13-18:
Adding alerts.

FIGURE 13-19:
Configuring
alerts.

TIP

Alerts are helpful when you have multiple conditions that need to be met while also achieving specific thresholds. Alerts can be changed based on delivery frequency or whenever a change in content occurs.

Only those users who configure an alert ever see it, and alerts are synchronized between the Power BI Services and Power BI Mobile apps. If you are looking to manage you alerts post-creation, here are some key capabilities, all of which are completed under the Manage Alerts, where you just created your alert.

>> If you want to delete an alert, you can select the Delete Alert Rule using the Trashcan icon.

>> If you want to disable an alert without deleting it, switch the Active toggle to Off. (See Figure 13-20.)

>> If you are looking to send yourself an email when these thresholds are hit, select Send Me an Email.

FIGURE 13-20:
Managing alerts.

REMEMBER

Only the user who configures an alert can receive alerts, so don't assume that everyone in an organization automatically receives notification. Furthermore, notifications are sent by email by default.

4

Oh, No! There's a Power BI Programming Language!

Chapter **14**

Digging Into DAX

Working with programming languages often scares even the most experienced developer from time to time. And guess what? That's no different with Power BI. In earlier chapters where code is needed, I have you dabble in a few equations (key phrase: *a few*). But now you get into the weeds a bit more.

First off, why is it so important to understand the workings of a programming language like Data Analysis Expressions (DAX)? Well, it turns out that this formula expression language is used for data analysis across many Microsoft products, not just Power BI — Excel's Analysis Service and its Power Pivot are just two examples, among many. DAX formulas integrate traditional functions, operators, and values to perform advanced calculations and querying on datasets while also supporting data in related tabular data model tables and columns. This chapter covers the conceptual framework of DAX. In the following two chapters, you have the chance to dig a bit deeper into language design and manipulation.

Discovering DAX

So, what is Data Analysis Expressions (DAX)? DAX is a type of programmatic syntax language that makes use of formulas and expressions to manipulate data in analysis tools such as Power BI. Functions, formulas, constants, and operators are used as part of DAX to create the necessary expressions. Simply put, DAX is an advanced version of Microsoft Excel in the sense that it uses formulas with sophisticated data manipulation capabilities as part of its business intelligence and data modeling toolset.

In many of the chapters of this book, I show you how to complete tasks without your having to write a single line of code. So why am I introducing you to programming? It boils down to this: All the functions that require no coding are performed by tools that have been programmed to complete set tasks. At times, however, you may need to manipulate data types but cannot do so with predefined actions configured by the tools in Power BI. The product produced by using a few drag and click out-of-the-box features may not be what you need, whether it's an issue with syntax, context, or function. That's when you introduce a syntax language such as DAX into the mix.

Peeking under the DAX hood

At its core, DAX combines three fundamental concepts: syntax, context, and functions. When combined, these inputs create the specific commands that yield the desired results, as described in this list:

>> **Syntax** refers to the components within the formula you make. It's the language used in the formula, such as the command, sign, operators, column or row, or tables. In other words, syntax is the programmatic structure.

>> **Context** refers to the target row incorporated into the formula for retrieval or calculation. You need to learn about two types: row and filter context.

>> **Functions** refer to the predefined and known commands in a system. These are the commands that are readily used to manipulate data without having to craft extended coding samples.

Establishing syntax

The very first thing you need to learn about DAX is the composition of a formula. In Figure 14-1, you find a sample formula for a measure.

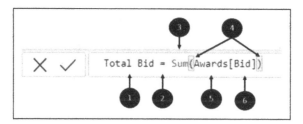

FIGURE 14-1:
A syntax example.

I've numbered these six components of note in Figure 14-1:

1. **The Measure name is** Total Bid.

2. **The equal-sign operator (=) indicates the beginning of the formula.**

   After the formula is calculated, the result is returned.

3. **The DAX function** SUM **is used in this formula, which adds all numbers in the** Awards[Bid] **column.**

   You will be reading a whole lot about functions in Chapter 15, so stay tuned.

4. **A parenthesis ( ) almost always surrounds an expression containing one or more arguments.**

   Arguments handle passing values to functions.

5. **The reference table is** Awards.

6. **The specific reference column** [Bid] **is found in the** Awards **table.**

   Using the specified argument, the SUM function aggregates all data for this specific column.

A calculated measure returns a value of all bids awarded. The formula also includes a *function* — a predefined formula. Formulas make it easier to complete complex calculations and manipulate large datasets, especially when various numbers, dates, times, and text are involved. One column name is Bid. Now, the column does belong to the Awards table, but including the table name along with a column name — *fully qualifying* a column name, in other words — is nonetheless a best practice.

TIP

When a table name has spaces, reserved keywords, or words with disallowed characters, be sure to use single quotation marks to enclose the table name. Also be sure to enclose any table in quotation marks if the table name has any non-ANSI alphanumeric characters.

WARNING

If a syntax error occurs in your formula, most of the time Power BI lets you know by displaying an error message. Sometimes, however, you may make a typographical error that Power BI doesn't flag — the result yields something quite different from what you might expect. Because the DAX editor in Power BI Desktop includes a built-in suggestion editor, I highly recommend using the editor to create correct formulas and ease your concerns.

Conceiving context

Context is a critical concept in DAX because it helps to shape the data dynamically. There are two contexts to be concerned about: row and filter:

» **Row context** is evaluated each time an expression is repeated in a table. That means, for each individual row, there's a different context. Row context exists either as a calculated column or a DAX function. Sample functions might be SUMX, AVERAGEX, or FILTER.

Suppose that a calculated column has been previously created. In that case, you can assume that the row context consists of the values in each individual row. That means, then, that the values in columns are related to a current row. Figure 14-2 provides an example of a row context.

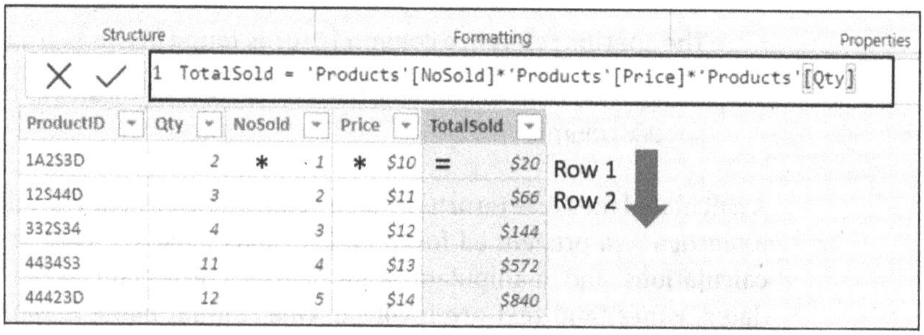

FIGURE 14-2:
A row context
example.

» **Filter context** is the application of those filters during the evaluation of measures or expressions. A filter can be applied directly to a column, like a filter on the Awarded column in the Opportunities table. In the case of Figure 14-3, the filter is applied to just those opportunities that are in process. Though the potential exists for several bars in your Bar chart, only one appears because a slicer filters all data except for the single condition In Process. The filters can be applied indirectly when model relationships affect other tables with foreign key relationships as well.

Formulating functions

Functions are those predefined formulas that perform complex calculations. When combining specific values, also known as arguments, a function produces an output in a particular order. Arguments take the form of other functions, formulas, expressions, column references, constants, numbers, text, and a variety of other options too numerous to mention here. (Chapter 15 spends a lot more time spelling out the 14 function types.)

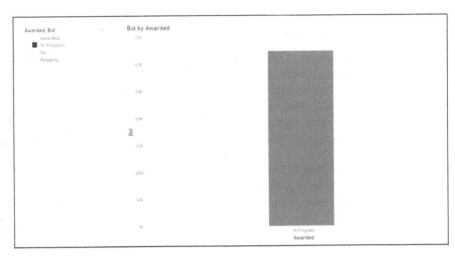

FIGURE 14-3:
A filter context
example.

Working with calculations

DAX formulas are used in measures, columns, tables, and row level security. To create new calculated measures or calculated columns, go to the Ribbon's Data View tab in Power BI. Once you navigate to the Data View tab, look for the Calculations area on the Ribbon's Home tab. You have four options, as shown in Figure 14-4, and this list describes what you can do by choosing them:

>> **New Measure:** Write a DAX expression from your data.

>> **Quick Measure:** Choose from a list of predefined calculations in Power BI.

>> **New Column:** Write a DAX expression that creates a new column in the selected table and calculates the values for each row.

>> **New Table:** Create a DAX expression to create a new table.

FIGURE 14-4:
DAX calculation
options.

The following sections lay out all four options so that you can better understand how to create measures, quick measures, calculated columns, and calculated tables.

Measures

Measures — also called *calculated measures* — help you develop insights into your data by addressing standard data analysis questions. Examples of measures might include *summarizations* (sum, average, minimum, maximum, and count, in other words). Measures are tied to fields. Each time you make a change to a field that includes a measure, you'll find that its calculations change. Of course, those changes are then (potentially) reflected in reports and dashboards.

In Power BI Desktop, a measure is created and displayed in either Report view or Data view. Each time you create a measure, it appears on the Fields pane with the Calculator icon. When you create a new measure, you can name it whatever you want. Later, you can add it to a visualization as you would any other field.

In the example shown in Figure 14-5, I've taken the Awards data and created a discount rate across the board for all awards at a rate of 8 percent. That means the calculated measure to be created is DiscountRate = SUM(Awards[Bid])*.92. (Figure 14-6 shows that the calculated field is now available as a new field called DiscountRate.)

FIGURE 14-5: A calculated measure in the DAX editor.

FIGURE 14-6: A calculated measure added to Fields pane.

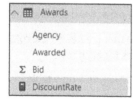

Quick measures

When looking to perform standard calculations quickly and easily, consider using quick measures because they reduce a significant amount of keyboard entry. A quick measure runs a set of DAX commands behind the scenes without your having to do any coding. You're asked to select the specific parameters using the graphical user interface dialog box. (See Figure 14-7.) When you finish, the results are presented to you in the form of a report.

FIGURE 14-7:
The Quick
Measures
dialog box.

You can create a quick measure in one of two ways: Select the Quick Measures but-ton on the Modeling toolbar or right-click any of the fields in the Fields pane and choose New Quick Measure from the menu that appears, as shown in Figure 14-8.

FIGURE 14-8:
Accessing the
New Quick
Measure option
via the Fields
pane.

Calculated columns

Let's assume that you already have a model. Sometimes, it isn't easy to simply load new data into a table and call it a day. That's why you should consider the use of *calculated columns*, a type of DAX formula that defines the columns' values. You can use the Calculated Columns feature to add new data to a table in your existing model. Rather than load the data using a data source, you create a DAX formula to do the work. Calculated columns are created using the New Column feature available under Report view or Data view.

TECHNICAL STUFF

Don't confuse calculated columns with custom columns. Though custom columns are created as part of a Power Query using the Add Column in Query Editor feature, a calculated column is created in Report view or Data view based on data that has already been loaded into your data model.

When you create a calculated column, the resulting product appears in the Fields pane. You'll find that the calculated column has an icon showing that its values are the result of a formula. As with measures, you can name the column however you want. Once the column is added to the list of fields found in the Fields pane, you can integrate the resulting product into a report visualization, as you would other fields.

In Figure 14-9, you can see the creation of a new column produced in Report view. The icon shows that a calculated column was created in the Fields pane. The resulting product is seen as *Profit is 10% of the Bid Amount*, as reflected in Figure 14-9.

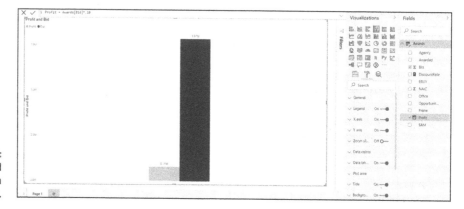

FIGURE 14-9: Calculated columns in Report view.

Calculated tables

When using Power BI, more than likely you're creating tables by importing data into your model using an external data source. There is, however, another way to create tables programmatically — by using calculated tables. That way, you can add new tables based on data already loaded into the data model. The idea here is to create a DAX formula to define the table's values rather than query and load the values into the table's columns from a source.

TIP

Calculated tables work best for more complex calculations and data you want to store as part of a data model rather than with the help of ad hoc calculations. In fact, combining tables with the use of statements such as JOIN, UNION, or CROSS JOIN is a great use case for calculated tables because calculated tables can have relationships with other tables.

Calculated table columns generally include data types and specific formatting; they also tend to belong to a specific category. As with other Power BI elements, you can name a column however you see fit and add it to a report, as with other fields. Each time the data changes in a table, the results are recalculated, assuming that a data refresh occurs. The exception is with the use of DirectQuery. In that case, tables reflect changes only after a dataset is refreshed in its entirety. If a table must use DirectQuery, it's best to have the calculated table in the Direct-Query instance for assured data freshness.

To create a calculated table, follow these steps:

1. **Choose Data View in the navigation bar on the left side of the Power BI screen.**

2. **Choose New Table in the Calculations area of the Ribbon's Home tab.**

3. **In the new screen that appears, click the New Calculations button, which allows to you create a DAX based calculation.**

4. **Enter the DAX expression that you want associated with the calculated table in the field, as seen in Figure 14-10.**

   As you are entering the expression, you'll see the calculated tables pre-populate on the screen. In this case, I've used the existing Awards Dataset to create a new calculated table called Listing. The table supplies insight on three items: agency, opportunity name, and bid amount.

5. **Once you are satisfied with your DAX entry, press Enter.**

   The expression is now committed as a new table to the existing dataset tables.

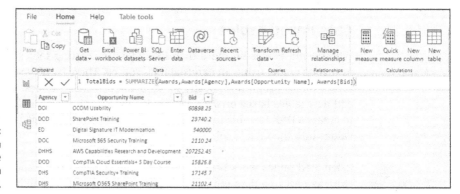

FIGURE 14-10:
Creating a
calculated table
from the Data
view.

Dealing with Data Types

Power Query lets you import data from a variety of data sources, and DAX expressions offer you the same flexibility. With DAX, each source can also support various data types, though the range is limited compared to Power Query. Figures 14-11 and 14-12 compare the differences between data types in DAX and Power Query. With DAX, when you import data into a model, the data is transformed into a tabular model data type.

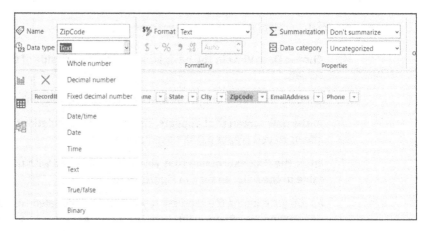

FIGURE 14-11:
DAX data types.

TIP

Figure 14-11 shows the DAX Data Type menu. Note that data types for DAX are somewhat different from those found in Power Query. (Refer to Figure 14-12.)

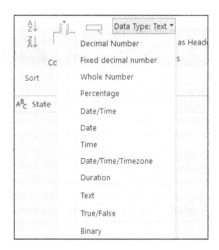

FIGURE 14-12:
Power Query data
types.

Each time model data is used as part of a calculation, data is transformed to a DAX data type, precisely for the output of a calculation. When you create a DAX formula, the terms you use determine which data type is returned. Table 14-1 illustrates the DAX data types.

TABLE 14-1 **DAX Data Types**

Model Data Type	Data Type in DAX	Description
Whole number	64-bit (8-byte) integer	Numbers without a decimal place. Can be an integer with either a positive or negative value. The negative range starts at 9,223,372,036,854,775,808 (–2^63) to a positive range not to exceed 9,223,372,036,854,775,807 (2^63-1).
Decimal number	64-bit (8-byte) real number	Real numbers with a wide range of parameters. Negative values can range from –1.79E +308 through –2.23E –308. Positive values range from 2.23E –308 through 1.79E + 308. The limit is 17 decimal digits.
Fixed decimal number	64-bit (8-byte) real number	Representative of monetary values. The range of values can be from –922,337,203,685,477.5808 to 922,337,203,685,477.5807. Four decimal digits can be used to ensure precision.
Date/Time	Date/Time	Date/time representation. The range begins after March 1, 1900, at 12:00 AM.
Date	Date	Just the date (no Time part). Upon conversion, the date value is the same as a Date/Time value without the digits to the correct placement.
Time	Time	Just the time (no Date part). Upon conversion, the time value is the same as a Date/Time value without the digits to the left placement.

(continued)

TABLE 14-1 *(continued)*

Model Data Type	Data Type in DAX	Description
Text	String	Unicode character data string. It can be an alphanumeric string represented in a text format. The maximum string length is 268,435,456.
Boolean	True/False	A Boolean value that is either TRUE or FALSE.
Binary	Binary	Used to represent any other data with a binary format not included on this list.
Blank	Blank	Considered the equivalent of a NULL value in SQL. It can use the BLANK function. To query, you can use the ISBLANK.

REMEMBER

Like importing data using Power Query, data types are set automatically. You should be familiar with how data types apply to DAX formulas. The most common reason for errors in a formula or result set is an improper data type. An example is the wrong operator being used with a data type in an argument.

Operating with Operators

There are four different operator types that can be used to create formulas in DAX. They're described in Table 14-2, with descriptions and examples for each one.

Arithmetic operators return numeric values based on performed arithmetic calculations. The arithmetic operators available in DAX are found in Table 14-2.

TABLE 14-2

Arithmetic Operators

Operator	Description	Example
+	Addition	4+2
–	Subtraction	4–2
*	Multiplication	4*2
/	Division	4/2
^	Exponent	4^2

Comparison operators return a TRUE or FALSE value based on comparison values. Table 14-3 shows you the DAX comparison operators.

TABLE 14-3

Comparison Operator

Operator	Description	Example
=	Equal to	[State]=" CA"
=_=	Equal to (strict)	[Country]="USA"
?*	Greater than	[Close Date] > "June 2000"
</	Less than	[Close Date] < "June 2000"
>=^	Greater than or equal to	[Price] >= 500
<=	Less than or equal to	[Price]<= 100
<>	Not equal to	[County] <> "CANADA"

A *logical operator* returns a single result when combining two or more expressions. Table 14-4 shows you the DAX logical operators.

TABLE 14-4

Logical Operators

Operator	What It Creates	Example
&&	An AND condition	([State] = "NJ") && ([Visitor] = "yes"))
||	An OR condition	(([State] = "NY") || ([Visitor] = "yes"))
IN	A logical OR condition or BETWEEN condition	'Product'[Size] IN { "Square", "Box", "Circle" }

REMEMBER

There is an ever so slight difference between an OR and AND comparison operator and OR and AND logical operator. With the comparison operator, you are evaluating numbers. With logical operators, you are evaluating text.

Text operators return a value based on concatenated operators that join two or more string values. Table 14-5 shows you the single DAX text operator.

TABLE 14-5

Text Operator

Operator	What It Does	Example
&	Connects two values to make a single text string	[City] & "," & [State]

Ordering operators

Ordering operators, formally known as *operator precedence* in DAX, help manage the order in which calculations are performed, which affects the value that's returned. In this, operator precedence in DAX follows the old mathematical rule of PEMDAS (flowing from left to right: parentheses, exponents, multiplication and division, and addition and subtraction) in specifying which order of operators is required to achieve the desired outcome.

All expressions evaluate a specific operation order. An expression always starts with an equal sign, which is meant to indicate the characters constituting the expression. After the equal sign, you find the elements that are calculated. Calculated elements are referred to as *operands*. Each operand is separated by the calculation operators. Though expressions are always read from left to right, the order in which elements are grouped can be fully manipulated if you use parentheses. Table 14-6 displays the operator order for a DAX equation.

TABLE 14-6

Operator Order

Operator	Description
^	Exponentiation
–	Sign (as in negative)
* and /	Multiplication and division
!	NOT (unary operator)
+ and –	Addition and subtraction
&	Connects strings (concatenation)
=,==,<,>,<=,>=,<>	Comparison

TECHNICAL STUFF

Frequently, you combine several operators for a formula. If the operators are equal in precedence, the order remains from left to right. Suppose that an expression contains a combination of multiplication or division operators as well as addition and subtraction operators. In that case, the calculation is evaluated based on the order in which they appear, which is from left to right.

Parentheses and order

In DAX like old school math, a simple bracket can change how a calculation turns out. Let's take a look at this equation. What's the difference between these two items?

= 2+2*3

= (2+2)*3

The first equation orders the data differently from the way the second equation does. The parentheses change the order of how the equation is calculated. In the first equation, 2*3 is calculated first. Then you add two, which equals 8. On the other hand, the parentheses in the second equation change the calculation order because 2+2 equals 4. You then multiply 4 times 3. The result is 12.

Making a Statement

There are four DAX statement types: DEFINE, EVALUATE, ORDER BY, and VAR. When trying to establish a DAX formula or function, you often need to define specific parameters or present the DAX expression a certain way, requiring a highly configurable query. You use one of these statement types to establish the DAX expression. Table 14-7 describes the four statement types.

TABLE 14-7 **Statements**

Statement Type	What It Does
DEFINE	Defines one or more entities that exist for the duration of a DAX entry exclusively
EVALUATE	Required to execute any type of DAX query
ORDER BY	Used, for one or more expressions, to sort results in a DAX query
VAR	Stores the result of an expression as a named variable and can be passed to just about any argument, including other measure expressions

Ensuring Compatibility

The DAX language is rooted in Microsoft Excel. Though many of the baseline computation engine features are the same, you need to be aware of a few differences. That's why DAX supplies a richer range of advanced features, including relational data store support and more data types than Excel within Power BI Desktop.

In any event, data types sometimes need a bit of coercion to properly work together. A general rule of thumb is that any operator's two operands on the left and right sides should have matching data types. Of course, if there are differences, DAX needs to convert the operator to a common data type to properly apply the operator. Two cases that require this behavior are when both operands convert to the largest possible data type and when operators are potentially applied.

Suppose that you have two numbers to combine. One number is from a formula such as =[Cost] * .50, and the result has decimals. The other value is an integer that's presented as a string.

Under these conditions, DAX converts both numbers to real numerical values. The values are converted into a numerical format, using the largest numerical format possible to store both kinds of numbers. Multiplication is then applied. There are, of course, exceptions: Depending on the data type, coercion may not be possible for comparison operations.

Chapter **15**

Fun with DAX Functions

I n Chapter 14, I talk about how functions are part of a formula named within a calculated expression. As the person coming up with the calculated expression, you're the one supplying the function with specific arguments — some required, some optional — that specify the type of input you're providing. (Such arguments are often referred to as parameters.) Each time a function is executed, a value is produced. With DAX, many function types allow you to perform calculations using dates and times, string-based conditionals, lookups, and relationship-based lookups. Of course, DAX also has standard calculation-based functions. The function is a prominent feature in DAX — learn to use functions well and you'll increase your productivity immensely. In this chapter, I describe more than 200 functions among the 14 categories to help make your DAX expressions more efficient.

Working with DAX Parameters and Naming Conventions

Like any programming language, DAX has a standardized parameter naming convention that helps facilitate language usage, especially when incorporating prefixes in the parameter name. (In fact, some DAX parameters allow you to use the prefix exclusively for names.) Table 15-1 explores the naming convention structure.

TABLE 15-1 **Parameter Naming**

Part	Parameter Name and Description
Expression	A DAX expression returning a single value. The expression may or may not be evaluated multiple times, depending on the row context.
Value	A DAX expression returning a single value. The value associated with the expression is evaluated exactly one time before other operators.
Table	A DAX expression returning table data.
tableName	Any existing table using standard DAX syntax, although it cannot be an expression.
columnName	An existing column using standard DAX syntax, usually fully qualified. It cannot be an expression.
Name	A string constant must be used to provide the name of a new object.
Order	Use *enumeration* — citing things one by one, in other words — to find the sort order.
Ties	Use enumeration to find the handling of the tie value.
Type	Use enumeration to find the PathItem (specific position from a string) and PathItemReverse (reverse specific position from a string) data types.

Prefixing parameter names

Each time you qualify a parameter, you may want to include a *prefix* — a specific unique value to differentiate a given parameter. An example might be adding the initials of a state in front of a parameter name. To qualify a parameter with a prefix, ensure that the prefix is descriptive based on the argument. Also, leave no ambiguity reading a parameter — for example:

> **Hide_ColumnName** references a column used to hide values in the DAX LOOKUPVALUE () function.

> **Seek_ColumnName** references a column used to show a value in the DAX LOOKUPVALUE() function.

TIP

Parameter names can sometimes be omitted. You would use only the prefix, assuming that it's clear enough to describe the parameter. Following this strategy may help avoid confusion later while reading the code. An example following this approach is DATE (Year_value, Month_value, Day_value).

Playing with parameters

To start out this chapter, I list the different types of functions available to you as well as a basic rule for naming a function using parameters. In Figure 15-1, you can find a sample function with fully qualified parameters.

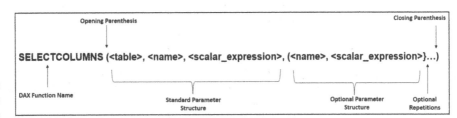

FIGURE 15-1:
A sample
function.

Each DAX function has a distinct parameter structure. In Figure 15-1, you'll notice that each parameter for a specific DAX function is incorporated as part of the table with a description. For the example provided, the DAX function SELECTCOLUMNS has the following attributes:

>> **Table:** The expression returns a table.

>> **Name:** The name given to a column; it requires double-quotes.

>> **scalar_expression:** It returns a scalar value, such as an integer or string.

Keeping a strict naming convention is essential with DAX functions, especially when it comes to the values for parameters. A table name is specific to what appears in a data model, as is the column name. Still, you find square brackets enclosing the column. An example is a Purchase [Purchase Amount].

TECHNICAL
STUFF

Using Formulas and Functions

If you've ever used formulas in Excel, you're likely familiar with DAX to some degree. The structure and design of Excel and DAX formulas are similar in nature, with a few exceptions:

>> **DAX functions reference complete columns and tables.** To reference a specific value in a table or column, you need to incorporate a filter.

>> **DAX has a variety of functions that return a table full of data instead of just a value.** Though the table isn't present in a report, it's used to input other functions.

>> **DAX includes more than just numeric functions.** In fact, you have features that include time intelligence and string-based data. Such formulas allow you to define or select data ranges and even perform calculations against one or more data ranges.

>> **DAX supports customized calculations, even for a single row of data.** You can use DAX for a current row or a series of rows by applying a parameter to perform calculations assuming a known context.

Because DAX is a functional language, any complete code sample including a formula contains a function. DAX formulas may be a combination of conditional statements, functions, and references. Furthermore, DAX formulas come in two flavors: numeric and non-numeric variations. Numeric data includes values such as integers, decimals, and currency-based values. Non-numeric is composed of strings and binary objects.

As you can see in the next section, 14 categories are composed of more than 250 DAX-based functions.

TECHNICAL STUFF

When reading a DAX expression, be sure to evaluate from the innermost function to the outermost. Expressions follow the operator rules as well, which makes crafting a DAX formula a task demanding precision.

Aggregate functions

"To aggregate" means "to combine many (often unrelated) items into one." That's why you should not be surprised that there is a function to combine into a single form. Aggregate functions cover scalar-based values such as count, sum, average, minimum, and maximum. You can use them for all rows in a column or table based on the expression. Table 15-2 includes all functions available for this function type.

TABLE 15-2 Aggregate Functions

Function	What You Can Do with It
APPROXIMATEDISTINCTCOUNT	Count the approximate number of distinct values in a column; can be used only with a Power BI DirectQuery table.
AVERAGE	Average all numbers in a given column.
AVERAGEA	Retrieve the average of all possible values in a given column, including handling all alphanumeric characters.
AVERAGEX	Calculate the average in a set of expressions within a table.

Function	What You Can Do with It
COUNT	Count the number of rows in the table when one or more specified columns has a nonblank value.
COUNTA	Count the number of values in a single column.
COUNTAX	Count the number of values that result from evaluating expressions on a per-row basis.
COUNTBLANK	Count the number of blank entries in a column.
COUNTROWS	Count the number of rows in a single table.
COUNTX	Count the values that result from evaluating an expression on a per-row basis for a table.
DISTINCTCOUNT	Count the number of distinct column values.
DISTINCTCOUNTNOBLANK	Count the number of distinct blank column values.
MAX	Return the largest column value or the largest value between two scalar expressions. The value ignores logical values; strings are compared in alphabetical order.
MAXA	Review the largest value in a column, not ignoring logical values and text.
MAXX	Review the largest result set value from evaluating an expression for each table row. Strings are compared in alphabetical order.
MIN	Review the smallest result set value in a column or the smaller value between two scalar expressions. The value ignores logical values. Strings are compared in alphabetical order.
MINA	Review the smallest value in a column. The value doesn't ignore logical values or text.
MINX	Review the smallest value from a set of results when evaluating an expression for each table row. Strings are compared in alphabetical order.
PRODUCT	Review the return of a product in a given column reference.
PRODUCTX	Review the returns of a product for an expression value in a table.
SUM	Add together all numbers in the column.
SUMX	Sum an expression using evaluation criteria for each row in a table.

Date-and-time functions

Date-and-time functions are derived from the datetime data type, which starts on March 1, 1900. All available date-and-time functions are listed in Table 15-3.

TABLE 15-3 Date-and-Time Functions

Function	What You Can Do with It
CALENDAR	Review a table with one column of all dates between a given StartDate and EndDate.
CALENDARAUTO	Review a table with one column of dates where values from the model are automatically calculated.
DATE	Review a specific date in datetime format.
DATEDIFF	Review the number of units, based on an interval, between a set of given input dates.
DATEVALUE	Convert a date in text format to a specific date in datetime format.
DAY	Review a number from 1 to 31, which represents the day of the month.
EDATE	Review the date considered the number of months before or after the given start date.
EOMONTH	Review the date in datetime format — precisely, the last day of the month before or after, specified by the number of months.
HOUR	Review the hour as a number from 0 to 23 (12:00 AM to 11:00 PM).
MINUTE	Review the number of minutes from 0 to 59.
MONTH	Review the month from 1(January) to 12 (December).
NOW	Review the current date and time in datetime format.
QUARTER	Review the quarter from 1 (January – March) to 4 (October – December).
SECOND	Review the number of seconds from 0 to 59.
TIME	Convert hours, minutes, and seconds as a number to a time using the datetime format.
TIMEVALUE	Convert a time using a text format to a time using a datetime format.
TODAY	Return the current date in datetime format.
UTCNOW	Return the current date and time in datetime format expressed in coordinated universal time (UTC).
UTCTODAY	Return the current date in datetime format expressed in coordinated universal time (UTC).
WEEKDAY	Identify the day of the week as a date. The range can be 1–7 or 0–6 based on the ReturnType parameter.
WEEKNUM	Identify the week number in the year as a number.
YEAR	Represent the year as a four-digit integer.
YEARFRAC	Break out the year as a fraction, representing the number of whole days between the start and end dates.

Filter functions

The filter function supports DAX returning specific data types, looking up values, and filtering by related value options. Filtering using the lookup functions works just like a database because it supports the use of tables and relationships. When you're concerned with context, the filtering functions let you manipulate data context by creating dynamic calculations. Table 15-4 offers you a list of all filter functions available in Power BI.

TABLE 15-4   **Filter Functions**

Function	What It Does
ALL	Returns all rows. All column values can be returned as well, assuming that filters are ignored even when applied.
ALLCROSSFILTERED	Clears all filters when applied to a specific table.
ALLEXCEPT	Returns all rows except those affected by a specific column filter.
ALLNOBLANKROW	Returns all rows except blank table rows or all column values. Any applied filters are ignored.
ALLSELECTED	Returns all rows in a table. Alternatively, when filters are ignored but applied within a query, all values in a column are applied. The filters remain intact even when applied from outside.
CALCULATE	Evaluates all expressions based on the context modified by one or more filters.
CALCULATETABLE	Evaluates all table expressions in a context modified by filters.
FILTER	Filters all tables that are returned.
KEEPFILTERS	Changes all instances of the CALCULATE and CALCULATETABLE function filtering semantics.
LOOKUPVALUE	Retrieves a value from a table.
REMOVEFILTERS	Clears filters based on a specified table or set of columns.
SELECTEDVALUE	Reviews the values when there is only one value in a given column; otherwise, alternative results are presented.

Financial functions

When calculating financial calculations such as rate of return, accrued interest, or depreciation rate, you would use a financial function. Table 15-5 lists all financial functions available in Power BI.

TABLE 15-5   Financial Functions

Function	What It Displays
ACCRINT	The accrued interest for a security that pays periodic interest.
ACCRINTM	The accrued interest for a security that pays interest at the maturity period.
AMORDEGRC	The depreciation for every accounting period. The function is specific for French accounting systems. If assets are purchased in the middle of an accounting cycle, prorated depreciation is applied to an account. The function is like AMORLINC. The exception is that the depreciation coefficient is applicable in calculating asset life dependency.
AMORLINC	The depreciation for every accounting period. The function is specific for French accounting systems. The prorated depreciation is applied to the account if assets are purchased in the middle of an accounting cycle.
COUPDAYBS	The number of days from the start of a coupon period to the settlement date.
COUPDAYS	The number of days for the coupon period containing an applicable settlement date.
COUPDAYSNC	The number of days from the start of the settlement date to the next coupon date.
COUPNCD	The next coupon date after the assigned settlement date.
COUPNUM	The number of coupons payable between two dates: the settlement date and the maturity date. The dates are rounded to the nearest whole value.
COUPPCD	The previous coupon date before the settlement date.
CUMIPMT	The cumulative interest paid on a loan instrument from the start period to the end period.
CUMPRINC	The cumulative principal paid on a loan instrument from the start period to the end period.
DB	The depreciation of an asset for a set period using a fixed-declining balance method.
DDB	The depreciation of an asset for a specified period using the double-declining balance method or another method as specified.
DISC	The discount rate of a specific security.
DOLLARDE	The dollar price expressed as an integer part and a fraction part, such as 9.25, into a dollar price expressed as a decimal number. Fractional dollar numbers are sometimes used for securities prices.
DOLLARFR	The dollar price, expressed as a decimal number where the dollar price is expressed as a combination of an integer part and a fraction part, such as 0.07. Unlike DOLLARDE, the first number in DOLLARFR format can be a 0 or another variation of a fraction while you'll never have a number that is anything but a whole number in DOLLARDE. DOLLARFR appears less frequently, but can be used for securities.
DURATION	The Macauley duration for an assumed par value of $100. In this case, duration is the weighted average of the present value of cash flows. This is used as a measure to determine bond prices in response to changing yields.

Function	What It Displays
EFFECT	The effective annual interest rate based on the nominal annual interest rate and the compounding periods per year.
FV	The future intended value of an investment based on its constant interest rate. FV can be any combination of interest rates: periodic, constant, or single lump sum.
INTRATE	The return for a fully invested security.
IPMT	The interest payment for a given period of an investment based on a periodic, constant payment and interest rate.
ISPMT	The calculated interest paid or received for a specific period of a loan or investment where principal payments are evenly distributed.
MDURATION	A modified Macauley duration for security where the assumed par value is $100.
NOMINAL	The nominal annual interest, given the effective interest rate and the number of compounding periods in a given year.
NPER	The number of periods for a given investment, assuming periodic, constant payments and both fixed or variable interest rates.
ODDFPRICE	The price per $100 face value of a given security having an odd first period.
ODDFYIELD	The security yield that has an odd first period.
ODDLPRICE	The price per $100 face value of a given security having an odd last period.
ODDLYIELD	A security yield that has an odd last period.
PDURATION	The number of periods required by an investment to achieve the desired value.
PMT	The principal payment of a loan based on a fixed payment and interest rate.
PPMT	The principal payment for a given period for an investment based on a periodic, constant payment and a constant interest rate.
PRICE	The price per $100 face value that pays periodic interest payments.
PRICEDISC	The price per $100 face value of a security that has been discounted.
PRICEMAT	The price per $100 face value of a security that may pay interest at maturity.
PV	The calculated present value of a loan or investment based on a fixed interest rate.
RATE	The interest rate per period of an annuity.
RECEIVED	A financial amount received at maturity for a fully invested security.
RRI	The interest rate equivalent for an investment and its growth trajectory.
SLN	The straight-line depreciation value of an asset for a single period.

(continued)

TABLE 15-5 *(continued)*

Function	What It Displays
SYD	The sum-of-years' digits depreciation value for an asset given a set period.
TBILLEQ	The bond equivalent of a Treasury bill note.
TBILLPRICE	The price per $100 face value on a Treasury bill note.
TBILLYIELD	The Treasury bill yield.
VDB	The depreciation of an asset for just about any defined period. VDB is also known as *declining variable balance.*
XIRR	The internal rate of return for a cash flow schedule that may not be consistent or periodic.
XNPV	The net present value for a cash flow schedule.
YIELD	The yield of a given security that pays periodic interest. You must use YIELD to calculate bond yield interest.
YIELDDISC	The annual yield of a given security with a discount.
YIELDMAT	The annual yield of a given security that pays interest at the maturity period.

Information functions

If you're looking for a function that evaluates a cell or row with an argument, information functions can decide whether the value matches the expected type. Table 15-6 displays all the information functions.

TABLE 15-6 **Information Functions**

Function	Description
COLUMNSTATISTICS	Displays statistics regarding every column in every table throughout a data model.
CONTAINS	Displays TRUE if at least one row exists where columns contain a specified value.
CONTAINSROW	Displays TRUE if at least one row exists where all columns have a specified value.
CONTAINSSTRING	Displays TRUE if one text string contains a replicate text string. Though not case-sensitive, it's accent-sensitive.
CONTAINSSTRINGEXACT	Displays TRUE if one text string contains another text string. CONTAINS-STRINGEXACT is case-sensitive and accent-sensitive.
CUSTOMDATA	Displays the value of a CUSTOMDATA connection string property, assuming that it's defined. Otherwise, it's left blank ( ).

Function	Description
HASONEFILTER	Displays TRUE when a specified table or column has only one value from a direct filter.
HASONEVALUE	Displays TRUE when a given column holds only a single value.
ISAFTER	Displays TRUE if a list of Value1 parameters equals that of Value2 parameters.
ISBLANK	Displays whether a value is blank. Otherwise, the value returned is TRUE or FALSE.
ISCROSSFILTERED	Displays TRUE if a specific table or column is cross-filtered.
ISEMPTY	Displays TRUE if the specific table is empty or the associative expressions are empty.
ISERROR	Evaluates whether a value is considered an error. Returns a value of TRUE or FALSE.
ISEVEN	Displays TRUE assuming that a number is even or FALSE if a number is odd.
ISFILTERED	Displays TRUE if a specific column has direct filters on it.
ISINSCOPE	Displays TRUE if specific columns have levels in a hierarchy of associative levels.
ISLOGICAL	Evaluates whether a value is logical based on the conditions defined. The value returned is TRUE or FALSE.
ISNONTEXT	Evaluates whether a value is *not* considered text. (Blank cells aren't considered text.) Returns TRUE or FALSE.
ISNUMBER	Evaluates whether a value is a number. Returns TRUE or FALSE.
ISODD	Evaluates whether a number is odd. Returns TRUE if odd or FALSE if even.
ISONORAFTER	A Boolean function; it considers the behavior of the START AT clause and returns TRUE for a row meeting every condition mentioned in a given parameter.
ISSELECTEDMEASURE	Evaluates whether a condition is TRUE based on a specified measure being evaluated.
ISSUBTOTAL	Displays TRUE when the current row contains the subtotal for a given column.
ISTEXT	Evaluates whether a value is text; returns TRUE or FALSE.
SELECTEDMEASURE	Displays the measure under evaluation.
SELECTEDMEASUREFOR-MATSTRING	Displays a format string for a given measure that's under evaluation.
SELECTEDMEASURENAME	Displays the name of a measure being evaluated.

(continued)

TABLE 15-6 *(continued)*

Function	Description
USERCULTURE	Displays the system-specific configurations of a given user, which includes their operating system and/or browser settings.
USERNAME	Displays the domain name and user credentials for a current user connection, following a formatting convention of domain name/username.
USEROBJECTID	Displays a current user ObjectID, or unique ID, which is made available by Azure Active Directory. This is made possible when the Azure Analysis Server and a user security identifier (SID) are qualified with Power BI.
USERPRINCIPALNAME	Displays the user principal's name.

Logical functions

Suppose that you need to respond to an expression based on information returned about the values. In that case, logical functions are a suitable choice. Some examples of logical functions are IS, AND, OR, and NOT. TRUE and FALSE are also logic operators. Power BI logical operators are described in Table 15-7.

TABLE 15-7   **Logical Functions**

Function	What It Does
AND	Evaluates whether all arguments are true; if that is the case, TRUE is returned as a response.
COALESCE	Displays the first argument that doesn't evaluate a blank value. If all arguments are blank, BLANK is the final response.
FALSE	Displays the logical response, FALSE.
IF	Evaluates whether a condition is met. If it can be met, the answer is TRUE; otherwise, it's FALSE.
IF.EAGER	Evaluates whether a condition is met based on varying IF conditions where TRUE or FALSE are both present. If the value is TRUE and another value is FALSE, one can use the function to clearly structure the condition for optimization.
IFERROR	Displays the value IF_ERROR when the first expression is an error and the value of the expression otherwise may or may not be accurate.
NOT	Evaluates when a condition converts from TRUE to FALSE or FALSE to TRUE.
OR	Displays TRUE if any condition can be met; otherwise, displays FALSE if none of the arguments can be met.
SWITCH	Displays a different result set depending on the value of an expression.
TRUE	Displays the logical value TRUE.

Mathematical and trigonometric functions

Math-based functions in DAX run the gamut of all standard mathematical operations, including trigonometric equations. This category has more than 30 options, as shown in Table 15-8.

TABLE 15-8   Mathematical and Trigonometric Functions

Function	What It Does
ABS	Displays the absolute value of a number.
ACOS	Displays the arccosine/inverse cosine of a number.
ACOSH	Displays the inverse hyperbolic cosine of a number. The number displayed must be greater than or equal to 1.
ACOT	Displays the principal value of the arccotangent/inverse cotangent of a number.
ACOTH	Displays the inverse hyperbolic cotangent of a number.
ASIN	Displays the arcsine, or inverse sine, of a number.
ASINH	Displays the inverse hyperbolic sine of a number.
ATAN	Displays the arctangent, or inverse tangent, of a number.
ATANH	Displays the inverse hyperbolic tangent of a number. The number evaluated must be between –1 and 1 but cannot be the actual value of –1 or 1 itself.
CEILING	Displays a value representing the nearest integer or measure of significance.
CONVERT	Converts an expression to a specific data type.
COS	Displays the cosine of the specific angle.
COSH	Displays the hyperbolic cosine of a given number.
COT	Displays the cotangent of an angle based on radians.
COTH	Displays the hyperbolic cotangent of a single hyperbolic angle.
CURRENCY	Displays a value as a currency data type.
DEGREES	Converts radians into degrees.
DIVIDE	Applies the safe divide function to handle divide-by-zero cases.
EVEN	Displays a number rounded up to the nearest even integer.
EXP	Displays *e* raised to the power of a given number.

(continued)

TABLE 15-8 *(continued)*

Function	What It Does
FACT	Displays the factorial of a number.
FLOOR	Supports the rounding of the number down, toward 0, to the nearest multiple of significance.
GCD	Displays the most significant common divisible value among two integers.
INT	Supports the rounding down of numbers to the nearest integer.
ISOCEILING	Supports the rounding up of numbers to the nearest integer or to the nearest multiple of significance.
LCM	Displays the least common multiple of integers.
LN	Displays the natural logarithm of a number.
LOG	Displays the logarithm of a number to the base you specify.
LOG10	Displays the base-10 logarithm of a number.
MOD	Displays the remainder of a number by a divisible value.
MROUND	Displays a number rounded to the desired multiple.
ODD	Rounds up a number to the nearest odd integer.
PI	Displays the value of π, up to 15 digits.
POWER	Displays the result of a number raised to a power.
QUOTIENT	Displays the integer portion of a division.
RADIANS	Converts degrees to radians.
RAND	Displays a random number greater than or equal to 0. The value must also be less than 1. The value is evenly distributed. Values change on a recalculation.
RANDBETWEEN	Displays a random number between two numbers specified.
ROUND	Displays a number that's rounded to a specific number of digits.
ROUNDDOWN	Displays a number that's always rounded down toward 0.
ROUNDUP	Always rounds up a number, away from 0.
SIGN	Displays the sign of a number: If the number is positive, it displays 1; if the number is 0, it displays 0; if the number is negative, it displays –1.
SIN	Displays the sine of the given angle.
SINH	Displays the hyperbolic sine of a number.

Function	What It Does
SQRT	Displays the square root of a number.
SQRTPI	Displays the square root of (number * π).
TAN	Displays the tangent of the given angle.
TANH	Displays the hyperbolic tangent of a number.
TRUNC	Displays a truncated number, which is presented as an integer by removing the decimal or fractional part of the number.

Other functions

Some functions don't fit into any specific category — ERROR and BLANK, for example. Table 15-9 displays all functions that don't fit elsewhere.

TABLE 15-9 **Other Functions**

Function	Description
BLANK	Displays a blank value.
EARLIER	Displays the value in the column before the specified number of table scans; the default is 1.
EARLIEST	Displays the value in the column for the first instance where row context exists.
ERROR	Displays a user specified error.
HASH	Displays a compute hash over a variable number based on input expressions, which returns an expression.
KEYWORDMATCH	Displays a TRUE condition if there's a match between the match expression and the text.

Parent-child functions

Parent-child functions are options to consider when dealing with hierarchical table sets and manipulating dates with a function. Table 15-10 presents all parent-child functions.

TABLE 15-10 **Parent-Child Functions**

Function	Description
PATH	Displays a string containing a delimited list of IDs. The PATH starts with the top/root of a hierarchy. It ends with a specified ID.
PATHCONTAINS	Displays TRUE if the specified item is contained within a specified path.
PATHITEM	Displays the *nth* item in the delimited list using the PATHITEM function.
PATHITEMREVERSE	Displays the *nth* item in the delimited list, which is produced by the PATH function. The path is calculated by counting backward in the path.
PATHLENGTH	Displays the number of items in a given path string.

Relationship functions

Relationship functions are appropriate if your business goal is to manage relationships between tables. You often find that these functions involve the integration between one or more tables. Table 15-11 describes the relationship functions.

TABLE 15-11 **Relationship Functions**

Function	Description
CROSSFILTER	Displays the cross-filtering direction to be used in a calculation to expose the relationship between two columns.
RELATED	Displays a corresponding value from another table.
RELATEDTABLE	Displays a corresponding table that's filtered so that it includes only related rows.
USERELATIONSHIP	Displays the specific relationship to be used in a calculation, such as the one that may exist between two column names.

Statistical functions

When dealing with statistical data and more complex mathematical complications that cannot be completed using other numeric libraries, you'll find statistical functions to be quite valuable. As shown in Table 15-12, some examples of statistical functions are distributions and probability data, including standard deviations.

TABLE 15-12   Statistical Functions

Function	Description
BETA.DIST	Displays the beta distribution.
BETA.INV	Displays the inverse of the beta cumulative probability density (BETA.DIST) function.
CHISQ.DIST	Displays the chi-squared distribution.
CHISQ.DIST.RT	Displays the right-tailed probability of a chi-squared distribution.
CHISQ.INV	Displays the inverse of the left-tailed probability of a chi-squared distribution.
CHISQ.INV.RT	Displays the inverse of the right-tailed probability of a chi-squared distribution.
COMBIN	Displays several combinations for a given number of items. Use COMBIN to determine the total possible group number for a given number of items.
COMBINA	Displays the number of combinations for a given number of items repetitiously.
CONFIDENCE.NORM	Using normal distribution displays the confidence interval for a population mean.
CONFIDENCE.T	Using a student t-distribution, CONFIDENCE.T displays the confidence interval for a population mean.
EXPON.DIST	Displays the exponential distribution.
GEOMEAN	Displays the geometric mean for a column reference.
GEOMEANX	Displays the geometric mean for an expression value in a table.
MEDIAN	Displays the 50th percentile for a column value.
MEDIANX	Displays the 50th percentile for a table expression.
NORM.DIST	Displays the normal distribution for a specific mean and standard deviation.
NORM.INV	Displays the inverse of the normal cumulative distribution for a mean and standard deviation.
NORM.S.DIST	Displays the standard normal distribution.
NORM.S.INV	Displays the inverse of the standard normal cumulative distribution. Distribution has a means of 0 and a standard deviation of 1.
PERCENTILE.EXC	Displays the *k-th* (exclusive) percentile of a value for a column.
PERCENTILE.INC	Displays the *k-th* (inclusive) percentile of a value for a column.
PERCENTILEX.EXC	Displays the *k-th* (exclusive) percentile of a value for a table.

(continued)

TABLE 15-12 *(continued)*

Function	Description
PERCENTILEX.INC	Displays the *k-th* (inclusive) percentile of a value for a table.
PERMUT	Displays the number of permutations for several objects that can be selected from several objects.
POISSON.DIST	Displays the Poisson distribution.
RANK.EQ	Displays rank number in a column of numbers. If a value has the same rank, the top rank of the set is the value displayed.
RANKX	Displays the rank of a single expression evaluated in its current context. Rank is based on a list of values for the expression evaluation for each row in a table.
SAMPLE	Displays a subset from a given table expression.
STDEV.P	Calculates the standard deviation based on an entire population using arguments while ignoring logical values and text.
STDEV.S	Estimates the standard deviation using a sample while ignoring logical values and text in the sampling.
STDEVX.P	Estimates the standard deviation for an entire population using results when evaluating an expression for each table row.
STDEVX.S	Estimates the standard deviation for a sample using results when evaluating an expression for each table row.
T.DIST	Displays a student's left-tailed *t*-distribution.
T.DIST.2T	Displays a two-tailed student's *t*-distribution.
T.DIST.RT	Displays a right-tailed student's *t*-distribution.
T.INV	Displays a left-tailed inverse of a student's *t*-distribution.
T.INV.2T	Displays the two-tailed inverse of a student's *t*-distribution.
VAR.P	Calculates variance based on the entire population while ignoring logical values and text in a population.
VAR.S	Estimates variance based on a sample while ignoring logical values and text in a sample.
VARX.P	Estimates variance based on an entire population, resulting from evaluating an expression for each row in a table.
VARX.S	Estimates variance based on a sampling that evaluates an expression for each row in a table.

Table manipulation functions

Think of table manipulation functions as another way to manipulate table data using DAX without having to deal with the data model. From JOIN statements to GROUPBY, you'll find many like-kind functions here that are common in enterprise relational database solutions such as Azure SQL Server for manipulating table data, as shown in Table 15-13.

TABLE 15-13   Table Manipulation Functions

Function	Description
ADDCOLUMNS	Displays a table with new columns applying DAX expressions.
ADDMISSINGITEMS	Adds back in rows with empty measure values.
CROSSJOIN	Displays a table that's a cross-join of two tables.
CURRENTGROUP	Offers a user access to the (sub)table representing the current group using the GROUPBY function.
DATATABLE	Displays a table with data defined inline.
DETAILROWS	Displays table data that corresponds to the DetailRows expression defined based on specific measures.
DISTINCT	Displays a one-column table assuming that a column contains a unique value.
EXCEPT	Displays the rows of a left-side table. The rows don't appear in a right-side table.
FILTERS	Displays a table based on a filter value applied directly to the specified column.
GENERATE	Displays the cross-join of the first table with these results if data is available. Referenced as a second table expression, the condition is evaluated for each row in the first table.
GENERATEALL	Displays the cross-join of the first table with these results, including rows when the second table expression is empty. Referenced as a second table expression, the condition is evaluated for each row in the first table.
GENERATESERIES	Displays a table with a single column populated. The table values are sequential values from start to finish.
GROUPBY	The condition sets up a summary whereby the input table groups the data by a specific column.
IGNORE	Allows a measure expression specified in a call to the SUMMARIZECOLUMNS function for one tag, which determines nonblank rows.
INTERSECT	Displays the rows of left-side table data that appear in the right-side table.

(continued)

TABLE 15-13 *(continued)*

Function	Description
NATURALINNERJOIN	Allows for a join on the left table with the right table using inner join semantics.
NATURALLEFT OUTERJOIN	Allows for a join on the left table with the right table using the left outer join semantics.
NONVISUAL	Marks a filter as NonVisual.
ROLLUP	Finds a subset of columns specified in the call to the SUMMARIZE function, because those should be calculated as groups of subtotals.
ROLLUPADDISSUBTOTAL	Finds a subset of columns specified in the call to the SUMMARIZECOLUMNS function, because those should be calculated as groups of subtotals.
ROLLUPGROUP	Finds a subset of columns specified in the call to the SUMMARIZE function, because those should be calculated as groups of subtotals.
ROLLUPISSUBTOTAL	Finds a subset of columns specific to the SUMMARIZECOLUMNS function that can be used in support of calculating group subtotals.
ROW	Displays a single row table with new columns specified by the DAX expressions.
SELECTCOLUMNS	Displays a table with selected columns and new columns, which can be specified by the DAX expressions.
SUBSTITUTEWITHINDEX	Displays a table standing for a semi-join of two tables supplied. The standard set of columns is replaced by a 0-based index column. An index column is based on rows within the second table sort based on the order of expressions.
SUMMARIZE	Displays a summary of the input table, grouped by specific columns.
SUMMARIZECOLUMNS	Displays a summary table for the requested totals over a set of groups.
TOPN	Displays a defined number of top rows according to a specified expression.
TOPNSKIP	Displays rows efficiency by skipping those that are unnecessary. In comparison to TOPN, the TOPNSKIP offers less flexibility but supplies better performance.
TREATAS	Supports columns where the input table is treated as columns from other tables. At the column level, you can filter out values not present in their respective output column.
UNION	Displays the union of tables whose columns match.
VALUES	Displays a single-column table of unique values when a column name is present. Assuming that a table name is provided, a table is displayed with the same columns and rows of the table. Duplicates with additional blank rows may be present.

Text functions

Like the set of text functions in the string function library found in Excel, the DAX text functions allow you to work with tables and columns in a tabular model. Table 15-14 incorporates all Power BI text functions.

TABLE 15-14   **Text Functions**

Function	What It Does
COMBINEVALUES	Displays a combined value based on a set of operands using a specific delimiter.
CONCATENATE	Joins two text strings as a single text string.
CONCATENATEX	Evaluates an expression for each row on a table. The result displays the concatenation of values in a single string result, separated by a specific delimiter.
EXACT	Determines whether two text strings are identical and displays TRUE or FALSE. EXACT is a case-sensitive term.
FIND	Displays the start position of a text string with another text string. FIND is case- and accent-sensitive.
FIXED	Rounds a number to a specific number of decimals. Displays the result as text using optional commas, when appropriate.
FORMAT	Transforms a value to the text by applying a specific number format.
LEFT	Displays a specific number of characters from the start of a text string.
LEN	Displays the number of characters in the text string.
LOWER	Converts all characters found in a text string to lowercase.
MID	Displays a string of characters from the middle of the text string, based on the string's starting position and length.
REPLACE	Displays part of a text string with a completely different text string.
REPT	Repeats text several times.
RIGHT	Displays a specific number of characters starting from the end of a text string.
SEARCH	Displays the starting position of a single text string within another text string.
SUBSTITUTE	Replaces existing text with new text inside a text string.
TRIM	Removes all spaces from a text string except for a single space between words or phrases.

(continued)

TABLE 15-14 *(continued)*

Function	What It Does
UNICHAR	Displays Unicode characters that are referenced by a given numeric value.
UNICODE	Displays a number corresponding to the first character within a string of text.
UPPER	Allows for the conversion of a text string to all uppercase letters.
VALUE	Allows for numerical text string conversion to an actual number.

Time intelligence functions

Time intelligence functions let you manipulate data based on time periods. Time ranges include days, months, quarters, and years. Table 15-15 lists all relevant Power BI time intelligence functions.

TABLE 15-15   Time Intelligence Functions

Function	Description
CLOSINGBALANCEMONTH	Evaluates a specific expression for the date corresponding to the end of the current month and after applying specific filters.
CLOSINGBALANCEQUARTER	Evaluates a specific expression for the date corresponding to the end of the current quarter and after applying specific filters.
CLOSINGBALANCEYEAR	Evaluates a specific expression for the date corresponding to the end of the current year and after applying specific filters.
DATEADD	Moves one or more dates by a specific interval.
DATESBETWEEN	Displays the dates between two given dates.
DATESINPERIOD	Displays the dates from the given period.
DATESMTD	Displays a set of dates in the month up to the last date visible in the filter context.
DATESQTD	Displays a set of dates in the quarter up to the last date visible in the filter context.
DATESYTD	Displays a set of dates in the year up to the last date visible in the filter context.
ENDOFMONTH	Displays the end of the month.
ENDOFQUARTER	Displays the end of the quarter.
ENDOFYEAR	Displays the end of the year.

Function	Description
FIRSTDATE	Displays the first nonblank date.
FIRSTNONBLANK	Displays the first value in the column for which the expression has a non-blank value.
FIRSTNONBLANKVALUE	Displays the first nonblank value of the expression evaluated for the column.
LASTDATE	Displays the last nonblank date.
LASTNONBLANK	Displays the last value in the column for which the expression has a non-blank value.
LASTNONBLANKVALUE	Displays the last nonblank value of the expression evaluated for the column.
NEXTDAY	Displays a subsequent day.
NEXTMONTH	Displays a subsequent month.
NEXTQUARTER	Displays the next quarter.
NEXTYEAR	Displays a subsequent year.
OPENINGBALANCEMONTH	Evaluates a specific expression for the date corresponding to the previous month's end after all filters are applied.
OPENINGBALANCEQUARTER	Evaluates a specific expression for the date corresponding to the previous quarter's end after all filters are applied.
OPENINGBALANCEYEAR	Evaluates a specific expression for the date corresponding to the previous year's end after all filters are applied.
PARALLELPERIOD	Displays a parallel period of dates by the given set of dates and a specified interval.
PREVIOUSDAY	Displays a previous day.
PREVIOUSMONTH	Displays a previous month.
PREVIOUSQUARTER	Displays a previous quarter.
PREVIOUSYEAR	Displays a previous year.
SAMEPERIODLASTYEAR	Displays a set of dates in the current selection from the previous year.
STARTOFMONTH	Displays the start of the month.
STARTOFQUARTER	Displays the start of the quarter.
STARTOFYEAR	Displays the start of the year.

(continued)

TABLE 15-15 *(continued)*

Function	Description
TOTALMTD	Evaluates a specific expression over a given period of time (interval), beginning on the first date of the month. The date ends with the last date in the specific date column, assuming that filters are applied.
TOTALQTD	Evaluates a specific expression over a given period of time (interval), beginning on the first date of the quarter. The date ends with the last date in the specific date column assuming filters are applied.
TOTALYTD	Evaluates a specific expression over a given period of time (interval), beginning on the first date of the year. The date ends with the last date in the specific date column assuming filters are applied.

Chapter **16**

Digging Deeper into DAX

n Chapters 14 and 15, I talk about the ABCs of DAX. In those chapters, I make several references to what it takes to create formulas so that you can create more sophisticated calculations to help drive better insights for an organization. This chapter closes the loop by helping you better understand the technical elements behind coding and debugging your DAX formulas in Power BI.

Working with Variables

One of the first things you learn in Programming 101 is how to use variables. Well, guess what? Variables are also a fundamental construct in DAX. You can declare DAX variables in your formula expressions. As long as you declare at least one variable, a RETURN clause is used to define the expression. The result then refers to the variable.

For many reasons, you'd want to use variables as you begin programming, whether for syntax, context, or functionality. Here are a few:

» Improved readability and maintenance of formulas

» Increased performance by allowing the user, developer, or observer to evaluate code once, as needed

>> Supports design-time testing of easy, targeted strategies for complex formulas, only returning *key variables* — those being called upon, in other words.

Writing DAX Formulas

If your data model is based on a calculation type, calculated table, or calculated column or is measured in Power BI, you'll find there is a standard convention for creating formulas.

A formula has a definite structure, starting with a defined name, followed by an equal symbol, which is then followed by a DAX formula. Here's an example:

```
<Calculation> = <DAX Formula>
```

Let's look at a hypothetical example. The definition of an `Awarded Status` calculated table that duplicates the Awarded table data is

```
Awarded Status = 'Awarded'
```

Understanding DAX formulas in depth

DAX formulas consist of a bit more than a few variables and an equal sign. Quite the contrary! First and foremost, a DAX expression is meant to return a result — either a table object or a scalar value. Let's break it down a bit further. If you have a calculated table formula, the result is a returned table object. In contrast, both calculated columns and measure formulas return singular values.

Let's take a step back for a moment. What can a formula have? A formula may have all the elements, as described in Table 16-1.

Extending formulas with measures

It's all fine and dandy to understand the *concept* of functions, formulas, and measures, but at some point, you need to bring the three together in Power BI Desktop to create extended calculations. That time is now.

One way to extend calculations is to use measures. DAX uses two types of measures: implicit and explicit. Most users like to start out by creating simple measures that summarize a single column or table. Then, over time, they realize that, as their data grows, they need to create more detailed measures based on other measures in their model.

TABLE 16-1	Formulas In Depth
Feature	**Description**
Function	Functions carry out specific goals. A function has an argument that allows the passing of a variable. The formula may use a function call and often needs functions inside one another. Function names are a type of formula with conditions that should always be followed by parentheses. Within each parenthesis, you have a variable passed.
Operator	Operators perform arithmetic calculations, compare values, work with strings, and test conditions of varying states.
Variables	Formulas may use variables to store results as part of a calculated expression.
Whitespace	With DAX, some characters can help users format formulas to make it easier to understand expressions. Different whitespace characters include spaces, tabs, and carriage returns. You don't necessarily need to include whitespace as part of your formula logic. It won't hurt performance. It will, however, have a positive impact on format style and consistency.
References to model objects	Formulas reference tables, columns, and measures. A formula cannot reference a hierarchy or a hierarchy level. Therefore, for a table reference, a table name must be enclosed within a single quotation mark. Likewise, a column reference requires an enclosure within square brackets. Under specific conditions, a column name can be preceded by its table name. Finally, measure names must always be enclosed within the square brackets.

Implicit and explicit measures

Implicit measures are automatic behaviors allowing visuals to summarize model column data. *Explicit data* (exclusively referred to as a measure) are calculations you can add to a model.

Anytime you see the sigma symbol (Σ) in the Fields pane, that should alert a user or data modeler that

>> The data is numeric.

>> The data will use the summarized column value in visualizations and fields to support summarization.

In Figure 16-1, the Awards table includes only fields that can be summarized, including the AwardID calculated column.

REMEMBER

You control how the column summarizes data, by setting the Summarization property either to Don't Summarize or to a specific aggregation function using DAX. When you set the Summarization property to Don't Summarize, the sigma symbol ignores the next column in the Fields pane.

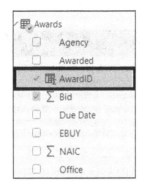

FIGURE 16-1:
The Fields pane,
showing a
calculated
column.

I've created a new Power BI report that includes a table containing three columns from the Awards table: Bid, Awarded, and Prime. The output of the table, shown in Figure 16-2, shows that I have various statuses I'm keeping track of, ranging from In-Progress to No to Pending to Yes. To decide how the column has been summarized, go to the Fields pane and choose the Bid field. You see that the pane now shows that the Bid field data will be summarized, as shown in Figure 16-3. Now, the data can be tabulated in other ways, but it likely won't supply an optimal response to the reader of the table.

Bid	Awarded	Prime
50,000.00	In-Progress	Yes
606,665.80	No	Yes
252,110.24	Pending	Yes
246,937.20	Yes	Yes
340,000.00	Pending	No
78,000.00	Yes	No
1,573,713.24		

FIGURE 16-2:
The table output.

Numeric columns using DAX functions offer a wide array of aggregation functions. You can program these programmatically or use a drop-down menu. The most often used numeric column options include these:

» Sum

» Average

» Minimum

» Maximum

» Count (distinct)

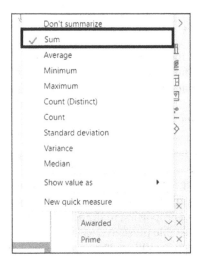

FIGURE 16-3:
Setting a
column's
calculation type.

>> Count

>> Standard deviation

>> Variance

>> Median

REMEMBER

You'll find when you are trying to format DAX calculations a phrase containing the word "distinct" now and again. Then there might be another choice that looks almost identical. What's the difference exactly? Take for example Count versus Count Distinct. The Count Distinct option only shows unique instances of a given value whereas Count shows results of all records.

Summarization of non-numeric data

Don't assume that numeric data can't be summarized. It can! By default, the only difference is that it won't have the sigma symbol (Σ) next to the non-numeric column in the field. Text columns are instead summarized for aggregations. Here are the example types:

>> First (alphabetical)

>> Last (alphabetical)

>> Count (Distinct)

>> Count

There are also data and Boolean columns that may allow for aggregations. These columns, however, will be used on a case-by-case basis.

Reasoning for implicit measures

You might argue that explicit measures are better for Power BI because they're calculation-driven — period. But the truth is that implicit measures are a bit easier to learn and use. They provide far more flexibility because report authors can use implicit measures to visualize data quickly. It takes a bit more effort with explicit measures when creating calculations.

Of course, every positive has a negative. Implicit measures allow the report author to create sloppy report designs, if they choose. That means aggregation can be done in the wrong way. The aggregated data may not be proper or suitable, based on the representative columns. In Figure 16-4, you can see an example of this scenario. The variance is well out of proportion to the actual values of any bid amount. In fact, if you look closely at the table presented earlier, in Figure 16-2, notice that the total bid pool is just shy of $1.6 million. The variance well exceeds this value.

Variance of Bid	Awarded	Prime ▾
625,000,000.00	In-Progress	Yes
9,086,058,333.85	No	Yes
15,362,333,278.21	Pending	Yes
11,834,263,253.16	Yes	Yes
0.00	Pending	No
0.00	Yes	No
12,794,741,006.68		

FIGURE 16-4: Bad data representation.

Simple and compound measures

You can write just about any DAX formula to add a measure to any table in your model. The only constraint you have is that a measure formula must return a scalar or single value.

TECHNICAL STUFF

Measures don't store values in the data model. Instead, measures are used at query time to return summarization instances of model data. Additionally, a measure cannot reference a table or column directly. That's why they must be passed to a table or column using a function to produce a summarization.

Measure complexity boils down to how many columns are aggregated. A simple measure aggregates the value of a single column. It does what implicit measures do automatically. In the example shown in Figure 16-5, you add a measure to the Awards table. Here's how:

1. **In the Fields pane, select the** Awards **table.**

2. **In the Calculations area of the Ribbon's Table Tools tab, click the New Measure icon, which allows you to begin creating a new DAX formula.**

3. **In the Formula bar, enter the following measure definition:**

```
AwardedOppty = SUM(Awards[Bid])
```

4. **When you finish, press Enter.**

   Notice that the Home Ribbon switches to the Measure Tools Ribbon, once you pressed enter so that you can format the formula, as shown in Figure 16-5.

FIGURE 16-5: Simple measure formation on the Ribbon.

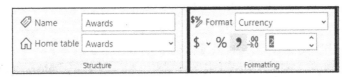

TIP

Change the formatting as soon as you possibly can. In this case, you change the number format to currency and set the decimal position to two. This helps create consistent values.

The measure is now properly structuring financial data by changing the formatting type to currency and decimal position two spots. Now, anytime you add financially oriented data like Awards, the same structure follows suit. To prove this statement, I created a new measure, TypicalBid:

```
TypicalBid = AVERAGE(Awards[Bid])
```

As soon as the new formula, TypicalBid, was entered into Power BI Desktop, the formula was recognized based on context. Changes that occurred included the switch to the currency format, given that the table was Awards and the column was Bids. You can see the results of a modified format type (currency) as seen in Figure 16-5, which is important because Power BI recognized the change automatically.

REMEMBER

If more than one measure is involved in the formulaic equation, such as Profit = Bid – Earned, it's known as a *compound measure*.

Comparing measures and columns

You've used both calculated columns and measures at this point. So, which should you choose and under which use case?

» Both calculated columns and measures allow you to add data to models.

» Both are defined by using DAX formulas.

» Both are referenced in DAX formulas by enclosing their names with parameters.

The differences, however, lie in their purpose, evaluation, and storage criteria. Table 16-2 explores the differences.

TABLE 16-2 ### Calculated Column versus Measures

	Calculated Columns	Measures
Purpose	Extends a table with new columns	Summarizes data models
Evaluation point	Row context at data refresh	Filter context at query time
Storage	Stores values for each row	Never stores values
Visualizations	Filters, group, and sort data	Designed for summarization

Syntax and context

DAX expressions analyze critical data for use in Power BI reports. These expressions must use specific syntax and context as a result. DAX expressions accept tables and columns as references. Keep these points in mind:

» DAX operators don't require users to repeatedly enter functions to create different expressions across tables.

» DAX operations apply to the entirety of selected data columns, not just a subset.

» With DAX, you can return the value of an entire table instead of returning a single value.

» DAX supports calculating date, time, and year variables from column data.

» With DAX, you can create as many as 64 nested functions in a single DAX expression.

The syntax of an expression

If you look at the following formula, you can see that there's a specific architecture to the equation taken from a table of data:

```
Profit = SUM(Sales([Earned]))
```

The equation has the following syntactical elements:

» Profit is the name of the measure or the calculated column.

» The equal sign (=), also known as the operator, marks the start of the function.

» SUM is the DAX function that adds all the numbers in the Sales([Earned]).

» Sales refers to the name of the table being analyzed.

» Earned is the column in the table that the SUM function will analyze.

» The parentheses ( ) enclose at least one argument.

As you craft equations and formulas, always make sure to adhere to a strict syntax that's in line with these principles.

Best Practices for DAX Coding and Debugging in Power BI

Power BI extends the use of DAX beyond what other Microsoft applications do — for a good reason! With DAX, your ability to visualize and augment data is increased exponentially. This chapter, along with Chapters 14 and 15, walks you through the basics of syntax, context, and functions. At the end of the day, however, you need to be laser-focused on optimization first because you don't want the code to become clunky.

DAX has many possible functions: It can become challenging to know where to start. It's undoubtedly hard to memorize the more than 250 functions I discuss in Chapter 15. But you should be familiar with how the 15 types of functions available to you are grouped and be able to sort your measures by category type. You should also be aware of things to avoid if you want to keep your formulas bug-free. The next few sections offer tips.

Using error functions properly

Anytime you're writing DAX expressions, there's a chance you may write evaluation-time errors. It's inevitable. Consider these two DAX functions to reduce any nerves:

» Use the ISERROR function to take a single expression and return a TRUE statement when the expression results in an error.

» Use the IFERROR function when there are two or more expressions. Should the first expression result in an error, the second expression is returned.

The ISERROR and IFERROR expressions can definitely be beneficial because they can contribute mightily to writing easy-to-understand expressions. Here's the downside: They can quickly degrade the performance of calculations. It can happen because the functions increase the number of hits to the system concurrently. Many of these errors are caused by unexpected BLANKs or zero values, so it's essential to know the data type conversion errors processing through the system.

Although you might be inclined to use the ISERROR and IFERROR functions, it's often better to use defensive strategies when developing your models and writing expressions. Consider the following:

» Ensure that the data incorporated into the data model is of a high quality.

» Use the IF function when you are looking to test a logical test expression which can decide whether an error result occurs.

» It is better to use IF rather than ISERROR and IFERROR as a defensive approach because it ensures quality data is loaded into a model and supports error handling more efficiently. While IF may result in added scans to a dataset, performance is better because of the added error handling built in.

» Use error-tolerant functions.

Avoiding converting blanks to values

You may be tempted to just leave things empty from time to time because there's simply no value realized from the expression. In these instances, where you find a value such as zero, you should rethink things before giving up. Consider the following measure, which explicitly turns a BLANK result into a 0:

```
Bid (No Blank) =

If (
    ISBLANK ([Bid]),
    0,
    [Bid]
    )
```

Here's another measure that converts BLANK results into zeroes:

```
Commissions =

DIVIDE([Commissions], [Sales], 0)
```

First, the DIVIDE function takes Commissions and measures it by the Sales measure. Should the result be zero or BLANK, the third argument — the alternate result, in other words — is then returned. In this example, the measure is guaranteed to always return a value because zero is passed as the alternate result. As you can see, both measure designs are inefficient and lead to poor report designs.

Power BI tries to retrieve all groupings within the filter context even when these items are added to report visualizations. The problem is that the result is a significant query leading to a slow report. Each example measure effectively turns a sparse calculation into a theatrical production, causing Power BI to sputter because the mundane tasks become a memory hog. The groupings, frankly, overwhelm the report user. That's why you want to be highly efficient with your use of the filter context, groupings, and variables. An example formula supplying more efficiency and appropriate use of variables includes this line:

```
Commission Payable = DIVIDE ([Commissions], [Sales])
```

TIP

In certain circumstances, you must configure a visualization to display all groupings. That means you should return values or BLANK within the filter context by enabling the Show Items with No Data option.

With DAX, there's only one condition when it's permissible to return a BLANK. That condition is when your measure is forced to return a BLANK because no meaningful value can be returned. This is an efficient approach, allowing Power BI to make reports faster.

Knowing the difference between operators and functions

Once upon a time, you learned basic mathematical formulas in school. Remember the difference between numerators and denominators? With DAX, it's a bit more technical. You need to know the difference between the function DIVIDE and the usage of the operator divide.

When using the DIVIDE function, you pass the numerator and denominator expression to get your result. You can also pass in a value that gets an alternate result:

```
DIVIDE(<numerator>, <denominator> [,<alternateresult>])
```

The DIVIDE function was deliberately created to handle division by zero. If an alternate is not passed in and the denominator is either zero or BLANK, the function should return a BLANK. The secondary use case is when an alternate result is passed in — it's returned instead of BLANK.

Referring to the IF, ISBLANK, or BLANK functions as discussed in Chapter 15, these do not stand on their own. You need a minimum of four DAX functions to complete the function properly. Such coding requirements are quite inefficient. Here's an example of an inefficient (and erroneous) code sample:

```
Bid Margin =
IF (
    OR (
        ISBLANK([Bids]),
        [Bids] == 0
    ),
    BLANK (),
    [Bids] / [Sales]
)
```

The reason why this code is inefficient is because the [Sales] is the denominator. Using [Bids], a numerator, will result in an infinite result of BLANK. As you can tell, the code is improperly formatted, causing unnecessary errors.

Here's an example using DIVIDE, which offers a far more efficient way of producing exactly the same formula:

```
Bid Margin =
DIVIDE([Bids], [Sales])
```

Given what you know from the review of these two equations, you should be in a position to follow these rules:

>> Use the DIVIDE function whenever the denominator is an expression that can return 0 or BLANK.

>> When the denominator is a constant value, use the divide operator, not the DIVIDE function. The division is 100 percent foolproof, and your expressions can perform better because no testing is needed.

>> Before you use the alternate value, think twice. You're often better to return a BLANK than anything at all.

>> Carefully consider whether the DIVIDE function should return an alternate value.

>> BLANK is often better for report visualizations because it helps eliminate groups when summarizations are BLANK. You can also focus your attention on groups where data exists.

>> When in doubt, you can configure visuals to display all groups that return values or BLANK within the filtered complex, by enabling the Show Items with No Data option.

Getting specific

A few letters with DAX make all the difference. You may need to write a DAX expression that tests whether a column can be filtered using a specific value. Over the years, DAX has used specific values, including IF, HASONEVALUE, and VALUES. For example, if you need to determine the sales tax for a customer in California, you may decide to use the following code:

```
CA State Tax =
IF (
    HASONEVALUE (Customer [State Tax]),
    IF (
        VALUES (Customer [State Tax]) = "California",
        [Sales] * 0.0725
    )
)
```

As presented here, the HASONEVALUE function returns a TRUE condition only if a single value of the STATE TAX column is visible in the current filter context. When it's TRUE, the VALUES function must be compared to the specific text "California". If that text condition is TRUE, the Sales measure is multiplied by 0.0725, or

7.25 percent, which is the state sales income tax in California. If the HASONEVALUE function returns FALSE, which may be the case because there's more than one value filter column, the first IF function returns a BLANK.

Using the technique as structured here is entirely defensive and prickly. It's needed because it can produce multiple value filters for the State Tax column. The VALUES function can return a table that produces a table of multiple rows. That said, when you compare a table of multiple rows to a scale value, the results yield a significant error.

Rather than use the trifecta of functions, why not just use a single filter, the SELECTEDVALUE function? Sometimes, simplicity, elegance, and efficiency do win the race. The same code equation using one function versus three can be written this way:

```
CA Sales Tax =
IF (
    SELECTEDVALUE (Customer [State Tax]) = "California",
    [Sales] * 0.0725
)
```

It's clean, simple, and pretty, indeed!

Knowing what to COUNT

You may need to write DAX expressions that count table rows every so often. There are a few ways to carry this out. Your first choice is to use the COUNT function to count column values. Another choice is to use the COUNTROWS function to count table rows. Both alternatives achieve the same result. There's one caveat: As long as the counted columns have no BLANKs, both will work.

In the first use case:

```
Bids Processed =
COUNT(Bids[BidDate])
```

The granularity shown in the Bid table is for one row per bid, and the BidDate column doesn't have a BLANK. The measure returns the correct result set.

```
Bids Processed =
COUNTROWS(Bids)
```

Again, efficiency and elegance win the race for a variety of reasons. Second, it doesn't consider BLANKs in any table column. The intention of the column is clarified because the function is self-descriptive.

Relationships matter

Anytime you look to review a pair of tables in Power BI, you can find many relationships. You may have many inactive relationships. However, only one active relationship at a time can be evaluated using DAX.

DAX code uses the active relationship by default. DAX can use a particular inactive relationship when associated with the USERELATIONSHIP function.

Keeping up with the context

In Chapter 14, I briefly touch on context. Let's reiterate the importance of context again, because it does matter. With DAX, you're completing a dynamic analysis. That's why it's essential to always consider the *context* — the data available for a calculation to be performed. You have these two options:

>> **Row context** applies whenever a DAX formula has functions that find a single row in a table. Think of a row context as targeting a specific row of data. It cannot reference any data outside the row without using functions. The row context is calculated at processing time rather than at run-time. You use the row context for generating calculated columns.

>> **Filter context** describes how you can filter across one or more calculations to decide specific results or values. The filter context doesn't replace the row context — it only extends the context. With the filter context, you can apply the ALL, RELATED, FILTER, and CALCULATED functions.

Preferring measures over columns

Earlier in this chapter, I discuss the differences between measures and columns. But here's the God's honest truth — measures always produce better DAX results in Power BI. Why? Because a measure is like a virtual calculation that lives on top of your model. A measure executes only when it needs to be used, whereas calculated columns are heavily integrated into the model.

Here are a few other reasons to use measures over calculated columns:

➤ Measures are lightweight and deployed when needed, whereas calculated columns are deployed unnecessarily when you run an equation that includes code.

➤ Though a calculated column can be used in a slicer, the column size increases along with the data model each time you run an operation. That isn't the case with the use of a measure. You see a measure executed only when called upon.

➤ One of the most powerful techniques for complicated calculation measurement is to measure branching and measure groups. Measure branching allows you to start with a core calculation and then build more complicated calculations from the base calculation, like a tree branch. Measure groups are like folders. Like-kind calculations are put in the same group to perform a task.

Suppose that you intend to perform nested calculations that require complex calculations. In that case, measure branching cuts out a significant chunk of the code, which improves calculation performance. Calculated columns don't improve calculation performance.

Measure groups keep reports clean and organized, helping you locate data quickly and more efficiently.

Seeing that structure matters

If there's anything I should be reiterating countless times as you reach the end of this chapter, it's the simple truth that structure matters. If you don't need something in your code, cut it out. If an internal column is in use, hide it rather than expose it in Power BI so that you don't need to expose it with DAX. If you want to call out a column using DAX as a variable, rename it so that it makes sense because all names should be user-friendly. And, whenever possible, use explicit measures because you'll be thankful for code readability and accelerated performance.

Chapter **17**

Sharing and the Power BI Workspace

After experiencing the entire data lifecycle across data sources, building visualizations, learning about DAX, and publishing reports, your next step, as a power user of Power BI, is to share the data from your desktop with everyone who is a stakeholder in your business. To do that, you have to switch gears and move to the web because you're unlikely to want users mangling your Power BI Desktop data. Instead, they should be using Power BI Services to carry out activities using a workspace, which is a crucial feature for collaboration and sharing. In this chapter, you learn about workspaces and how you can collaborate, share, and accelerate your business operations with monitoring tools, all available using Power BI Services.

Working Together in a Workspace

Picture yourself in an art museum. You can explore visuals and read anecdotal tales about each work by yourself or with others by your side. A Power BI workspace, available in Power BI Services, is analogous to curating content for a museum, but of course it's data! A workspace is created by a Power BI designer to manage a collection of dashboards and reports. Think of a workspace as a filing cabinet. The designer can share the workspace with users based on roles, responsibilities, and permissions. In fact, the designer can even build an app by bundling together targeted collections of dashboards and reports and distributing them to their organization, whether that involves just a few users or an entire community. These apps, called *template* apps, are distributable on a variety of devices, including desktop and smartphone.

Defining the types of workspaces

The idea behind a Power BI workspace is that it should contain all content specific to an app. When designers create an app, they bundle all the content assets necessary for use and deployment and make it available in the workspace. The content might include anything from datasets to dashboards to reports.

REMEMBER

A workspace may not necessarily include all content types. It may contain reports, datasets, or dashboards exclusively. It depends on the business purpose and how the designer wants to share and collaborate with other users.

The workspaces shown in Figure 17-1 are intended for sharing and collaboration using a collaboration scheme with others. You access them via your My Workspace (see Figure 17-2), as it is your desktop on the Internet for Power BI. You can publish data from Power BI Desktop to Power BI Services. Then, you can organize, store, and share those assets just published online to one or more workspaces that you might intend to use for collaboration. In Figure 17-3, you find assets that were originally created in Power BI Desktop now available in a workspace associated with the Pipeline Identification project.

It might be difficult at first to understand why it's necessary to transition from the Power BI Desktop to Power BI Services. The key selling point is often workspaces, the sharing and collaboration features in Power BI Services. Workspaces provide the following benefits — you can

>> Sustain focused collaboration among a small or globally dispersed team

>> Use workspaces to house reports and dashboards for one team or multiple teams

>> Streamline the sharing and presentation of reports and dashboards by housing them in a single environment

>> Maintain security by controlling access to datasets, reports, and dashboards

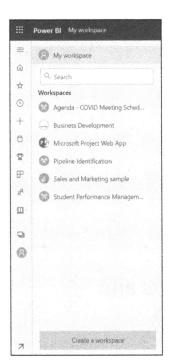

FIGURE 17-1:
A list of
workspace apps.

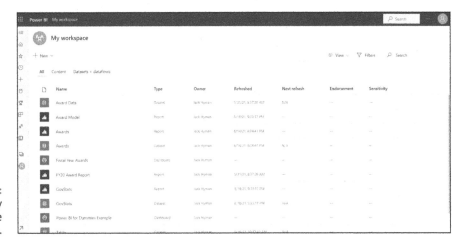

FIGURE 17-2:
The My
Workspace
interface.

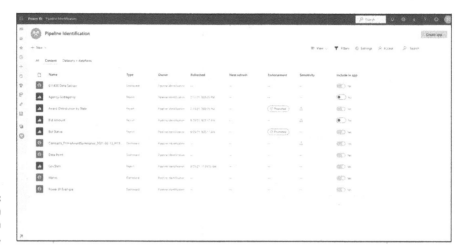

FIGURE 17-3:
The content of a
workspace in
Power BI.

Figuring out the nuts and bolts of workspaces

When you go into Power BI Services, you're introduced to the Power BI Services navigation menu. (See Figure 17-4.) To no one's surprise, data ingestion and access are a big part of Services.

- Show the navigation pane
- Home
- Favorites
- Recent
- Create
- Datasets
- Goals
- Apps
- Share With Me
- Learn
- Workspaces
- My Workspaces
- Get Data

FIGURE 17-4:
The navigation
menu in Power BI
Services.

At the bottom of the list, you find workspaces-related features. A user has a single My Workspace but can have many workspaces within My Workspace. Just keep in mind that a user can be active in only one workspace at a given time — the one highlighted in the navigation.

Creating and configuring the workspace

Creating a workspace requires that you configure a few items, including its branding, name, description, access, storage, license mode, app type, and security settings. To complete this configuration, follow these steps:

1. **Click the Workspace icon on the Power BI navigation menu.**

2. **On the menu that appears, click the Create a Workspace button. (See Figure 17-5.)**

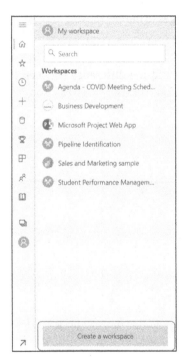

FIGURE 17-5:
The Create a Workspace button.

3. **In the new window that appears on the right side, use the settings to configure the new workspace.**

   Here are your options, divided between Standard (see Figure 17-6) and Advanced (see Figure 17-7):

   - *Upload:* Save a photo from your desktop to customize the workspace experience.

- *Workspace Name:* Name the workspace based on its content and datasets. Treat this name as you would for a file collection.

- *Description:* Describe the purpose of the workspace.

- *Contact List:* Workspace admins or assigned users receive notifications about updates in each Power BI workspace.

- *Workspace OneDrive:* This allows a user to configure a Microsoft 365 group whose OneDrive shared library is available to assigned workspace users.

- *License Mode:* Select the license type assigning the right to access content in the workspace. An organization may have access to one type (Pro) or more than one type (Premium-based).

- *Develop a Template App:* Select the check box if you want the workspace to become an app.

- *Security settings:* Selecting this check box allows administrators and contributors to make changes to the workspace.

4. **When you finish, click Save.**

TIP

For a refresher on license types and the difference between Pro and Premium-based licensing, see Chapter 3.

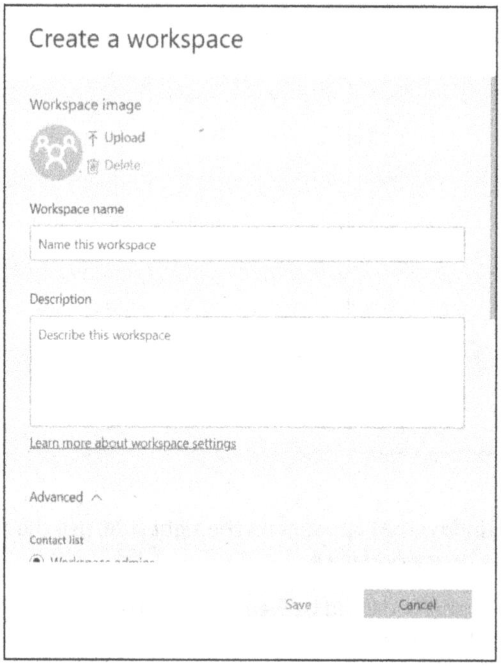

Create a workspace

Workspace image

⼿ Upload

🗑 Delete

Workspace name

    Name this workspace

Description

    Describe this workspace

Learn more about workspace settings

Advanced ⌃

Contact list

◉ Workspace admins

Save   Cancel

FIGURE 17-6: Configuring the standard features of a workspace.

FIGURE 17-7:
Configuring the
advanced
features of a
workspace.

Wandering into access management

A big part of sharing and collaborating starts with access management. You must configure who gains access to workspaces and each of the content assets inside the workspaces. You as the designer can assign four distinct role types: admin, member, contributor, or viewer. To change access, follow these steps:

1. **Click the Workspace icon on the Power BI navigation menu.**

2. **Choose the workspace you want to modify from the menu that appears.**

3. **On the right side of the workspace label, select the three vertical dots.**

4. **Click Workspace Access from the menu that appears, as seen in Figure 17-8.**

   Doing so brings up the Workspace Access pane on the right side of the screen, as shown in Figure 17-8.

5. **Enter the email addresses or group accounts of those whose access you want to control along with the workspace roles you want to assign them.**

6. **When you finish, click Close.**

FIGURE 17-8:
Assigning
workspace
access.

REMEMBER

When you create a user group, everyone in that user group gets assigned to the group. Assuming that a user is a part of several user groups, that person is assigned the highest permission level based on their assigned role. However, if you embed the user groups, all contained users get permission.

WARNING

Your ability to interact with data in workspaces is significantly limited unless you have a Pro or Premium license. You can either view and interact with items or read data stored in workspace dataflows — nothing less, nothing more.

Dealing with settings and storage

Remember all those settings you configured when you first created a workspace? You can modify them at any time, including changing the storage type from Pro to Premium per User, Premium per Capacity, or Embedded. Also, if you're looking to delete a workspace, you can do so under Premium. To make these changes, follow these steps:

1. **Click the Workspace icon on the Power BI navigation menu.**

2. **Choose the workspace you want to modify from the menu that appears.**

3. **On the right side of the workspace label, click the three vertical dots.**

4. **Click Workspace Settings. (Refer to Figure 17-8.)**

   Doing so brings up the Workspace Settings pane on the right side of the screen.

5. **Go to the Premium tab.**

6. **Select the capacity choice that best reflects your need.**

7. **When you finish, click Save.**

TECHNICAL STUFF

You might be wondering what exactly the Embedded option involves. Suppose that you've used an enterprise application or visited a website and seen analytics features embedded. In that case, Power BI might just be the solution behind the application or website. The Embedded choice allows you to build an app so that a customer does not need to authenticate.

Creating and Configuring Apps

Unsurprisingly, you need to have some content in a workspace in order to create and configure an app for distribution. Think of our recipe analogy for baking a cake. You decide you are going to create an app workspace, which allows for all of your workspace assets to be rolled up into a stand-alone deployable application. Then, you apply the icing, which in this case is assigning the collaborator-specific roles. Of course, you may even want to add a dash of a few extra content components as you see fit, such as reports, dashboards, datasets, dataflows, and files imported into Power BI Services. Unlike a Power BI workspace, which is intended for a finite number of users for collaboration, an app is intended for a broader number of users after it's published. An *app* is a published, read-only view of data. Apps provide mass distribution to those who want access to analytic insights. There is a catch, though; you must have, at minimum, a Pro license to consume and view an app. Alternatively, the app must be supported by one of the two Premium capacity types in an organization.

To add any type of content into an app workspace once set up, select the New button and then choose the content you want to add. (See Figure 17-9.)

Each time you add content, it's added to the Workspace list. You can then choose to include the item in the app, as shown in Figure 17-10. You'd select the slider to show whether it should be included. Once you're ready to package the app for distribution, press the Create an App button in the upper right corner.

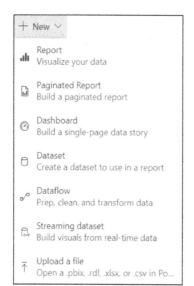

FIGURE 17-9:
Adding new content to a workspace.

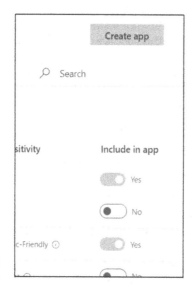

FIGURE 17-10:
Creating an app.

Slicing and Dicing Data

As users consume your reports, dashboards, and datasets, you might want to know *how* they consume these content assets. That's why Microsoft has integrated monitoring and alternate data analysis tools within Power BI for those users who have Pro and Premium licensing to evaluate such metrics.

You can slice and dice usage data in several ways. Options include analyzing data in Excel as well as accessing a high-level view of your data with the Quick Insights report. You can also use metrics reports to understand who is accessing and viewing your reports and dashboards. Click the three vertical dots next to any reports or dashboards within a workspace to access these capabilities. You see two options: one for dashboards (see Figure 17-11) and another for reports (see Figure 17-12).

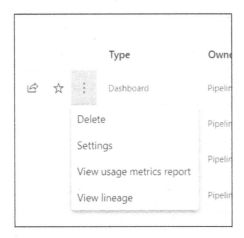

FIGURE 17-11:
The Dashboard
menu under
Workspaces.

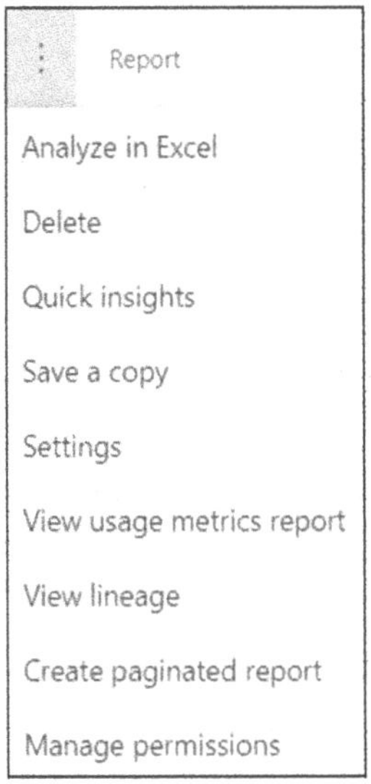

FIGURE 17-12:
The Report
menu under
Workspaces.

Analyzing in Excel

Sometimes, Power BI may be just a bit too much for a user to evaluate enterprise data comfortably. Users may want to review a subset of data — so we return to Microsoft Excel. With the Analyze in Excel option, you can import Power BI datasets into Excel. Then you can choose to view and interact with the dataset side-by-side or independently. Whether your business goal is to create a PivotTable, chart, table, or Excel output, you need to have the Excel Add-On feature from Power BI downloaded. Don't be alarmed when you see a prompt the first time you try to analyze in Excel, similar to the one you see in Figure 17-13. Once the add-on is downloaded to the computer, you can begin evaluating your datasets.

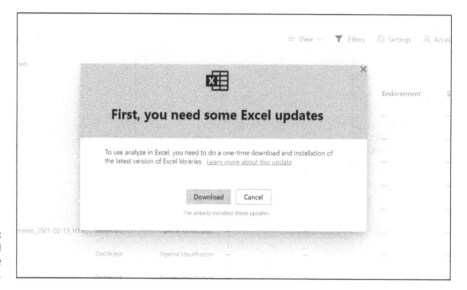

FIGURE 17-13:
The Download prompt for the Excel add-on.

Benefiting from Quick Insights

Perhaps you want a quick snapshot of a dataset. Or maybe you're looking for patterns, trends, and ambiguities in your data. The anomalies in the data can be challenging to find if you're first starting out and don't know where to start looking. However, Power BI at least attempts to do the hard work for you. Its artificial intelligence engine finds critical trends, patterns, indicators, and anomalies in your data. With Quick Insights, Power BI automatically produces the top trends it believes are essential in each dataset for a user to consider evaluating. In the example shown in Figure 17-14, you have one federal agency, the State Department, obligating the lowest dollar amount for COVID-19-related projects relative to other federal agencies. Similarly, for counties in Virginia, a greater allocation of dollars was given to Fairfax and Stafford relative to others.

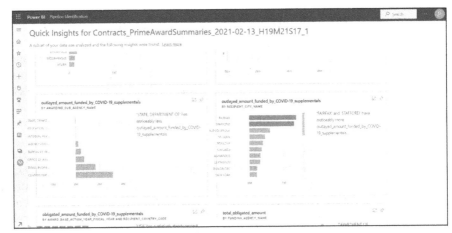

FIGURE 17-14:
The Quick
Insights feature.

Using Usage Metric reports

Ever want to know how popular a report or dashboard is? Or perhaps who accessed an item in a workspace today, this week, or over time? Microsoft recognized that data access metrics help improve a designer's ability to deliver best-in-class analytics. The Usage Metrics report can help users analyze data points, including distribution types, views, viewers, viewer rank, views per day, and unique views per day, as shown in Figure 17-15.

FIGURE 17-15:
A usage metrics
report.

Working with paginated reports

Earlier in this chapter, I show you how to create, update, and delete reports as stand-alone content assets in Power BI Desktop and Services. The stand-alone report is optimized for data exploration and interactivity. Another type of report, however, is specific to Power BI Pro and Premium users. That report is the *paginated* report, which can be shared directly or as part of a Power BI app.

Unlike web-based reports, paginated reports are meant for print based consumption. That means they're formatted to fit well on paper. In fact, you might call the presentation of these reports pixel-perfect. Suppose that you're looking to render a highly sophisticated business report PDF, such as a year-end report or profit-and-loss statement. In that case, a paginated report is an excellent choice.

TIP

If you're given access to a paginated report, you can freely share a report with others. Also, you have the option to subscribe yourself and others to a report.

REMEMBER

Though viewing a paginated report is possible as a Pro or Premium user, publishing requires a Premium license.

In certain reporting frameworks, you're collating many reports to create a single report. That isn't the case with Power BI — in fact, a report designer is creating a report definition. The definition contains no data; it merely tells you where to acquire the data, which data to obtain from those sources, and how to display the data from those sources. After configuring those three parameters, you run the report, at which time the report processes the definition. The result: a report that displays the data. As with other reports, you click the three dots next to the report and choose Create Paginated Report to get started with developing a user-friendly report.

Troubleshooting the Use of Data Lineage

Business intelligence projects can get complex pretty quickly. Following the flow of data from one source to its destination might even be a challenge. Suppose that you've built a relatively complex, advanced analytical project that contains several data sources and maintains numerous reports and dashboards. Each of these assets clearly has a variety of dependencies. As you review these assets, you might come upon questions such as, "What will happen to this report if I make a change to this data point?" Or you may want to better understand how a change you might make will reflect in a dataset.

Data lineage simplifies many complex processes by breaking down processes into more manageable steps. Think of it as your little detective! With data lineage, you can see the path your data takes from start to completion, which is crucial when you're scratching your head, having hit many roadblocks. Whether you're managing a workspace with a single report or dashboard or one with many, make sure that the impact of a single change in a dataset is recognized by referring to the data lineage to track those changes. A bonus is that you can resolve many data-refresh concerns with data lineage as well.

To access data lineage information, follow these steps:

1. **Go to the workspace you're targeting.**

2. **Click View.**

3. **Choose Lineage from the menu that appears. (See Figure 17-16.)**

   Lineage view appears, as shown in Figure 17-17.

FIGURE 17-16: Gaining access to data lineage.

As with other workspace features, only specific roles can access Lineage view. You must be an admin, a contributor, or a member to see Lineage view. Also, you must have a Power BI Pro or Premium license using an app-based workspace to make use of the view.

Once you select Lineage, the view of all items found within the workspace appears on the canvas. Figure 17-17, for example, shows the data lineage for the Pipeline Identification workspace.

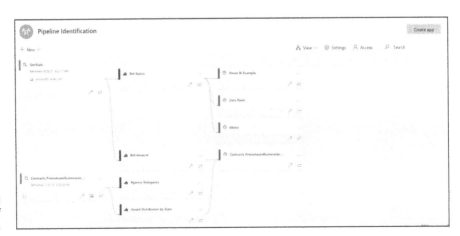

FIGURE 17-17: An example of data lineage.

Lineage view provides a synopsis of all artifacts found in your workspace — datasets, dataflows, reports, and dashboards, for example. As shown in Figures 17-18 through 17-21, each of the cards on the canvas as represented in Lineage view is a separate asset. The arrows between each of the cards explain the dataflows among assets. Data flows from left to right, letting you observe data as it goes from the source to the destination. Generally, the flow tells a story, such as the one in this list:

>> A source produces one or more datasets. (See Figure 17-18.)

>> Reports are generated from datasets. (See Figure 17-19.)

>> A collection of reports presenting a snapshot in time results in the creation of a dashboard. (See Figure 17-20.)

>> Data flows in particular directions. (See Figure 17-21.)

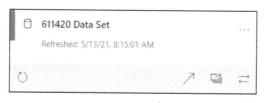

FIGURE 17-18: Example of a Dataset card.

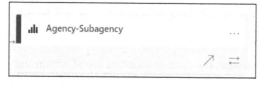

FIGURE 17-19: A Report card.

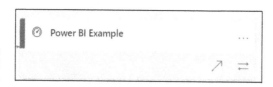

FIGURE 17-20: A Dashboard card.

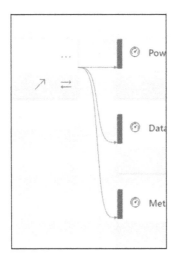

FIGURE 17-21:
Arrows between
each asset in a
workspace.

Datasets, Dataflows, and Lineage

It's not uncommon for datasets and dataflows to be associated with external sources. Some examples may include databases or datasets found in external workspaces. You see that — when reviewing the Dataset card, as shown in Figure 17-22 — a user can drill down to evaluate different factors by choosing one of these three commands. Each command reveals a different aspect of the dataset:

>> **View Details and Related Reports:** This command displays all reports tied to the associated datasets or dataflow.

>> **Shows Impact Across Workspace:** This command provides you with an impact analysis of how the dataset or dataflow impacts workspace activity. (See Figure 17-23.)

>> **Show Lineage**: This command provides you with a micro-level view of the dataset.

More Options

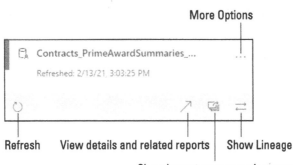

Refresh   View details and related reports   Show Lineage

Show impact across workspaces

FIGURE 17-22:
Drilling down into
a Dataset card.

FIGURE 17-23:
Showing the
impact of an
action across a
workspace.

Defending Your Data Turf

Can you imagine a sensitive report or dashboard being exposed to an unauthorized user group in your organization? That won't go over too well, because that global exposure can potentially harm your data and information security practices. Microsoft integrated a way to codify protection for your data analytics assets. Called *sensitivity labels,* this feature (which is available across the Microsoft 365 product family and integrates with Power BI) allows users to apply labels to reports, dashboards, datasets, dataflows, and .pbix files. Such labels guard sensitive content against unauthorized access. It is incumbent on you to label your data correctly to ensure that only authorized users access your data.

Though information protection might seem nonnegotiable, your organization must have a few implementation prerequisites in place first, such as a Power BI Pro or Premium per User license. For sensitivity labels to work, edit permissions must be enabled for all content you want to label in the workspace. Before edit permissions can even be accessed, a systems administrator must enable sensitivity labels in Settings for users to apply such permissions in the Power BI workspaces. (See Figure 17-24; more on sensitivity labels in a few paragraphs.)

TIP

You must be part of the security group authorized to apply the sensitivity labels; otherwise, access is disabled.

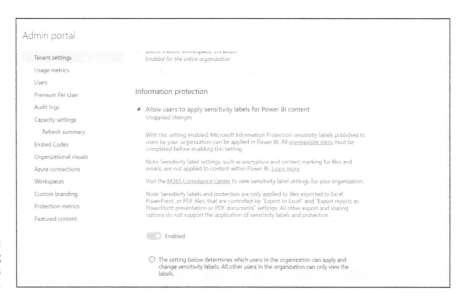

FIGURE 17-24:
Enabling
sensitivity labels
in Power BI.

REMEMBER

Data protection must be enabled for your instance of Power BI so that sensitivity labels can appear. Otherwise, you won't find any sensitivity labels in the Sensitivity column in List view of dashboards, reports, datasets, or dataflows with your workspace.

WARNING

Your systems administrator must configure sensitivity labels in the Microsoft Information Protect Admin console, separate from Power BI Admin. This step must be completed before sensitivity labels can be enabled and usable by any user.

To make changes to a sensitivity label on a report or a dashboard, Follow these steps:

1. Go to the report or dashboard you want to edit.

2. Click the three vertical dots.

3. Choose Settings from the menu that appears.

4. Locate the Sensitivity Label section in the Settings pane that appears, (See Figure 17-25.)

5. Choose the appropriate sensitivity label.

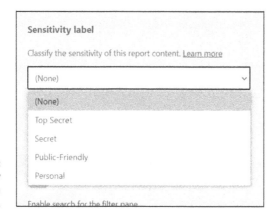

FIGURE 17-25:
The Sensitivity
Label drop-down
menu.

6. **When you finish, click Save.**

In your workspace, the sensitivity label appears in the column under the appropriate report or dashboard, as shown in Figure 17-26.

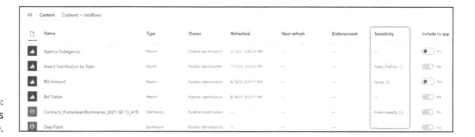

FIGURE 17-26:
Sensitivity labels
in a workspace.

ON THE WEB

To learn how to configure sensitivity labels in Microsoft 365's information protection admin console, go to https://docs.microsoft.com/en-us/microsoft-365/compliance/create-sensitivity-labels.

5
Enhancing Your Power BI Experience

Transition from Power BI Desktop to Power BI Services to share and collaborate with organizational stakeholders using workspaces.

Gain insights from your data by using the Power BI Services prebuilt reporting and dashboarding solutions.

Establish best practices and approaches to ensure that your datasets are always secure and refreshed for the most relevant experience.

Explore ways to extend Power BI with other Microsoft applications, including Power Apps, Power Automate, OneDrive, SharePoint 365, and Dynamics 365.

Chapter **18**

Making Your Data Shine

Old data does an organization no good if newer, more relevant data is available. And, let's be honest, if the data is stale and lacks integrity, will the analysts who actively use Power BI to crunch numbers be able to create new compelling reports, observe dashboards, and craft complex calculations? I doubt it. Ensuring that your Power BI datasets are second to none and performing like the workhorses you dream of for your teams is what every user aims for. That's why Microsoft has integrated several data-refresh and -security features into Power BI. In this chapter, you see how to design, configure, and deploy enterprise Power BI datasets for data freshness and fine-grain security.

Establishing a Schedule

What good is data if it's not kept clean and up to date? Some data analysts might prefer to refresh data manually in Power BI Desktop and Services. Still, this approach is illogical when you need to ensure that data is periodically updated for data relevancy.

Rolling out the scheduled refresh

When you have your data ducks all in a row and simply want to craft an online refresh schedule, you set up that activity in Power BI Services. To create a schedule update, follow these steps:

1. **Go to the Datasets+Dataflows tab in a workspace.**

2. **Locate a dataset and then click the Schedule Refresh button.**

   This takes you to another screen, where you have the option to configure the schedule refresh.

3. **In the Scheduled Refresh pane (see Figure 18-1), modify the schedule to accommodate your refresh schedule.**

4. **When you finish, click Apply.**

FIGURE 18-1:
The Scheduled
Refresh pane.

REMEMBER

Power BI is your little corner of the world, whereas Power BI Services is for sharing.

You can change the frequency, time zone, and time of your scheduled refreshes using the Scheduled Refresh settings. Any schedule notifications can then be sent to a specific email address or Active Directory group available.

The above example assumes you've already established a data gateway. If you haven't, pay close attention to the next section.

Refreshing on-premises data

Another common use case for refreshing involves accessing on-premises data. For that task, you need to use a *data gateway* — a type of bridge that supports connection details and credentials. You download and install a data gateway from Power BI Services by going to the Settings menu at the top of the Power BI Services home page. (You know, our friend the Cog icon). Once there, choose Settings ➪ Download ➪ Data Gateway, as shown in Figure 18-2.

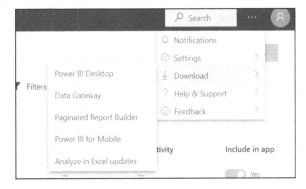

FIGURE 18-2:
Downloading a
data gateway.

There are two gateway modes: standard and personal. Here's how they differ:

» **Standard mode**: When you require multiple people to access the gateway, Standard mode is suitable. You can also use a Standard mode data gateway with other Microsoft services, especially the Power Platform family. A data source can be added only once, so it's an excellent choice for corporate environments looking for data integrity. You have the choice to apply generic credentials for data sources as well.

» **Personal mode:** In this mode, only a single user can use a gateway. Also, the gateway can only be used by Power BI. If sharing isn't needed, Personal mode is a possibility. Otherwise, your only choice is Standard mode.

Assuming that you've installed the gateway or the Power BI Services group administration has granted you access as a gateway user, you're now authorized to use the gateway to refresh datasets that use on-premises datasets.

For each gateway, you can select a different dataset on the Datasets settings menu. To make these changes, follow these configuration steps:

1. **Go to the Datasets tab in a workspace.**

2. **Select a dataset to review.**

3. **Hover the cursor over the dataset in the list.**

4. **When the settings for the dataset you've selected appear in the pane on the right, as shown in Figure 18-3, click the Gateway Connection option on the right.**

   You will then see a list of data sources along with associated data gateways.

5. **For each data gateway, select a data source that you'd like to map to, as shown in Figure 18-4.**

FIGURE 18-3:
Data gateway options.

REMEMBER

Each time you create a data source, you need to provide data source credentials in the Data Source section. This means that you need to edit the credentials securely so that they can be cached in Power BI Services.

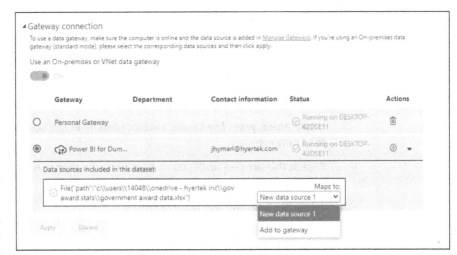

FIGURE 18-4:
Modifying data
gateways.

Protecting the Data Fortress

Data is precious. Not everyone should gain access to it. If it's on your desktop, it's generally restricted to you unless you share your computer. As soon as the data hits the Internet, though, all bets are off. You need to protect the crown jewels of your organization. That means datasets, reports, and dashboards may need focused security settings. That's why you want to implement row level security (RLS) with Power BI to restrict data access so that unauthorized users don't gain unauthorized access to data. With RLS, filters restrict data access at the row level. You can define the filters within a role. Members of an assigned workspace have access to the Power BI Services datasets, assuming that you're within the provisioned security group.

TECHNICAL STUFF

Configuring RLS can occur in a number of different places. You can configure RLS in Power BI Desktop or by using DirectQuery with SQL Server, for example. When using Analysis Services or Azure Analysis Services live connections, you configure RLS in your model. Try to avoid configuring security with Power BI Desktop — your configurations won't appear in the live connection dataset.

Configuring for group membership

To create group memberships, you need to define roles and rules within Power BI Desktop first. Once you're ready to publish, those details are associated with the data model that's published. To configure these roles and rules, start in Power BI Desktop and Follow these steps:

1. **Select the Model tab.**

2. **Locate the Manage Roles button.**

3. **Under Roles, press the Create button, then fill in the box with the name for a new role.**

4. **Repeat this process until you've added the number of roles you feel are sufficient.**

5. **Select the Role and the Table of choice.**

6. **Select the ellipses to the right of the Role or Table label to open a pane for creating a DAX Expression to filter against.**

   A sample condition is presented in Figure 18-5.

7. **Once you have created all the role requirements you intend to use in Power BI Services, click Save.**

REMEMBER

You don't assign users roles within Power BI Desktop. That happens in Power BI Services. You enable the security assignment in Power Desktop with the use of DAX Expressions.

Making role assignments in Power BI Services

You can't just "set it and forget" when it comes to role assignments in Power BI Desktop. You are simply creating a blueprint for security when published to Power BI Services. After all, you are continually publishing data to the Internet. Then, you assign users and groups access to reports, datasets, and dashboards in a workspace for sharing and collaboration. As time goes on, your role in Power BI Services is as much to administer security for users to access content as it will be a data expert for this very reason.

You need to go to the dataset first and then find the security settings for that dataset in the workspace settings. If you haven't previously defined roles, you see a message like the one shown in Figure 18-6.

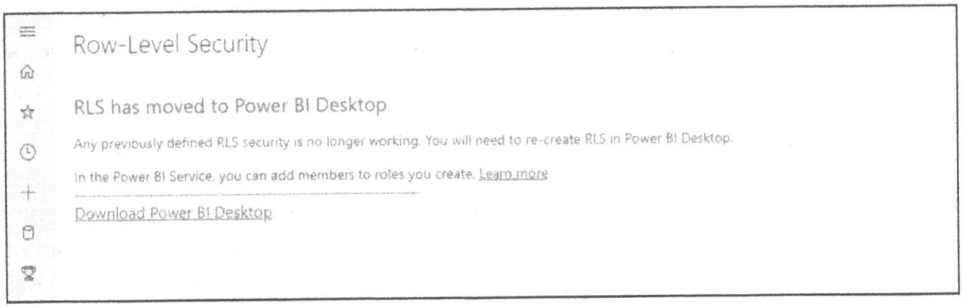

FIGURE 18-6: An RLS error message.

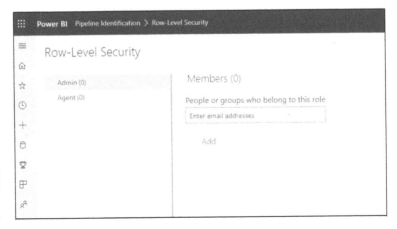

Once you've configured your RLS and published the model to Power BI Services, the result will be similar to what you see in Figure 18-7. On the left, you find the roles for this particular dataset. The numbers in the parentheses show how many members each role has. On the right side, you can control each member group and its associated roles.

FIGURE 18-7: Row level security in Power BI Services.

Taking care of one or two users is a piece of cake, but how about a few hundred or several thousand users? No cake here. The reason is simple. The same users might be using the same row level security settings for datasets, which means assigning those users to exactly the same security groups as members within an assigned row. Under these conditions, you can create a single security group once and then your work is done.

Sharing the Data Love

Power BI Services allows for collaboration between various users and groups. It's not just about sharing datasets — it's also about sharing reports and apps. You can share data at scale in several ways, including the ones described in this list:

» **Workspaces:** When publishing to Power BI Services, you can publish to a workspace. Once you've published to a workspace, you automatically gain access to datasets you've published. As to other users, you can assign roles, assuming you have the licensing to do so, on a case-by-case, basis.

» **Apps:** If you make your dataset available to others via an app, you need to grant the app users Build permission. In fact, all users must have the same Build permissions; it's an all or nothing situation here. Go to the Permissions tab when you create an app and use the settings to assign permissions, as shown in Figure 18-8.

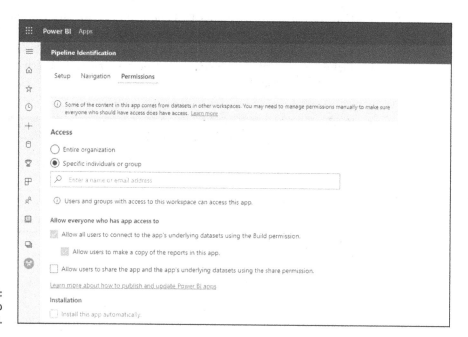

FIGURE 18-8: Setting app permissions.

REMEMBER If you were to revoke app access for a user of a security group using the Permissions tab, it doesn't automatically revoke their access to the dataset. Deleting access requires managing permissions to the actual dataset, not merely the app.

Refreshing Data in Baby Steps

Datasets come in all shapes and sizes. You find some that are minuscule and others that weigh in at several gigabytes, even as Power BI attempts to compress the data in real time. Power BI does its very best to mitigate speed, resource usage, and reliability issues. A way around all three of these is the use of incremental refresh.

An *incremental refresh* allows you to refresh a subset of data, resulting in a quicker, more reliable refresh with lower resource use and consumption. Suppose that you know your data will scale well into gigabyte territory. In that case, consider planning for an incremental refresh as part of your deployment strategy early on. For an incremental refresh of that kind to work in Power BI Services, it must be configured in Power BI Desktop. In broad steps, here's what needs to be done:

1. **Create a RangeStart and RangeEnd parameter.**

2. **Filter by using the RangeStart and RangeEnd parameters.**

3. **Define an incremental refresh policy.**

The next few sections dig a little deeper into each step of the process.

Creating RangeStart and RangeEnd parameters

Creating the incremental refresh parameters in Power BI Desktop for filtering is the first step in ensuring that your data always sparkles and shines. Those two parameters that need to be created are RangeStart and RangeEnd. Like DAX parameters, these parameters are case-sensitive. If you try to use other parameter names, you will be out of luck.

Here's what you need to do:

1. **Go to Power Query to begin this process.**

2. **Once in Power Query, click Manage Parameters on the Power BI Ribbon's Home tab and choose New Parameter from the menu that appears.**

3. **On the Parameters pane, enter** RangeStart **in the Name field.**

4. **Choose Date/Time from the Type drop-down menu and Any Value from the Suggested Value drop-down menu.**

5. **Enter the following date in the Current Value field:** 01/01/2021.

   Power Query might change the format of this value later, depending on your system settings. Don't panic! Also, the dates you enter are based on your personal needs — they aren't set in stone.

6. **Repeat the Steps for RangeEnd.**

   The Current Value field date should be 12/31/2023. Your date format may vary, depending on your system formatting scheme in Power BI.

An example of what you've just entered into Power Query appears in Figure 18-9.

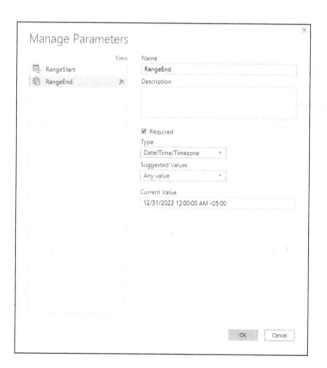

FIGURE 18-9:
Managing
parameters.

Filtering by RangeStart and RangeEnd

In order to support an incremental refresh, you need to configure a filter using the RangeStart and RangeEnd parameters. Suppose you are looking to learn each time a file is updated with new award date, whether it is a win, loss, or update to details.

Using the date data in the file, your team will be able to recognize these changes. Here's how, using Power BI Desktop:

1. **Go to the Power Query Editor.**

2. **Click to select the Awards table from the list of queries.**

3. **Select the Date Due column header and then choose the Date/Time Filter option from the menu that appears.**

   You are going to initiate a filter for the Awards column.

4. **Drill down to the Custom Filter option.**

   You are now going to set the Incremental Refresh parameters. You will need to make a few modifications from the previous section, though.

5. **When the Filter Rows interface appears, make sure Basic is selected, then choose the Is After or Equal To option from the first drop-down menu.**

6. **Click on the Calendar icon.**

   Doing so brings up a Date, Parameter, or New Parameter menu.

7. **Choose the New Parameter option.**

8. **In the new pane that appears, click RangeStart.**

9. **Change the Date type from Date/Time to Date, and then press OK.**

   You've now established the first parameter for the filter.

10. **Choose the Is Before or Equal To option from the bottom drop-down menu.**

11. **Click on the Calendar icon**

    Doing so brings up a Date, Parameter, or New Parameter menu (again).

12. **In the new pane that appears, click RangeEnd.**

13. **Change the Date type from Date/Time to Date, and then press OK.**

    You've now established the second parameter for the filter.

    At this stage, you successfully created the filter conditions which should mimic those in Figure 18-10.

14. **Click the OK button.**

15. **Click the Ribbon's Close & Apply button to exit the Power Query Editor.**

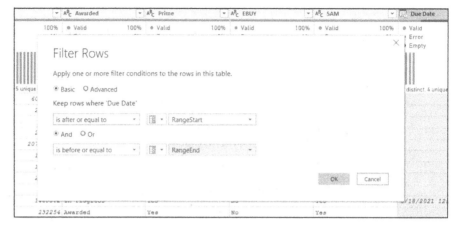

FIGURE 18-10:
Filtering rows
using the
RangeStart and
RangeEnd
parameters.

Establishing the Incremental Refresh policy

Anytime you put a filter in place for an incremental refresh, you need to complete one more step — to define the execution policy. In the example that's presented, where you have a column Due Date in the table Awards, you can create the policy by following these steps:

1. **Go to the Fields pane of Power BI Desktop and right-click the table you want to refresh incrementally.**

2. **Select Incremental Refresh from the menu that appears. (See Figure 18-11).**

   Be sure to select the correct table from the drop-down menu.

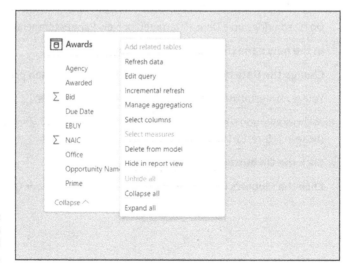

FIGURE 18-11:
Setting up an
incremental
refresh.

3. **In the new screen that appears, switch the Incremental Refresh toggle to On.**

4. **Select the periods in which data must be stored and refreshed.**

REMEMBER

Storing data means keeping it housed permanently; updating it for relevancy is a *refresh*.

You can select the check boxes to detect data changes or only refresh during complete days.

5. **Select the Apply All button when complete.**

Treating Data Like Gold

Have you been in a situation where you've worked on a dataset for a very long time and now, when it's ready for prime time, you want to tell the world that it's ready for showtime? Sure, you won't win any gold, silver, or bronze medals. Still, you can increase your dataset visibility for others to access, by way of endorsement techniques.

To an analyst, a dataset is a dataset. An analyst wants to be assured that a dataset is reliable, practical, and accurate. Some datasets may be created as a test, whereas others are meant for production and are considered truth sources.

Data at the end of the day translates back into code when it's searched, no matter which business intelligence tool — including Power BI Desktop or Power BI Services — you may be using. That's why you enforce the use of dataset endorsements. In other words, let the report's creator know exactly which datasets are reliable and ready for consumption.

You can endorse several content assets in Power BI, including datasets, dataflows, reports, and apps. You can implement endorsements in two ways:

>> **Promoting:** When content is designated as promoted, it receives a badge signifying that the content is ready for use by other users. Contributing members of a workspace who have access to the content where it resides can promote the content. The goal of content promotion is reusability.

>> **Certifying:** Certification shows that a content asset is recommended for usage because it's highly reliable, curated, and well maintained. A Power BI admin must assign users the designation to certify content within a group.

REMEMBER

Regardless of the content type, the process of endorsement is the same.

To configure an endorsement, follow these steps:

1. **Go to Power BI Services.**

2. **Locate the workspace that includes the content asset (dataset, dataflow, report, or app) that you want to promote.**

3. **Click the three vertical dots to the left side of the content type.**

4. **Choose Settings.**

   A Settings pane appears on the right side of the screen,

5. **Scroll down the pane to the Endorsement section.**

   Under Endorsement, you have four options to pick from: None, Promoted, Certify, and Feature on Home, as shown in Figure 18-12.

6. **Pick the appropriate choice for promoting your data.**

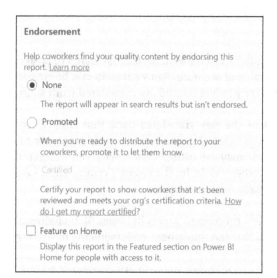

FIGURE 18-12:
Configuring
endorsements.

Notice that, in Figure 18-12, the Certified option is grayed-out. That's because the system administrator must enable endorsements for the specific user or group before they're allowed to configure any content within a given workspace. An example of two items promoted is shown in Figure 18-13.

FIGURE 18-13:
Endorsements
listed in a Power
BI workspace.

Configuring for Big Data

Can you imagine a dataset growing beyond 10 gigabytes (GB)? In the Big Data world, this use case happens daily. Once upon a time, though, hard caps were applied to what a tool such as Power BI could handle. Imagine a production business intelligence system running and suddenly one day it stops because it reaches a kilobyte overcapacity. That won't go over well. Enterprise-class customers who are running Power BI Premium can use a feature to extend the life of a dataset, enabling large dataset formats. The benefits are plentiful.

>> Datasets can grow beyond 10 gigabytes.

>> When using XML for Analysis (XMLA), write operations are faster. (For more on XMLA, see Chapter 5.)

There are two ways datasets can grow using this method: individually or as a default in the Premium workspace. If you decide to grow a dataset individually, follow these steps:

1. **Go to Power BI Services.**

2. **Locate the workspace that includes the dataset you want to grow.**

3. **Click the three vertical dots to the left side of the dataset type.**

4. **Click Settings.**

5. **Assuming that you have a Premium license, scroll down to the section of the page titled Large Dataset Storage Format.**

6. **Under Large Dataset Storage Format, set the toggle to On and click Apply, as shown in Figure 18-14.**

REMEMBER

If you see the large dataset storage format grayed-out, you lack either the license for Premium or the permission to change capacity such as this in your environment.

Configurations across an entire workspace require a slightly different approach —
follow these steps:

1. **Go to Settings in your workspace.**

2. **Locate the Premium section.**

3. **Navigate to the License drop-down menu. (See Figure 18-15.)**

4. **Depending on your Premium license type, select Premium per User or Premium per Capacity under the License Mode heading.**

   In this case, you select Premium per User.

5. **Choose Large Dataset Storage Format from the Default Storage Format drop-down menu. (Refer to Figure 18-15.)**

6. **Click the Save button.**

You're now configured for big data across your entire workspace.

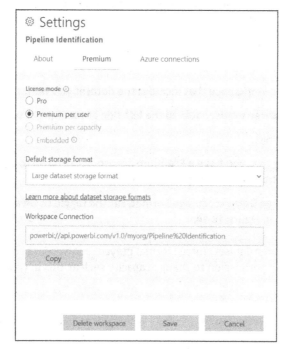

FIGURE 18-15:
Configuring a
large dataset for
a workspace.

Chapter **19**

Extending the Power BI Experience

It comes as no surprise that Microsoft considers Power BI its premiere enterprise business intelligence product. Power BI is a big part of the company's Power Platform suite of products, a robust set of applications that act as the glue to automate processes, build solutions, analyze data, and create virtual agents. Power BI "checks the box" when it comes to analyzing data. In this chapter, you discover how Microsoft has tightly integrated user-friendly collaboration and data-sharing capabilities between mobile, collaboration, automation, and application management features with Power BI.

Linking Power Platform and Power BI

The Microsoft Power Platform is a set of applications allowing users like yourself to automate processes, build solutions, analyze data, and create virtual agents. Microsoft has realized that data is everywhere. The belief that organizations can harness and gain insights into their data intelligently using a streamlined approach is where Power Platform came from. Power Platform has four major components:

>> **Power BI**: The enterprise business analytics tools

>> **Power Apps:** The application development solution to create low- to no-code apps, primarily for mobile consumption

>> **Power Automate:** Formerly known as Microsoft Flow; handles process automation and workflow generation

>> **Power Virtual Agents:** Help users create intelligent virtual bots

REMEMBER

When you use Power Platform, you can connect to more than 300 data connectors. (Microsoft is constantly adding data connectors to the platform during its quarterly product releases as well.) Power Platform also supports artificial intelligence (AI) ingestion to handle built-in logic for use in conjunction with Microsoft Dataverse, formerly known as Common Data Services. Dataverse is a primary data-collection repository for all applications using Power Platform. As you can see in Figure 19-1, the data connection opportunities in Power Platform are significant.

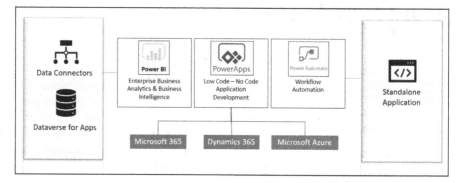

FIGURE 19-1:
Data connector options in Power Platform.

Powering Up with Power Apps

If you like the idea of building applications that don't take months or years to code, consider the low-code, no-code development solution known as Power Apps. The Power Apps platform allows you to build a highly graphical, data-centric application requiring little to no code. In fact, even a novice developer can build a highly complex, data driven application that includes logic for a business wishing to integrate other Power Platform solutions across different device form-factors, including smartphones and tablets.

With Power Apps, you can build either canvas driven apps or model driven apps. A *canvas* driven app allows a user to design and develop task-specific apps with design flexibility. A *model* driven app, on the other hand, allows users to design and develop component-focused apps using existing data sources based on business processes.

It should come as no surprise that security is an integral part of Power Apps, and for that matter, Power Platform as well. A user manages enterprise security through Azure Active Directory to enable policies, especially when multifactor authentication is necessary.

When organizations require audit logs and analytics, including tracking data loss and prevention policies, you need to access all the data by way of the admin controls, which, of course, requires access through the Power Apps admin center, now called the Power Platform Admin Center. To access it, go to the Power Apps Admin Center, where all other applications are administered in Microsoft 365, as shown in Figure 19-2. Once there, locate the list of all app admin environments, and then click the Power Apps link. You're then presented with a list of options similar to the one you see in Figure 19-3.

All admin centers

	Name	Description
	Azure Active Directory	Go deep with identity management. Enable multi-factor authentication, self-service password reset, and edit company branding.
	Compliance	Manage your compliance needs using integrated solutions for data governance, encryption, access control, eDiscovery, and more.
	Endpoint Manager	A single management experience for the End User Computing team in IT to ensure employees' Microsoft 365 devices and apps are secured, managed, and current.
	Exchange	Manage advanced email settings, such as quarantine, encryption, and mail flow rules.
	Power Automate	Manage the automation of repetitive and time-consuming tasks in the Power Platform admin center, where you can set up connections to web services, files, or cloud-based data and put them to work.
	Office configuration	Manage, configure, and monitor deployment of Microsoft 365 Apps for your organization.
	Search & intelligence	Manage Microsoft Search settings including services and content that are available for people in your organization. Make finding internal tools, documents, and people just as easy as searching the web in Bing.
	Stream	Choose how Microsoft Stream works for your organization.
	Power Apps	Use the Power Platform admin center to manage activity, licenses, and policies for user-generated Power Apps, which can connect to your data and work across web and mobile.
	Power BI	This admin center enables Power BI service admins to manage a Power BI tenant for your organization. The portal includes items such as usage metrics and settings.
	Security	Get visibility into your security state, investigate and protect against threats, get recommendations on how to increase your security, and more.
	SharePoint	Manage sites, sharing, storage, and more for SharePoint and OneDrive. Migrate files and sites to Microsoft 365.
	Dynamics 365 Apps	Use the Dynamics 365 admin center to manage your environment, manage capacity, monitor usage and perform other admin operations.

FIGURE 19-2:
A list of admin centers in Microsoft 365.

FIGURE 19-3:
Options for your
Power Platform
Admin Center.

**TECHNICAL
STUFF**

Believe it or not, the Power Platform Admin Center covers core functionality for Power Apps, Power BI, and Power Automate. It used to be that Power Apps had its own admin center. No more! Don't get confused by the labeling — the Power Platform Admin Center has exactly the same set of tools.

REMEMBER

You can connect to just about any data source in the Power Platform and integrate the data across the existing systems to be extended across solutions. This doesn't require the use of Dataverse, though. The data can remain in the applications themselves. For example, you can utilize the data within SharePoint 365 or Dynamics 365 and inherently connect the data to an app you've built, so the information is consumable.

Creating Power App visuals with Power BI

Power BI enables data insights and decision-making. At the same time, Power Apps allows users to build and use apps that connect to their business data. Users can use the Power Apps visual function to pass context-aware data to the canvas app, which updates in real time as you make changes in your reports. To use a Power Apps visual with Power BI, you must follow these steps:

1. **Ensure that you're using the latest version of Power BI Desktop.**

   By default, the Power Apps visual is available with Power BI Services. If you're using Power BI Desktop and it doesn't appear, upgrade to the latest version.

2. **Each time you want to integrate a Power Apps visual, you add it to your report and then set the associated data fields from the Visualizations pane, as shown in Figure 19-4.**

   You can either choose an existing app or create a new app based on the Power Apps visualization you've just embedded onto the report page. Regardless, the report must be published to Power BI Services and opened in the browser.

FIGURE 19-4:
The Power Apps
Data field.

3. **Once you double-click the Power BI visual that was embedded into the report, select the desired option — existing or new — as indicated in Figure 19-5.**

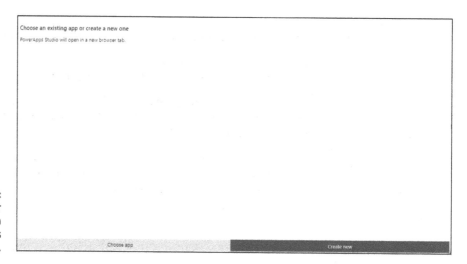
Choose an existing app or create a new one
PowerApps Studio will open in a new browser tab.

Choose app   Create new

FIGURE 19-5:
Creating or
selecting a
Power Apps
environment.

4. **If you decide to create a new app, select the correct environment, assuming that you have more than one environment available. Otherwise, proceed with creating your new app.**

TECHNICAL STUFF

Some organizations have more than one tenant of Power Platform, hence, they could have a sandbox and production environment of Power Apps and even Power BI. Small organizations usually have just one, though. It's usually those organizations who license Power BI for Premium per Capacity who fall into this camp.

If you've elected to create a new app, you're redirected to Power App Studio, which does the hard work for you — therefore, little to no code is required.

5. **You're asked to select either a form or a gallery view — your choice doesn't matter at this point. You can press the Skip button.**

As shown in Figure 19-6, the newly created app appears in Power App Data Studio.

If you decide to select an existing app, the visual prompts you to open the app in Power Apps. The visual sets up the required components in the app so that Power BI can communicate with the Power App.

If you decide to create a new app, Power Apps creates a new one with all components prewired — and the low-code all ready for you to operate. Your only responsibility post-creation is to add the external data source you can access in the Power Apps visual using Power App Data Studio.

TECHNICAL STUFF

Whether you are creating a new app or using an existing app within a Power Apps report, you need to make sure that the PowerBI Integration. Refresh() function appears as part of the app.

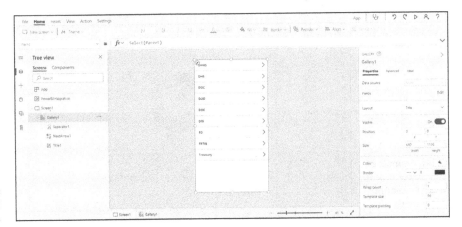

FIGURE 19-6:
A newly created
Power App.

**TECHNICAL
STUFF**

Not every app is configured the same way at this point. Depending on how you've named your data fields in Power BI and labeled your fields in Power Apps, you might see some variation. In the example, the Agency Lookup points to a source that's coded similarly to this:

```
LookUp(Agency,Agency_Name=First(PowerBIIntegration.Data).
    Agency_Name)
```

At this point, the Power BI report and the instance of the Power App Studio you've launched share a live data connection.

6. **Using this open connection, you can filter and change any data in a report to see how the updated data reflects immediately in the app within Power App Studio.**

7. **Choose File ⇨ Save As from the main menu to save and publish the app to the Power Apps instance under your top-level domain.**

8. **In the new screen that appears, choose The Cloud as your save location, name the app in the Name field, and then click Save.**

9. **Test your Power App by going to the associated Power BI report.**

Users can now gain insight from data between your report and the Power App instance, as shown in Figure 19-7, by selecting the report you've just saved and shared — the Power App is now embedded into the report. You can complete a drill-down report of the data inside the report.

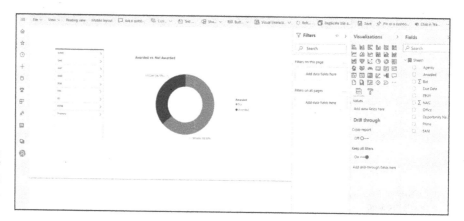

FIGURE 19-7:
An example of
Power BI and
Power Apps
integration.

Acknowledging the limitations of Power Apps/Power BI integration

If you're looking to heavily integrate Power Apps and Power BI, consider the size of your dataset first. Believe it or not, this solution has some significant scalability limitations. In various conditions, integration simply can't happen, either. There's an extensive laundry list of features that Power BI and Power Apps can't do presently. For example, the following conditions may prevent you from using Power Apps visuals with Power BI:

» The maximum number of records that can be passed using the PowerBIIntegration object is limited to 1,000.

» Power Apps visuals don't support multilevel embedding, especially when the visuals are in a secondary cloud setting (SharePoint or Teams, for example) with Power BI.

» Changing a data field with a visual requires a modification within the Power BI Services. If you don't update the service and propagate the change to Power Apps, the app responds haphazardly.

» While you'll be able to view reports and apps on a screen together, your Power App data must remain separate from your report off screen.

» Power BI Report Server doesn't support Power Apps visuals.

Introducing the Power BI Mobile app

Power BI allows users to consume analytics on just about any device: desktop, smartphone, tablet, or even smartwatch. Depending on the operating system, you can connect and interact with your data in the cloud or on-premises in various ways, as outlined in Table 19-1.

TABLE 19-1   **Power BI Mobile Support**

Operating System	Capability
Apple iOS phone and watch	Power BI supports specific mobile layouts for IOS phone and watch. You can also use the Q&A virtual analyst wizard with this edition.
Apple iOS tablet	When you're using Power BI for iPad, the mobile app displays more than just the specific formatted reports — it offers dashboards and reports the way they were formatted for the Power BI Services. In addition, you can view Report Server and Reporting Services KPIs using the iPad. Integrated into the app is the ability to set data alerts to notify users when dashboard changes occur beyond the set limits.
Google Android OS Phone	Similar to the iPhone, the Android phone edition offers exclusive views as part of its mobile reporting. Users can filter reports using various geographic-specific filters. In addition, a QR code feature exclusive to Android allows users to go directly to the dashboard and report data.
Google Android OS Tablet	All the Apple tablet/iPad capabilities are comparable to the Google Android OS tablet. One notable feature is the ability to tag favorite dashboards and reports so that users can access them quickly, along with their favorite Power BI Report Server and Report Service KPIs and reports.
Windows OS	Power BI Mobile runs on any Windows mobile-based device, including Windows 10 phones, tablets, and Surface devices. Like other mobile platforms, there is specific Windows-based functionality, such as pinning dashboards to the Windows OS Start menu from the Power BI Mobile app. You can also run Power BI in presentation mode using Surface Hub and the Power BI Mobile app for Windows 10.

WARNING   Microsoft no longer supports Windows 10 Mobile as of March 2021. The focus now is exclusively on Windows OS–based productivity, including smart devices such as Surface tablets and laptops. Microsoft doesn't think of these devices as mobile-based devices, because they run the whole Windows OS operating system.

REMEMBER   You always create your reports initially using Power BI Desktop. Those reports are then sent to the Power BI Services along with the creation of dashboards.

Integrating OneDrive and Power BI

OneDrive is an online document file storage platform. In fact, it's the same repository used in SharePoint, but with fewer bells and whistles. With OneDrive, versioning and sharing of files are limited to the filing cabinet mentality. SharePoint is more focused on collaboration for businesses in the scope of websites and intranets — OneDrive is focused on files and folders. Many users can collaborate simultaneously, including complete complex workflows, auditing, template, and auditing controls across both applications. With OneDrive, you can't create websites or social collaboration solutions, and that's the big selling point for SharePoint. For the purposes of Power BI, however, OneDrive's focus is perfectly fine. Sometimes you need for a document to reside in a centralized repository. At other times, it can simply reside on a local user's desktop.

Because OneDrive doesn't allow for documents to be publishable to the web, how are you supposed to share a Power BI file? The trick is to make the document discoverable to a specific audience by providing them access to the file. In this example, you see how to connect OneDrive to Power BI for data sharing and file consumption. Follow these steps:

1. **Point your browser to your OneDrive for Business location.**

2. **Locate the Excel file containing the data you need.**

3. **Right-click the file and choose Open in App or Open in Browser from the menu that appears, as shown in Figure 19-8.**

   Open in App leverages the Desktop Client toolset while Open in Browser opens OneDrive in your web browser of choice.

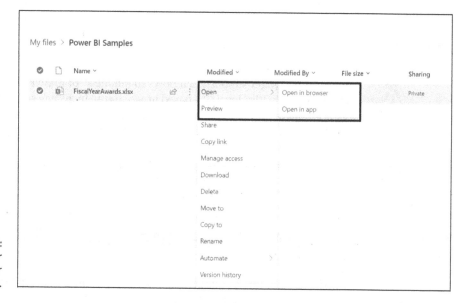

FIGURE 19-8:
Select either
Open in App or
Open in Browser.

4. **In Excel, choose File ⇨ Info.**

   The Info pane appears.

5. **Click the Copy Path button. (See Figure 19-9.)**

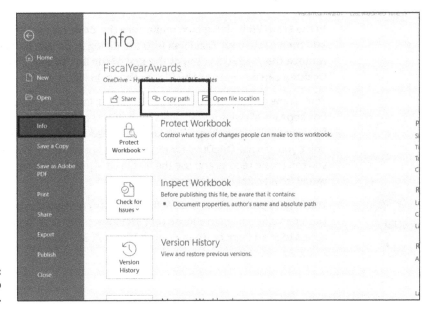

FIGURE 19-9:
The Info option to
Copy Path.

6. **Open Power BI Desktop and then click the Get Data option on the Ribbon's Home tab.**

7. **Choose Web from the menu that appears. (See Figure 19-10.)**

FIGURE 19-10:
The Get Data
from Web option.

8. **In the From Web dialog box, make sure the Basic radio button is selected, and then paste your Excel link into the dialog box's URL field. You should remove the** `?web=1 string` **at the end of the link so that Power BI Desktop can navigate to the file, as shown in Figure 19-11.**

   You've now connected the file to your Power BI instance. A navigator dialog box appears, allowing you to select from the list of tables, sheets, and ranges found in the Excel workbook you just connected to in the example. At this point, you can use OneDrive for Business just like any other Excel file. In fact, you can create reports and use the files in OneDrive for datasets like you would for any other data source.

TIP

You may be prompted for your Active Directory credentials as part of Step 8. Don't panic. You need to choose your Windows credentials for on-premise access to SharePoint or to your online Microsoft 365 Account.

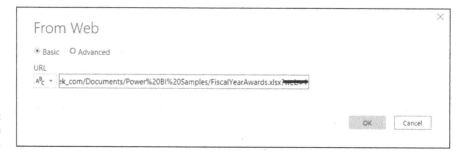

FIGURE 19-11:
The basic option to add the URL.

Collaboration, SharePoint, and Power BI

SharePoint 365, which is part of the Microsoft 365 (formerly Office 365) suite of tools, allows users to collaborate with other members of an organization, by way of the creation of intranet sites, web pages, document libraries, and lists. As part of the user experience, a user can add a *web part*, which is a tiny stand-alone application, to provide relevant, targeted content. The content can run the gamut from visuals, news, or communications. One of those web parts available to users for data integration is the Power BI web part, within the modern SharePoint user experience.

Differentiating between the classic and modern SharePoint experience

Microsoft has transformed the SharePoint experience into a modern-ready experience pushing for modularity, reusability, and mobile versus the mentality of code-everything. This means that there are limits to the kinds of visual customizations that can be completed across the entire user experience.

Does this mean that Microsoft has abandoned the classic experience, not allowing users to code intranet sites and web pages? Not quite yet. But there are, of course, features you don't get with the classic experience that come supplied with the modern experience. However, with the trade-off of more minor customization comes a more intuitive data driven experience for collaboration. One example is the Power BI web part. This feature isn't natively available with the modern experience; it requires the classic experience. You need to do a significant amount of hand-coding to integrate even simple features. On the other hand, for the modern experience, adding a Power BI web part is as simple as drag, drop, and click.

Integrating Power BI into SharePoint 365

Before you do anything in SharePoint, you need to configure Power BI to present your reports using the Power BI web part. To complete these actions, you need to open Power BI Services and then go to the report you want to present in SharePoint. To complete these actions, follow these steps:

1. **Go to Power BI Services.**

2. **Locate the report you want to present in SharePoint Online.**

   Reports are found under individual workspaces.

3. **Go to the individual report you'd like to embed by selecting Choose File ⇨ Embed Report ⇨ SharePoint Online from the main menu, as shown in Figure 19-12.**

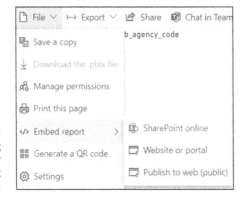

FIGURE 19-12: Configuring Power BI for SharePoint Online.

4. **Copy the link that shows up in the Embed Link for SharePoint dialog box.**

   You use this link to embed your report in the Power BI web part. (See Figure 19-13.) I show you exactly how in the next section.

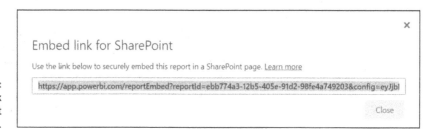

FIGURE 19-13:
Embedded link
for SharePoint
Online.

Viewing Power BI reports in SharePoint

The next part of your Power BI integration experience requires you to go to your SharePoint Online instance. In the following steps, you configure the Power BI web part to display the report you just configured for SharePoint Online:

1. **Go to any SharePoint web page that incorporates SharePoint's modern experience.**

2. **Locate the plus (+) sign (see Figure 19-14) on the page where you want to add the Power BI web part.**

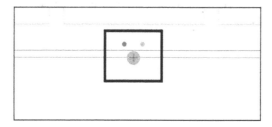

FIGURE 19-14:
Adding a web
part on a Modern
SharePoint web
page.

3. **Click the plus sign and select your web part.**

4. **You want to pick the Power BI web part,** as shown in Figure 19-15.

5. **After the Power BI web part is provisionally placed on your SharePoint page, click the Add Report button. (See Figure 19-16.)**

   A panel appears on the right side of the screen, as shown in Figure 19-17.

FIGURE 19-15:
A web part
catalog.

Data analysis

Microsoft Forms   Power BI   Quick chart   Site activity

FIGURE 19-16:
Power BI web
part initialization.

Power BI

Include a Power BI report on your page.

Add report

Power BI ✕

You can display reports from Power BI by pasting the link below.

Power BI report link

Paste the report link here.

Learn more

Page name

Display

Show navigation pane
⬤ On

Show filter pane
⬤ Off

Show action bar
⬤ On

FIGURE 19-17:
The Power BI
Report Configura-
tion panel.

6. **Paste the URL you copied from Power BI Services in the previous section, "Integrating Power BI into SharePoint 365," into the panel's Power BI Report Link field.**

7. **Press the Enter key so that the changes can take effect.**

   You now see the report embedded into SharePoint Online, as shown in Figure 19-18. Interestingly, the name of each report page carries over from Power BI.

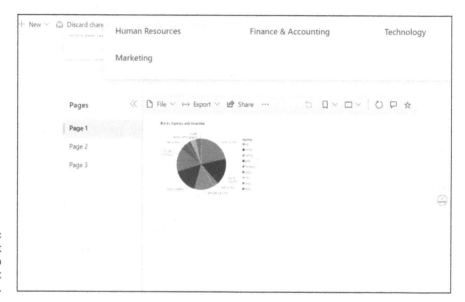

FIGURE 19-18:
A Power BI report
embedded into
SharePoint
Online.

You can configure the layout, start page (if there are multiple report pages), navigation page, filtering options, and Action bar for each Power BI report web part within the SharePoint Online Power BI web part.

Automating Workflows with Power BI

Power Automate, formerly known as Microsoft Flow, helps organizations automate processes that might be simple. Some of these tasks might even be time-consuming. Still, with an automated workflow, you can reduce errors as well as nonessential tasks. Power Automate is the powerful workflow engine that allows you to connect not only Microsoft-based systems together but third-party applications as well.

With Power Automate, there's a single source of truth. In fact, you can automate and build business processes across applications and services you may have deployed long ago or may just be completing as part of a new IT implementation. And, when Power BI is part of the equation, scenarios can vary from simple data automation to very advanced processes requiring branching and trigger actions. For example, with Power Automate, a workflow might be created to establish an approval process. Or, perhaps when data is added to Power BI, users can be notified about the changes in the system.

Configuring prebuilt workflows for Power BI

Not all configurations for Power BI actually occur in Power BI. The hard work happens in Power Automate. You're simply connecting to Power BI for the configurable activities. To begin creating a workflow, launch Microsoft 365's Power Automate app. (See Figure 19-19.)

FIGURE 19-19:
Accessing Power Automate from the Microsoft 365 console.

Once Power Automate launches, you're presented with several ways to create a flow. The most efficient way to create a Power BI flow is by entering *Power BI* in the Search box on the right side of the screen, as shown in Figure 19-20.

After you press Enter, all prebuilt Power BI templates appear, as shown in Figure 19-21.

Microsoft has more than 40 prebuilt templates (as of this writing) for integration into Power Automate.

TIP

FIGURE 19-20:
Searching for
Power BI on the
Power Automate
landing page.

FIGURE 19-21:
The Power
Automate
prebuilt Power BI
templates.

To configure a sample prebuilt workflow, follow these steps:

1. **Click to select the Update an Excel Table from Power BI workflow template (see Figure 19-22), one of the most sought-out workflows for Power BI.**

2. **Open the template and click the Flow option.**

   A screen appears for configuring all the accounts you need to authenticate.

   In this case, you need to authenticate for Power BI and Excel.

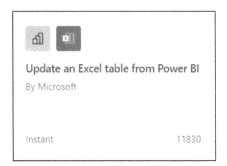

FIGURE 19-22:
The Update an
Excel Table from
Power BI
workflow
template.

3. **After making sure you have the proper accounts selected, click Continue. (See Figure 19-23.)**

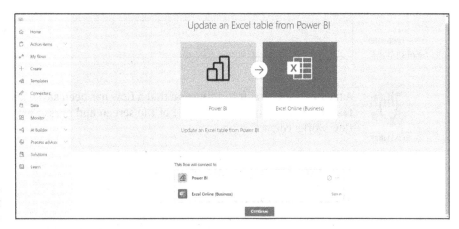

FIGURE 19-23:
Configuring
accounts.

4. **After you press Continue, you're prompted to map the fields from the Excel source to your Power BI data source.**

   In this case, I'm mapping for a file found in OneDrive with user-related data where a match in Power BI exists to update a row, as shown in Figure 19-24.

5. **Assuming that you've configured all the fields and no errors appear after testing your flow (press the Test button first — see Figure 19-25), click the Save button — again, see Figure 19-25) when you're ready to complete your flow.**

TIP

I can't stress enough the phrase "test your work carefully" before you save your flow so that it can run live from the onset. The worst thing you can do is have errors, resulting in unnecessary activities to those who are meant to use them. I mean after all, who wants to wake up with a full inbox of useless emails and text messages, right?

FIGURE 19-24:
Mapping fields
for Power
Automate Flow.

FIGURE 19-25:
The Test and
Save options.

REMEMBER

A message appears, informing you that a flow has been saved and that it should be tested. Go to the upper-right side of the screen and press Test to ensure that the flow works correctly.

Using the Power Automate Visual with Power BI

Within Power BI, you can add a handy visualization option called Power Automate Visual. Here's how:

1. **With a report open in Power BI, select the visual you want from the Visualizations pane (see Figure 19-26) and drag it to the Services canvas.**

FIGURE 19-26:
Adding Power
Automate Visual
to the Power BI
canvas.

2. **After the visual is added to the canvas, select the field that you want to act as your Power Automate trigger.**

   In this case, the trigger is Awarded.

3. **Once the field is selected, click the three ellipses (More Options) in the upper right corner of the Power Automate dialog box on the canvas, and then choose Edit from the menu that appears.**

   Power Automate launches in your browser.

   You have the option to use one of the prebuilt flows, search for a flow, or create your own flow.

4. **For this flow, create a list item in SharePoint Online by double clicking the prebuilt flow.**

5. **After selecting a prebuilt flow, click the Create an Item for a SharePoint List from Power BI, as shown in Figure 19-27.**

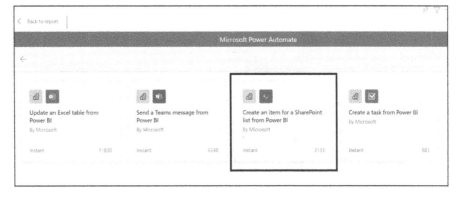

FIGURE 19-27: Creating a SharePoint item for a List from Power BI.

6. **On the new screen that appears, validate the authentication credentials for both Power BI and SharePoint and then click Continue.**

7. **Locate the SharePoint site collection, site, or subsite along with the list you want to map your fields to. When you finish mapping your SharePoint list data to the flow, click Save, as shown in Figure 19-28.**

8. **After clicking Save, you'll want to head back to the report by selecting Back to Report on the left side.**

   You'll find that your Run Flow button has now been added to the report, as shown in Figure 19-29.

FIGURE 19-28:
Mapping fields
for Power BI
SharePoint Flow.

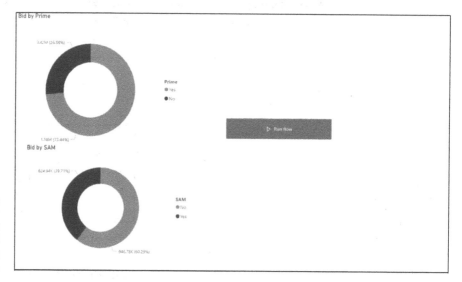

FIGURE 19-29:
A Power
Automate button
for Power BI
attached to a
report.

Unleashing Dynamics 365 for Data Analytics

There are many flavors to Dynamics 365. Whether you're a user of Dynamic 365 CRM, Sales, Finance, Operations, HR, Business Central, or another module, Power BI can help you evaluate your data with greater depth than Dynamics 365 alone. Embedded in Dynamics 365 are countless ways to slice and dice your data based on available industry metrics. Still, many organizations need to compare data outside of what Dynamics 365 offers. Often, the data must be aggregated with third-party systems. Regardless of the circumstances, the way to ingest data into Power BI Desktop for evaluation and analysis is exactly how it works in Chapter 6. All of the options for Dynamics 365 are found under Online Services. (See Figure 19-30.) Select the application you want to ingest data from into Power BI and follow the prompts after clicking Connect.

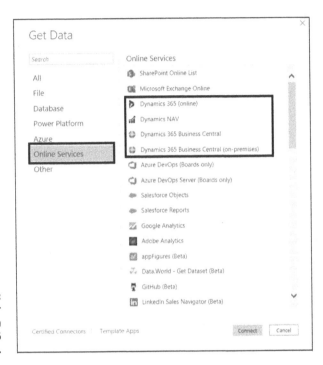

FIGURE 19-30:
The menu for selecting a Dynamics 365 Instance.

Here's what happens after selecting a particular Dynamics application:

1. **You're either asked to enter the URL for your organization's instance of Dynamics CRM or asked to log in for Dynamics 365 (all other applications).**

   In this case, login credentials are provided.

2. **Once you're logged in, select which tables from the Production instances you want to transform and load by checking each item on the left.**

3. **Once ready, select Transform Data.**

4. **Your Dynamics 365 Business Central Data has been imported into Power BI for evaluation using Power Query Editor.**

Now you can create reports using the tables and data just imported into Power BI without having to depend on Dynamics 365.

6

The Part of Tens

Chapter 20

Ten Ways to Optimize DAX Using Power BI

The Data Analysis Expressions (DAX) language is a formula expression language used across many Microsoft products. If you've ever used products such as Analysis Services, Power Pivot in Excel, or Power BI, you already know a smidgeon about DAX. The functions, operators, and values to perform advanced calculations and the queries on data in relational tables in Power BI are, in many cases, the same ones used in other Microsoft products. However, with Power BI, Microsoft has created specific niche DAX features available only for its enterprise business intelligence product.

In this chapter, I show you how to take into consideration those special features found only in Power BI. Furthermore, you see some key ways to perfect your DAX code while using Power BI.

Focusing on Logic

Performance optimization is the key to modeling data, database delivery, and data extraction. That's why, when you design a high quality database layer, you are, in effect, setting the path for an optimized data model that supports data efficiency with DAX.

When creating the data model and database layer, focus on ensuring that the fields are correctly mapped, have an intended purpose, and lack redundancy. This not only helps you minimize your need for calculated columns, calculated tables, and measures with DAX but also provides a generally faster overall output experience with Power BI. Don't be a glutton for performance challenges by calculating in more complex activity, resulting in a slow DAX environment.

DirectQuery mode with DAX, for example, has some significant limits. Make sure the model has absolutely no logical references. If you're using DirectQuery, it already means taking a hit to performance because of its automation, so adding DAX expressions creates a significant lag.

Import Model mode, on the other hand, brings with it its own challenges. Because this mode supports in-memory models, you need to avoid business logic that feeds a data model arbitrarily. The random use of feeds just slows down the processing speed of a model. You can certainly use filters within a view, but if you do so, be sure to minimize the required logic when deploying the filters. (In this context, *minimizing the filter logic* means not implementing the same filter many times across the same environment.)

Whether you're following the DirectQuery mode or Import Model mode, a solid approach to implementing logic is putting logic in stored procedures that create tables, enabling your models to reuse the logic. By doing this, you can create the same set of tables and create a single source of truth. Also, you should implement indexes — ideally, clustered columnstores — when applying large tables.

Formatting Your Code

It's not uncommon for you to have your own quirky way of naming code. Everyone has their own systems. If your code is only for you, it's probably okay to break a few rules here and there. Notice the word *few*, not *all*. Why is that? Just because the code is for you now doesn't mean that you won't later share the sample with someone else.

Throughout this book, you may notice that everything I cite maps clearly to a table, column, or row. Every variable is meaningful and relevant for the code sample. Common courtesy is making sure that others aren't baffled when trying to read your DAX code. In fact, you don't want to open your own code sample one day and scratch your head while you wonder what you wrote.

Your first goal is to format all your code consistently and document meticulously. Here's an example of well documented, formatted code:

```
Total Orders =
    IF (ISFILTERED ('Date Ranges'[Date Range]),
        CALCULATE (COUNTROWS ('Order Data'),
            FILTER ('Order Table',
            'Order Table'[Submit Date] >= [Commit Date]
            && 'Order Table'[Submit Date] <= [Ship
            Date]) ),
                COUNTROWS ('Order Data') )
```

Following these best practices can help you keep your code clean:

>> Always indent a new row if you're referencing a new function or measure.

>> Place spaces before and after both open and closed brackets to ensure the context of the data is realized.

>> Always place spaces around operators such as +, -, and = for the purpose of readability.

>> Don't overcomplicate your code with unnecessary variables, functions, and formulas.

>> Never create items arbitrarily or give a table the same name you might call a measure. It just confuses you or other developers.

>> Never include a column name unless you reference the table where it originated.

Keeping the Structure Simple (KISS)

You may remember the phrase "Keep it simple" in some incarnation from when you were much younger. That statement applies to Power BI and DAX as well: The more complicated you make tables and columns, the more likely you are to experience two problems. First, you see an immediate performance hit when it comes to getting results. Second, it's difficult to decide what's necessary versus what's arbitrary data.

Simply put, it's important to include only those tables and columns absolutely needed in your model to explore a business issue. When you add more code than necessary, you're causing excess memory usage and increased user complexity, and you're likely to unintentionally increase data volume. All these items lead to decreased performance. You're trying to decrease the number of columns in a model and the number of rows.

Less is more — your goal is to find precision and accuracy.

As you work through the reengineering of your data to achieve simplicity, you likely need to rework fact tables where columns have been removed — the tables need to be reaggregated. Under almost all conditions, the smaller the model, the better the performance.

One condition that may prohibit data reduction involves unique IDs. An example is a primary key such as TransactionID or ProductID, which is being used to simply count items. These types of columns create prohibitive circumstances for creating lightweight models. The lesson here is simple: Think twice before using unique data and using DAX.

Staying Clear of Certain Functions

Have you ever heard the old saying, "I wouldn't touch it with a ten-foot pole?" It applies to certain functions because the impact on Power BI performance and the potential data output can be detrimental to your dataset. Avoid essential functions such as SEARCH, IFERROR, CONTAINS, and INTERSECT. "Why?" you ask? Let's dig a little bit:

A good practice to ensure that you're being cost efficient and business savvy is to use the Best Practices Analyzer (BPA) along the way as you select DAX functions. As you utilize BPA, check for the true worth in using this same function, which often lacks efficiency and is cost prohibitive.

SEARCH is one of the costliest functions to use in terms of memory and processing load because it requires the system to scan each row for a given value. In other words, there are no search shortcuts. A way to tackle searching with DAX more efficiently is to create a column in your database. Afterward, you bring the column into the model as a data column. SEARCH must perform operations on the fly; therefore, for functions, there's a need to leverage SEARCH when potentially using measures. If you can't create a new column in a database, consider creating a calculated column. You need to have the measurements refer to the column.

IFERROR is a benign function in Microsoft Excel. When it's used in Power BI, though, you're likely to experience performance issues. Using more simplistic functions such as DIVIDE, which resolves divide-by-zero errors more easily using built-in processes without errors, mitigates many errors and supports faster performance.

Using functions that require excess parsing, especially when virtually mapping relationships, can be highly inefficient. Again, the concern relates to performance concerns. The more you parse data, the higher the performance degradation appears to the user. It's not uncommon to use CONTAINS or INTERSECT for virtual relationships. Both require heavy interaction among table relationships. That's why you should consider using a nimbler function such as TREATAS. Whereas with CONTAINS and INTERSECT, you parse through the entire dataset, TREATAS all but filters out column data to a finite set of data from a specific set of columns.

Making Your Measures Meaningful

There is a time and place for using specific DAX features. And the use of measures is no different. Sure, you can compute columns using a calculated column, but doesn't it make more sense to look for data efficiency? Introducing measures into the mix yields no negative performance hit to a data model. Considering that you can't manipulate data in some cases by using calculated columns on their own, measures are a solid alternative approach. Many mathematical, statistics, and trigonometric calculations require measures, because they can't be completed using a calculated table alone.

Whether you are trying to work with basic DAX functions or are authoring complex DAX function code, you *must* understand that Power BI does allow users to aggregate columns implicitly. In Power BI, implicit measures can be helpful when you want to quickly test how a visualization might perform. Another option is to create an explicit measure by using DAX. In such a situation, your intent is to create focused calculations. Here are reasons that it might make sense for you to create repeatable measures for DAX, even if it's slightly more complex. Consider the dataset by applying *either* of the following schools of thought:

>> **Power BI should behave like Excel.** That means using implicit measures in conjunction with workbook data. That means the heavy use of two functions: SUM for numerical data and COUNT for text data. When you use the Power BI Desktop, any numeric columns can use the Summarize By property.

>> **Power BI should explicitly define all measures.** By explicitly defining measures, the model supports data control because the developer is coding the behavior. Though this method may offer more developer flexibility, it may not always yield the exact results you want at first. Revisions may be required but can yield significant results if perfected over time.

Filtering with a Purpose

The FILTER function is overused. Though its primary purpose is to filter columns based on measure values, think long and hard about why you want to use the filter. If filtering is intended for just a column value, there's no need to use the FILTER function. In fact, your Power BI performance degrades when using the FILTER function when the purpose is not clearly defined. Let's look at a few examples, starting with something you should *not* be doing:

```
BID = CALCULATE ([PROFIT], FILTER ('State', 'State'
    [Country] = "United States"))
```

Avoid the logic used in this example — you're filtering each row unnecessarily. Now, here are two potential options that are more suitable:

Option #1

```
BID = CALCULATE ([PROFIT], 'State'[Country], "United
    States")
```

Option #2

```
BID = CALCULATE ([PROFIT], KEEPFILTERS ('State'[Country] =
    "United States"))
```

Both options are solid choices; however, the results are different. Compared with the original query, the second option performs the same way. The difference is that the code is far more efficient because the filter is applied to the column directly rather than to the entire table. In the first option, the code sample is awkward because it shows the United States' profitability in all areas. You'd consider using this option under particular circumstances, such as when you need a value to show regardless of a specific filter having to be applied.

Transforming Data Purposefully

DAX doesn't mean Data *Transformation* Expressions — it's meant for analysis. Keep Power BI capabilities in the proper swim lane, which means if you want to transform your data, spend as much time as possible doing this in Power Query. The more time you spend extracting, transforming, and loading your data in

Power Query before you import it into a Power BI model, the less you need to do later. Models that do the heavy transformative activities before import lead to fast resource processing and optimization.

Once your data is transformed into the best possible state in terms of preparation before load, you can then analyze the data after it's ingested into Power BI. Follow these guidelines before you ingest your data in Power BI, using DAX to transform datasets as a primary utility. Your data should be

>> In a suitable format for analysis

>> Completely loaded into the model using an optimal data model format.

>> Cleansed, merged, and split as much as humanly possible, because doing this work in DAX only adds unnecessary steps

REMEMBER

It's okay to spend more time preparing your data than analyzing it, because getting the best possible format during transformation minimizes later analysis.

Playing Hide-and-Seek with Your Columns

By now, you probably realize that filtering an entire table can have profound performance implications, not only with Power BI but also when implementing DAX. The reason has to do with parsing each table row: It's incredibly time-consuming and often yields marginal output. Instead, you can choose a better way to manage data in your tables, not only for DAX but also for Power BI in general. Follow these best practices:

>> **Whatever you do, avoid filtering an entire table.** You run the risk of stalled performance. Suppose that you're paying for database bandwidth using Azure, AWS, GCP, or IBM Cloud. In that case, you're in for a bit of sticker shock if your transactional volume is significant.

>> **Remove all columns that you know you won't use.** Having columns in a table "just because" adds an unnecessary tax to query performance.

>> **Focus on filtering using a column-based approach.** An even better tactic is to filter only those few columns that you know have relevant data. If you can remove the remaining columns from the dataset, do it. You'll likely have high performing results.

Using All Those Fabulous Functions

I wouldn't have spent almost an entire chapter outlining more than 250 functions if they weren't a fabulous resource for Power BI and DAX. They're genuinely a code reduction lifesaver because they are named formulas within an expression. A function generally has a required, optional parameter as an input. Each time a function is executed, a value is returned. And these functions require little to no code, unlike other development efforts.

DAX functions run the gamut from calculating dates and times to calculating data associated with strings, lookups, and iterating over tables to perform recursive table activities. With DAX in Power BI, your ability to code data reaches far beyond what Excel offers in supporting mathematical calculations— the following list gives you some clues:

- >> Only DAX in Power BI lets you reference a complete column or table — perhaps you want to use only particular values from those columns or tables. You can apply a filter function to a formula.

- >> Suppose that you want to customize calculation-based data on a row-by-row basis. In that case, certain DAX functions enable you to use current row values. You can also use row data as a parameter value.

- >> Only the variables you can use with DAX allow you to perform calculations that vary by context.

- >> DAX allows you to return a function across a table and its dataset, not just a single value. Though the table may not be displayed in a reporting client, the table provides input to other functions.

- >> DAX has a specific function type for business users, called *time intelligence* functions. These functions are unique because they let you home in on select date ranges and perform complex calculations based on a series of dates, including date ranges.

Rinse, Repeat, Recycle

Functions and measures allow you to be incredibly efficient when it comes to writing well-written code. That's why there's no reason to write long blocks of code to carry out a menial activity. For example, you're trying to calculate a single value. You're better off splitting your calculations into smaller blocks than creating a long equation — for two reasons:

» Repetition helps you avoid performance errors.

» Code efficiency is apparent because you quickly see a pattern after a few equations are written, given that reuse is alive and well.

TIP

One way to ensure that repeatability and code consistency is followed is by using variables. When you use variables, they offer several benefits, such as helping you ensure robust documentation and avoid making unnecessary errors while repeating the coding cycle.

Chapter **21**

Ten Ways to Make Compelling Reports Accessible and User-Friendly

The ability to read reports and visualizations in Power BI should not be limited to those people who can distinguish colors or have the ability to read unaided. How about users who are color-blind or even those who require assistive technologies to help them interpret data? They should not be left in the dark just because they have a unique requirement. With Power BI, you can incorporate numerous capabilities seamlessly with little effort to make reports accessible for numerous audience types.

In this chapter, I describe ten ways to accommodate audiences that require special needs when interpreting Power BI data using accessible methods.

Navigating the Keyboard

Report authors should not worry that users will be subjected to using a mouse or keyboard to view data in Power BI thanks to built-in support for accessibility-rich features. Report users can also walk through data points in visuals, go-between page tables, and review interactive capabilities, including cross-highlighting data, filtering, and slicing data using their keyboard or with a mouse as well.

The user can navigate a report by using the focus shortcuts that show up to indicate where the user is in the report at any given time. Depending on the browser being used, focus abilities do vary. For example, the use of Apple Safari, Google Chrome, and Microsoft Edge differ.

To access frequently used keyboard shortcuts, press the question mark (?) key in Power BI to display a keyboard shortcut dialog list.

Having a Screen Reader As Your Companion

Microsoft has made it possible for users requiring visual accommodations to use a screen reader as a companion. Every object in Power BI with keyboard navigation also has an alternative compatible option for screen readers. That means report consumers can navigate all visualization, including titles, visual types, alt text, and any textual information integrated into the visualizations.

Standing Out with Contrast

Power BI supports the integration of high contrast themes for most, if not all, of its visualizations. High contrast allows for a limited number of colors, which makes an interface easier to use for those with visual challenges. Those with photosensitivity or visual impairments benefit significantly from using high contrast models on their computers. Those in low light environments also benefit tremendously, given the limited color scheme required to view visualizations.

When using high contrast features in Windows, Power BI Desktop automatically detects which high contrast theme is utilized and applies the setting that best suits the visualization. Once published to Power BI Services, the high contrast colors carry over to the following environment, as shown in Figure 21-1.

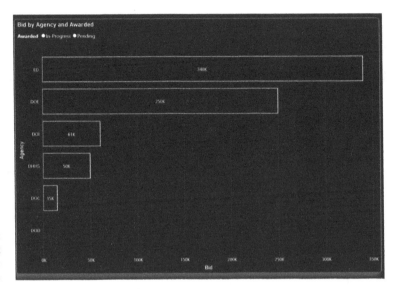

FIGURE 21-1:
A high contrast theme in Power BI.

REMEMBER

Unlike Power BI Desktop automatically detecting the high contrast settings, Power BI Services does its best to detect the appropriate settings based on the browser being utilized. You can set the theme manually by going to the Power BI Services in the upper right corner and choosing View⇨ High Contrast Colors from the menu there. You can then select the applicable report theme from the choices given.

Recognizing Size Matters (with Focus Mode)

Each visual is set to a default size when generated. Sometimes, you may want to increase the size to help those who need to see the finer-grain detail, whether it's the dots on a plot chart or smaller text. To increase the readability of a visual in a dashboard, you can expand a visual to fill up more screen space by clicking the Focus Mode icon at the top right-hand side of a report, as shown in Figure 21-2.

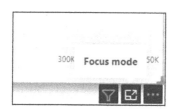

FIGURE 21-2:
Changing the
focus.

Switching between Data Tables and Visualizations

Sometimes, an individual who might be color-blind or have visual challenges may not perceive nuances in visual data. It may very well be easier for them to tell apparent differences using textual data. In these cases, having access to tabular alternatives is ideal. You can show tabular data in one of two ways: Either press Alt-Shift-F11 on the keyboard to bring up table data or click More Options and then choose the Show as a Table option found on the report. The only difference between the two options is that the keyboard-based option is screen-reader-friendly. Figure 21-3 shows an example of table output.

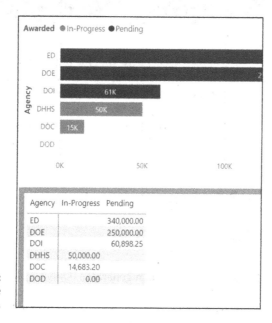

FIGURE 21-3:
Data table
output.

A Little Extra Text Goes a Long Way

Not every feature implemented by a report designer may be readable by a screen reader, especially when manually created by the report designer. When visuals and images are created manually, a best practice is to add alternative text (alt text) descriptions. Providing alternative text gives anyone requiring assistance the opportunity to interpret visuals, images, shapes, and text boxes using textual descriptors.

To provide this alternative text, you have to create the descriptions for each item by selecting the objects (in Design mode) using Power BI Desktop in the Visualizations pane. Here's how:

1. **Go to the Format selection.**

2. **Expand the General Tab.**

3. **Scroll to the bottom and fill in the Alt Text box with the text you've chosen, as shown in Figure 21-4.**

4. **When done, press Enter.**

   Be aware that there's a cap on how many characters you're limited to with alt text: You cannot enter more than 250 characters.

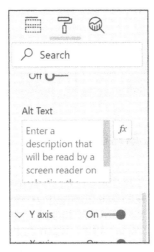

FIGURE 21-4: Adding alt text.

Be as descriptive as possible when describing your findings in the box while also conserving your use of words. A specific feature unique to Power BI is that alt text data can be made dynamic. In particular, you can include DAX measures and conditional formatting. As values change, the alt text reflects the values to better describe the conditions the end user is viewing.

Setting Rank and Tab Order

When you cannot visualize items on a screen and are dependent on a keyboard or screen reader, the end user might be at the mercy of the Report tabs. That's why it's also essential that a report designer manipulate the tab order to match the way users visually process report visuals. A best practice is to remove any unnecessary decorative elements such as shapes or images that are only there to add anecdotal asides to a report.

To set the tab order, go to the Ribbon's View tab and click the Selection icon in the Show Panes area of the tab to display the Selection pane. When the pane appears, move each item around using the up and down arrows, as shown in Figure 21-5.

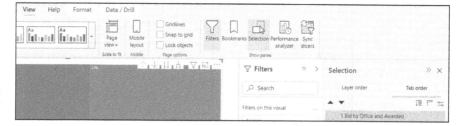

FIGURE 21-5:
Setting the tab order.

It's All About Titles and Labels

Though a visual is an important asset, the title and labels surrounding the visuals are just as crucial — they're the road signs that orient the reader by describing the context of the content. An excellent visual never includes confusing language, such as acronyms or jargon, even in report titles, legends, headers, footers, or labels. In the example found in Figure 21-6, the header is explicit in that it describes the specific purpose of the visual. The labels for the bar graph mimic the title that the unit of measurement states, which is thousands for each federal agency bid.

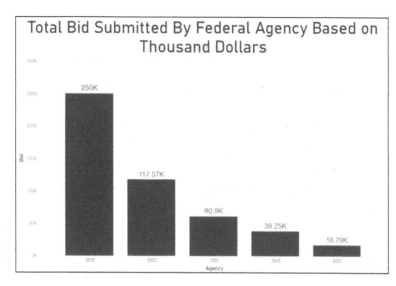

FIGURE 21-6:
Representative
titles and labels
for a visual.

A visual can have a few labels or many. You have the option to turn on and off the labels for each series in your visual. In fact, you can even select the position for each label so that they appear either above or below the series. Labels can also be different colors and sizes, too, which is essential, considering that you want it to be easy to see whether the data is difficult to read in the first place. Figure 21-7 and Figure 21-8 are exemplars of quite different approaches.

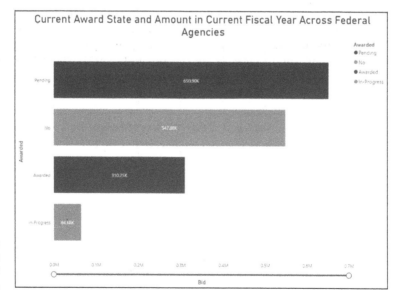

FIGURE 21-7:
Title and labels
that are highly
configured.

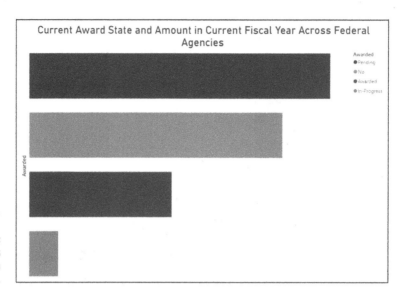

Current Award State and Amount in Current Fiscal Year Across Federal Agencies

Awarded
● Pending
● No
● Awarded
● In-Progress

Awarded

FIGURE 21-8:
Title and labels
with minimum
configuration.

Leaving Your Markers

Some of your report viewers might be color-blind. In these cases, you should avoid using color to express conditional formatting of information points. Instead, use markers to convey different series-based data. A variety of data series such as line, area, scatter, and bubble visuals can all convey data markers using shapes as part of each line to break up the data points in a data series. A set of data points help to decipher values with ease. Figure 21-9 supplies an example of implementing markers for three states: awarded opportunities, bidding opportunities, and lost opportunities over seven months. In Figure 21-10, you can see how you can access the Markers configuration area along with the options to configure shapes.

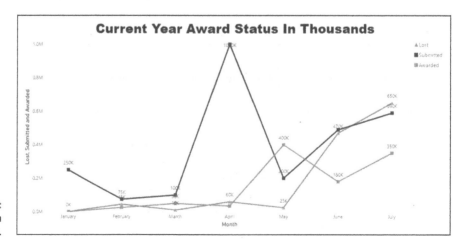

Current Year Award Status In Thousands

▲ Lost
■ Submitted
■ Awarded

Lost, Submitted and Awarded

Month

FIGURE 21-9:
Working with
markers.

FIGURE 21-10:
Configuring
markers in the
Visualizations
pane.

Keeping with a Theme

Not every theme offered by Microsoft, or for that matter designed by a report designer, is end user–friendly. Sometimes, a consumer of reports may have reverse colors (red/brown, green/orange. blue/purple), whereas others may be color-blind. In other instances, some users may have issues with decoding shading, which results in contrast challenges between text and background colors. Suppose that you're familiar with Section 508 Compliance, WCAG 2.0+, or USA Web Design System Guidelines. In that case, they all have certain principles that indicate some level of contrast that mirrors a ratio of 4:5:1. Several tools are available to the public to test for contrast and accessibility on the web for free. That said, there is variation among report reviewers when it comes to color deficiency.

The best approach is to minimize the use of many colors. That's why Microsoft has developed specific themes that help reduce the creation of inaccessible reports. For example, a user with vision challenges will have difficulty distinguishing between green and red, green and brown, blue and purple, or green and orange. (Bear in mind, these are just a few poor color pairings; there are many more.) When using these combinations, data will likely be misconstrued. Therefore, using a color scheme that is limited to one or two colors that are highly contrasting versus a color scheme that is quite similar is the best approach.

To access Microsoft's predefined themes in Power BI (including color-blind-friendly themes), go to the Themes area on the Ribbon's View Tab and click the down arrow. You have several options to pick from, including the Power BI themes, theme gallery, browser themes, and current theme customization, as shown in Figure 21-11.

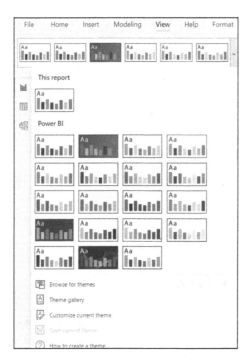

FIGURE 21-11:
Report theme
options.

Index

A

access management, 311–312
actionable decisions, 22
action-based controls, 219
Active Directory (Azure), 96
Add a Tile menu, 236
Add Alert Rule, 244
Add Data Fields text boxes, 222
Adobe, Microsoft connectors to, 95
Advanced Editor button, 121
Advanced Filtering, 222
After Deletion view, 157
aggregate functions, 268–269
Aggregate Per Category, 135
Aggregated Column, 179
aggregations, 174–181
AI (artificial intelligence)
  Power BI as having built-in AI capabilities, 29, 44
  Power Platform as supporting, 344
alerts, setting of, 244–246
Alt Text box, 383–384
Alt-Text (General section), 215, 216
Analysis Cube (Azure), 98
Analysis Services (Azure), 62, 97, 98, 99
analysis stage (of data), 30, 53–54
analytics, 31, 200–201, 236, 364–365
anomalies, in data, 104–107
Append Queries As New, 116
Applied Steps, 72, 157, 158
apps
  accessing reports from, 59
  canvas driven app, 345
  creating and configuring of, 313–314
  model driven app, 345
  setting app permissions, 334
  template app, 62, 306
Apps menu, 59
AppSource marketplace, 211–212
Area charts, 193, 194
arithmetic operators, 260

artificial intelligence (AI)
  Power BI as having built-in AI capabilities, 29, 44
  Power Platform as supporting, 344
ascending order (A-Z), 162
Ask a Question About Your Data screen, 243
Assume Referential Integrity check box, 142
authentication method, 90
automatic page refresh, 224
automatic relationships, 159–160
auto-update features, 37
Azure, linking of Power BI with, 46
Azure Active Directory, 96
Azure Analysis Cube, 98
Azure Analysis Services, 62, 97, 98, 99
Azure Cosmos DB, 51, 92–93
Azure Data Lake, 17, 18
Azure HDInsight, 51
Azure SQL Database, 51, 90
Azure SQL Server, 88, 91
Azure Streams (Azure Stream Analytics), 236
Azure Synapse Analytics, 51

B

Background (formatting), 214
background color, setting of, 218
bad data representation, 294
Bar charts, 188–194, 216–217
Basic Filtering, 222
Before Deletion view, 157
Best Practices Analyzer (BPA), 372
big data, configuring for, 341–342
Borders (formatting), 214, 218
bring your own key (BYOK), 44
business analyst, role of, 24, 27
business intelligence (BI), defined, 21–22

C

calculated columns, 256, 292, 296
calculated measures, 254

K

key influencers, working with, 207–208

key performance indicators (KPIs), 203

keyboard shortcuts, 380

keys, finding and creating appropriate ones for joins, 111–113

L

labels, 384, 385, 386

languages
- Data Analysis eXpression Language (DAX). *See* Data Analysis eXpression Language (DAX)
- M (short for mash-up), 108, 121
- Python scripting editor, 208–210
- R scripting editor, 208–210

Large Dataset Storage Format, 341–342

left anti join type, 116

left outer join type, 116

legend, configuring of, 216

let and **in** statement, 122

license, Microsoft's use of term, 35, 38

licensing
- capacity-based license, 38
- comparison of options for, 39–40
- content and collaboration as driving, 39–40
- deciding which option is best suited for you, 38–44
- defined, 35
- options for, 35
- per-user license, 38

Line charts, 193–195

list, use of term in SharePoint, 87

Live Connection, 76, 77, 78–79, 99

LiveConnect, 62

local datasets, 76

local storage, 77

Lock aspect (formatting), 214, 218

Lock option (field level), 222, 223

logical functions, 276

logical operators, 261

M

M (language), 108, 121–123

M Query Editor interface, 122

Maintain layer order (General section), 215, 216

Make This Relationship Active check box, 142

Manage Aggregations, 180

Manage Alerts, 244

Manage Parameters, 335

Manage Relationships, 148, 160

Manage Roles, 148

management stage (with data), 30

manual relationships, 160

many-to-many (M:M), 142, 143, 170, 171

many-to-one (M:1), 142, 143, 170, 171

Map example, 201

maps, 200–202

markers, working with, 386–387

Match Entire Cell Content option, 108

mathematical and trigonometric functions, 277–279

Mathematical Operations, 135

matrices, 206

Maximum option (Data Labels), 220

MDX (multidimensional expressions), 98, 134

Measure Tools Ribbon, 295

measures
- also called calculated measures, 254
- as another name for formulas, 52
- comparing of with columns, 296
- compound measure, 295
- defined, 134
- explicit measures, 291–293
- extending formulas with, 290–295
- implicit measures, 291–293, 294
- making them meaningful, 373
- preferring of over columns, 303–304
- role of, 254
- simple and compound ones, 294
- simple measure formation on Ribbon, 295
- swapping numeric columns with measures and variables, 169–170

Merge Columns option, 113

Merge interface, 113

Merge Query, 117

metadata, 10, 161–162

metrics, forecasting of, 88

Microsoft
- as adding data connectors to Power Platform, 344
- connectors to applications developed and managed by other vendors, 95
- Dataverse, 81, 147, 344

URL, basic option for adding of, 354
Usage Metrics reports, 317
USERELATIONSHIP function, 303

V

values
  avoiding converting blanks to, 298–299
  distinct values, 171
  error values, 125
  replacement of, 108–110
  specific ones in DAX, 301–302
  storing values with measures, 134–136
VAR statement, 263
variables, 169–170, 289–290
version, Microsoft's use of term, 35
video, on dashboard, 236
View As button, 148
View Details and Related Reports command, 321
View Error hyperlink, 125
View Native Query, 79
Visual Error icon, 219
Visual Header settings, 219
Visual Header Tooltip icon, 220
Visual Warning icon, 219
Visualization canvas, 184
visualization configurations, 215–220
visualization stage (with data), 29
Visualization tile, 238–240
visualizations
  additional options for, 211–212
  choosing of, 185
  creating of, 184–185
  dealing with table-based and complex ones, 205–208
  options for, 22
  switching between data tables and visualizations, 382
Visualizations pane, 184, 185, 186, 197, 208, 209, 213, 214, 387
visuals
  examples of, 53
  sources of, 54

W

Wallpaper (formatting), 224
Waterfall charts, 195–196
web content, on dashboard, 236
web part, 354, 356, 357
Width (General section), 215, 216
Workspace Access, 311
Workspace section (Power BI Services), 227, 228
Workspace Settings, 312
workspaces
  adding new content to, 314
  arrows between each asset in, 321
  assigning workspace access, 312
  configuring advanced features of, 311
  configuring standard features of, 310
  content of, 308
  creating and configuring of, 309
  defined, 16
  defining types of, 306
  figuring out nuts and bolts of, 308–313
  saving dataset and visualizations in report to, 226
  showing impact of an action across, 322
  working together in, 305–313
  workspace apps, 307

X

XML for Analysis (XMLA), leveraging, 81–83
X-Position (General section), 215, 216

Y

Y-Position (General section), 215, 216

Z

zip File, 228

About the Author

Jack Hyman is the founder of HyerTek, a Washington, DC-based technology consulting and training services firm specializing in cloud computing, business intelligence, learning management, and enterprise application advisory needs for federal, state, and private sector organizations in the United States and Canada. He is an enterprise technology expert with over 20 years of digital and cloud transformation experience, collaborative computing, usability engineering, blockchain, and systems integration. During his extensive IT career, Jack has led U.S. federal government agencies and global enterprises through multiyear technology transformation projects. Before founding HyerTek, Jack worked for Oracle and IBM. He has authored many books, provided peer-review guidance for scholarly journals, and developed training courseware with an emphasis on Microsoft technologies. Since 2004, he has served as an adjunct faculty member at George Washington University, American University, and the University of the Cumberlands. Hyman holds a PhD in Information Systems from Nova Southeastern University.

Dedication

To my children, Jeremy & Emily: I hope you always love learning as much as I do.

Author's Acknowledgments

Many folks were involved in the making of *Microsoft Power BI For Dummies*. I want to thank key members of the team. Thanks to Acquisition Editor, Steve Hayes, for giving me the opportunity to write this book (and so many other Dummies projects over the years). A great big thanks to Senior Project Editor, Paul Levesque, for keeping me in check throughout this project with his most excellent suggestions for writing a strong text and ensuring the project stayed in sync. To Copy Editor, Becky Whitney, your help ensuring the book was written well and full of style is much appreciated. Also, thanks to Carole Jelen of Waterside Productions for bringing me yet another exciting project to share with the world. And finally, my wife Debbie and kids, Jeremy, and Emily for allowing me to take on yet another labor of love.

Publisher's Acknowledgments

Acquisitions Editor: Steven Hayes

Senior Project Editor: Paul Levesque

Copy Editor: Becky Whitney

Tech Editor: Scott Proctor

Production Editor: Tamilmani Varadharaj

Cover Image: © NicoElNino/Shutterstock